A LOT

Can Happen in the Middle of

NOWHERE

The Untold Story
of the Making of *Fargo*

TODD MELBY

Foreword by William H. Macy

MINNESOTA
HISTORICAL
SOCIETY PRESS

mnhspress.org

The Minnesota Historical Society Press is a member of the Association of University Presses.

Manufactured in the United States of America

10 9 8 7 6 5 4 3 2 1

♾ The paper used in this publication meets the minimum requirements of the American National Standard for Information Sciences— Permanence for Printed Library Materials, ANSI Z39.48–1984.

International Standard Book Number
ISBN: 978-1-68134-188-0 (paper)
ISBN: 978-1-68134-189-7 (e-book)

Library of Congress Control Number: 2020950775

This and other Minnesota Historical Society Press books are available from popular e-book vendors.

A LOT

Can Happen in the Middle of

NOWHERE

Contents

Foreword

It's common for an actor to be asked, "Did you know the film would turn out so well when you read the script?" The truthful answer is usually no. And if you're young or new in your career, there is the nagging thought that the film can't be that good if they're casting me. But I knew *Fargo* would be magnificent from my first reading of the script. A great script, talented directors, and a wonderful part ... well, duh. I was in my little cabin in the middle of Vermont when I got the call, and I had no one to tell. I went outside and screamed for twenty minutes.

I remember the set as being very calm and quiet. We were called to Minnesota before shooting began to rehearse and work with Liz Himelstein on the accent. But Minnesota had one of its freakish winter warm spells, and Joel and Ethan Coen were out looking for snow. I kept trying to get Peter Stormare and Steve Buscemi to go out and get in trouble with me in Minneapolis, but they always turned me down, preferring to stay in and work on the script. I remember the guys at the Oldsmobile dealership, where we shot for nearly a week, really wanted to sell me a Toronado. I remember sitting at the dealership office desk, doodling on a pad while a shot was being set up, and Ethan looked at my doodles, laughed, and decided to shoot them in the film. I remember Roger Deakins's quiet shorthand with his crew as he set up his magical lighting. I remember Joel, Buddha-like, while Ethan paced the set. Ethan's big note to me was to always stomp the snow off my shoes when I walked into the Lundegaard house. I don't remember a note from Joel. I remember the lovely music in the dialogue.

Toward the end of shooting, production came to me, knowing I had a few acres in Vermont, and asked if I wanted to buy the wood chipper. It was an excellent one, and I had admired it. But they had taken the thing apart in order to make the leg-in-the-chipper gag work, and I said no. I really regret that decision.

Fargo changed everything for me, and I will always be grateful to Joel and Ethan. I recently came upon the film while channel surfing. I watched the whole thing, and I loved it. It was difficult to recognize my young self, but Jerry Lundegaard was just as I remembered him.

Directing has been described as building a boat while you're in the water. The director is asked hundreds of questions during the prep weeks and through shooting. *Which actor do you want to cast? Do you like the green shirt or the red one? Where do you want to put the camera?* As mundane as some of the questions are, and no matter how long the day has been or how behind schedule you might be, the director had better think long and hard before answering, because at some point he or she will sit in an editing room and stare at that damn red shirt, knowing that it will be red until the end of time. This book will give you a glimpse into some of the thousands of questions Joel and Ethan had to answer, and you will delight in how masterful their answers were.

William H. Macy
Hollywood, California

Preface

Movies aren't escapism for me. I don't just show up at the multiplex or flip on Netflix hoping to find something worth watching. I stalk trailers, reviews, listings, and special screenings like a gambler studying *The Racing Form*. At age eight, I talked my mother into buying me a ticket to *2001: A Space Odyssey*. At nineteen, I watched *All That Jazz* six times. At thirty-four, I took the day off work to attend a midafternoon screening of *Pulp Fiction*. At age fifty-two, I messed up. Instead of flying to San Francisco for a rare, five-and-a-half-hour screening of Abel Gance's 1927 silent epic, *Napoléon*, I hunkered down in North Dakota to report on an oil boom.

Seemed like a good idea at the time.

In the mid-eighties, the Coen Brothers got my attention with *Blood Simple*, an eerie thriller that seduced me on a Saturday night and wooed me back to the theater the next afternoon. On my second viewing, I snuggled in just three rows from the screen so the rain on the windshield, the bullets through the wall, the knife through the hand, and the shovel to the head would seem that much closer. *Blood Simple* and the Coen Brothers captivated me like a beguiling dame in a Raymond Chandler novel. A decade or so later, when I learned the pair had made *Fargo*, I knew where I'd be on opening night.

The Coens didn't film *Fargo* in North Dakota's largest city. The plan was to film Minneapolis scenes in Minneapolis and its suburbs, many of the locations not far from Joel and Ethan's childhood home in St. Louis Park. The prairie on the edge of the suburbs, on the outskirts of places like Chaska and Eden Prairie, would serve as stand-ins for rural highways prowled by Marge Gunderson, the film's pregnant heroine. However, in early 1995, Minneapolis lacked snow. So the Coens caravanned to Grand Forks, North Dakota, bunked at the Holiday Inn, and made excursions to Minnesota and North Dakota landscapes near the Canadian border so *Fargo* would look like the white, desolate Fargo of their imagination.

Lots of the suburban scenes in *Fargo* were shot along the I-394 corridor to the west of Minneapolis, in a series of middle-class malls, automobile showrooms, and corporate office towers tucked next to cloverleafs. Continue west on I-394, and the road narrows to two lanes and gets a new name: US Route 12. That road winds its way across western Minnesota, South Dakota, Standing Rock Sioux Reservation, and, hundreds of miles later, to a little prairie town where I was born.

Hettinger, North Dakota, is a city of about 1,221 souls in the arid western part of the state. During the winter of 1942, when my father was six years old, photographer John F. Vachon arrived. The US Library of Congress owns nineteen of Vachon's black-and-white negatives from his visit. One shows a Hettinger shoe repairman proudly leaning on a snow shovel, having just cleared the sidewalk in front of his shop. Others feature abandoned farm equipment on a deserted road near a church, a lonely two-story house surrounded by snow, and a bird's-eye view of a solitary figure in a dark coat trudging through Hettinger's quiet streets on an overcast winter day. My favorite is "Hettinger, North Dakota (vicinity). U.S. Highway 12." A diamond-shaped sign indicates the road curves to the right, only the pavement is damn near invisible. Fierce winds have covered the highway with white snow and clumps of dirt. On the left side of the frame, a series of telephone poles hint at the city's connection to the outside world. But on this day, locals are trapped inside, far away from civilization.

This is pretty much the way Ethan Coen views Minneapolis, the city I now call home.

In the only earnest introduction to an early Coen Brothers screenplay, Ethan writes that *Fargo* "evokes the abstract landscape of our childhood—a bleak, windswept tundra, resembling Siberia except for its Ford dealerships and Hardee's restaurants."

Photographer John Vachon captured the stark landscape of the North Dakota prairie on the outskirts of Hettinger in 1942. (Library of Congress, Prints & Photographs Division, FSA/OWI Collection)

The Coens hit their mark.

Fargo paints North Dakota and Minnesota as icy hellscapes for dunderheads. Still, I can't help liking the film. Marge and Norm are sweet. Jerry is venal, but geez, how else was he going to confront his father-in-law—talk to him? That funny-looking guy *is* kinda funny looking. And Mr. Mohra, the man with the broom sweeping his driveway near the end of the movie? I love reciting his lines to friends ("Where can a guy find some action? I'm going crazy out dere at the lake"), showing off my best Norwegian American accent.

Indeed, listening to the accents in *Fargo* reminds me of my maternal grandmother, Ruth A. Olson, hobbling around her South Dakota kitchen. Ruth, and her husband, John, raised hundreds of beef cattle and six kids west of the Missouri River. They sold the cows for slaughter and sent the kids off to a one-room schoolhouse on horseback. My grandmother's maiden name was Thorstenson, although every member of her genera-tion pronounced it TOR-sten-son. My great-grandparents Peter Johan Thorstenson and Anna Sophie Birkland immigrated from Norway in 1882 and 1885, respectively. After pairing up, they married and had ten children. A few of them had doozies for names: August, Alfa Meniva, Hjalmer, and Sisilie.

My father's family was a mix of Norwegian and German immigrants to North Dakota and Minnesota, so the roots of the *Fargo* accent aren't that different from my family's roots: a mix of Norwegian, Swedish, and German immigrant influences. I've got no Swede in me, except for my love of "I Been a Swede from North Dakota," an upbeat folk song. Popu-larized by Yumpin' Yiminy in 1932, the ditty tells the story of a hick from the sticks who comes to the big city to party.

I bin a Swede from Nort' Dakota
Work on farmstead 'bout two yare
Tink I go to Minnesota
Take in the big Minneapolis fair

I buy me a suit, I buy me a bottle
Dress me up way out of sight
Yump on the tail of a Yim Hill wagon
Yesus Chreest, I feel for fight

I go down to Seven Corners
Where Salvation Army play
One dem vomans come to me
Dis is what dat voman say

She say, "Will you work for Yesus?"
I say, "How much Yesus pay?"
She say, "Yesus don't pay nothing."
I say, "I won't work today."

There are at least two other versions of the song; all drop the "th" in "north," "this," and "that" for hard "t" sounds, and switch out "j"s and "w"s for "y"s and "v"s. And why not? It's funny to hear "Jesus" pronounced "Yesus," especially when the Swede doesn't care about getting into heaven if it doesn't pay a dime.

⋈

In writing this book, I traveled to Los Angeles to read multiple drafts of the screenplay. I talked to actors who got their big breaks in *Fargo*, and a few who didn't. I talked to a stuntwoman who bashed her head into a doorjamb while blinded by a shower curtain. I learned about the cassette tapes Ethan gave the film's dialect coach, then I obsessively tracked down the man who recorded them. When a casting specialist told me she video-taped auditions, I nagged her for copies until she rifled through boxes in a barn to find them. When she finally mailed the unedited tapes to me, I opened them with the zeal of a child on Christmas morning. I also talked to dozens of cast and crew members and combed through ephemera, in-cluding behind-the-scenes photographs, daily call sheets, newspaper clip-pings, and an obscure French film journal. All offered insight into Joel and Ethan Coen's fierce work ethic and meticulous creative strivings.

Fargo is the movie that catapulted careers. For Minnesotans, the film shed light on our passive-aggressiveness, our smug sense of self-righteousness, and our bone-chilling winters, which must be confronted, scraper in hand, even when our father-in-law refuses to fund that well-researched business proposal.

chapter 1

Homey and Exotic

Writing Fargo

"Scenarists are inevitably amateurs, boobies, and hacks."

—RODERICK JAYNES

"We tell the story the way we want."

—ETHAN COEN

Joel Coen gripped the movie camera with one hand, peered through the viewfinder, then reached around the front for the focusing ring. The ring encircled the lens and had nubby indentations on it, making it easy to find. With a brief turn of the ring, an image came into focus.

It was Ethan, his younger, curly-headed brother, gripping a homemade spear, preparing to take a star turn in a backyard movie.

The night before, the boys had plopped themselves in front of the family television set at 1425 Flag Avenue in St. Louis Park, Minnesota, to watch *The Naked Prey*, a mid-sixties movie about a white man fighting for his life against black men with spears. Set in South Africa, the film stars Cornel Wilde as one of several ivory-seeking tourists who upset the locals and are captured, then punished. Wilde, a wiry, bearded man, is singled out to be hunted for sport. Wearing only a loincloth, Wilde is chased across the plains by tribesmen, who heave spears at his torso and try to stick him with sharp knives.

Even with multiple commercial interruptions, *The Naked Prey* made a vivid impression on the teenagers. The next day, Joel and Ethan made

...wn version of the chase movie. With Ethan in the role of "Native with a Spear," the boys coaxed a friend to join them, and they set about acting and recording the tale in the woods behind their suburban Minneapolis house. Since they had no editing equipment, the Coens bounced between points of view, recording the pursuer and then the pursued, one after another, on and on, until the film inside the Vivitar Super 8 camera was filled.

"We would shoot one side of the chase, then run over someplace else and shoot the other side," Joel recalled. "The big advantage to that is when you get it back from the drugstore, the movie is finished."

As boys, the Coens watched all kinds of moving images flicker before their impressionable eyes. Joel remembers seeing both campy (*Sons of Hercules in the Land of Darkness*) and Italian surrealist (*8 1/2*) movies on local television. At the U Film Society, a concrete bunker of a theater at the University of Minnesota, they saw the Marx Brothers and European imports. "I think the fact that we were watching movies that way, where there was no distinction that was being made between essentially very sophisticated, auteur-driven European films and the crassest commercial movies that were being made, we made no distinctions in our minds either," Joel recalled. "They were just different ways of expressing yourself."

In the ensuing months and years of their youth, they'd dream up all sorts of scenarios, then act them out in front of the whirring Super 8. And since Joel was nearly three years older than Ethan, he often pointed the camera at his shorter sibling, who, dressed as a "native" or a lumberjack or an international statesman, tried to appear menacing, silly, or important. They got friends to join them too. Mark Zimering, who grew up to become an endocrinologist, costarred in the *The Naked Prey* remake, which the Coens titled either *Zeimers in Zambezi* or *Zeimers in Zambia* (accounts differ), and *Lumberjacks at Play*, another original drugstore short featuring goofy lumberjacks.

"For *Lumberjacks at Play*, [Joel] had a lumberjack in a plaid shirt going to work with a briefcase full of pancakes and a hacksaw," Zimering said. "They liked pancakes a lot, and so the lumberjacks would eat the pancakes, and then vomit."

When the camera wasn't on, the Coens and Zimering headed to the kitchen to experiment with strange culinary combinations. "We spent a lot of time in the refrigerator, experimenting with stuff like cranberry juice and ketchup, trying to trick the other person into drinking it," he said. "Vomiting was a recurring motif—probably because it showed up well against the snow."

Another short also focused on food: *The Banana Film*. It claimed to be a story of a "man with the uncanny ability to smell bananas." Then there was *Would That I Could Circumambulate* and *My Pits Smell Sublime*. Occasionally a movie would have loftier ambitions. The short about the international statesman was inspired by Richard Nixon's globe-trotting secretary of state. Titled *Henry Kissinger: Man on the Go*, the movie showcased Ethan dressed in a suit, clutching a briefcase, and walking briskly around Minneapolis–St. Paul International Airport.

Before loading the Super 8 with film and pressing the shutter release trigger, Joel and Ethan didn't write a single sentence, but that wasn't for a lack of inspiration. They grew up watching writers battle with words.

Their father, Edward Coen, worked as a professor of economics at the University of Minnesota. Their mother, Rena Coen, earned an undergraduate degree at Barnard College and a master's at Yale University before moving to Minnesota. Like Edward, she also wanted a doctorate degree. So after giving birth to Deborah in 1952, Joel in 1954, and Ethan in 1957, Rena returned to college. She juggled kids, cooking, and studying art history at the University of Minnesota. By the time Rena finished her doctoral thesis—"The Indian as the Noble Savage in Nineteenth Century American Art"—Joel was fourteen and Ethan was eleven.

"It's true that they grew up in a house with an art historian and Joel is very interested in art history," Rena said. "But they also grew up in a house with scribblers. Both Ed and I write all the time, and they're writers too. I don't know if they were influenced by our writing, but it wasn't something strange to them."

They're writers too.

During the first phase of their career—from 1984's *Blood Simple* to 2001's *The Man Who Wasn't There*—all of Joel and Ethan's films bubbled up from inside their brains, not the imaginations of novelists or other screenwriters. They don't talk much about writing, probably because reporters don't ask, but screenwriter William Goldman once did. The Coens told him a few things, like how they refuse to work from an outline or know how the screenplay ends when they begin.

"The rule is, we type scene A without knowing what scene B is going to be," Ethan said. "Or for that matter, we type scene R without knowing what scene S is going to be."

Unlike Joel and Ethan, Goldman never directed or edited a film, which may be why he's critical of the public perceptions of how movies are made. Most movies about movies depict principal photography, those long days and sleepless nights when cinematographers are hunched behind cameras and boom operators hold long poles with bulbous microphones over the heads of strikingly beautiful actors bathed in flattering light. It's glamorous, it's enticing, and yet, it's only a fraction of what it takes to make a really good movie. Goldman dreaded this part of moviemaking because this is when interlopers are lurking and reporters are hovering, mouths agape, before disappearing to write features about an actor or a director, thinking they've seen *the thing* happen.

"Shooting is all most people know—from those awful articles in magazines or stories on the tube that purport to be on the inside but are only bullshit," Goldman wrote. "The movie company knows who is watching and they behave accordingly. Stars do not misbehave when the enemy is about. Directors do not admit their terrors when the enemy is about. Writers, to give us our due, are not even there when the enemy is about."

Goldman, who died in 2018, wrote *Butch Cassidy and the Sundance Kid, The Princess Bride, Marathon Man,* and *All the President's Men,* among others. He also wrote tell-all books about Hollywood, including *Which Lie Did I Tell? More Adventures in the Screen Trade.* That book includes a mini-analysis of *Fargo* as well as *Chinatown,* the 1974 movie about greed, incest, and murder in 1930s Los Angeles. Most people know *Chinatown* for its stars Jack Nicholson and Faye Dunaway and its director Roman Polanski—all of whom were nominated for an Academy Award. Too few know it for

Joel and Ethan Coen during shooting for *Fargo* in the woods near Square Lake in Washington County, Minnesota. (Photo by Lauri Gaffin)

its writer, Robert Towne, who *won* the Academy Award for Best Original Screenplay and is credited with writing more than a dozen other films.

"It's that stupid auteur theory again, that the director is the author of the film," said Billy Wilder, director and cowriter of many Hollywood classics, including *Sunset Blvd., The Apartment,* and *Double Indemnity.* "But what does the director shoot—the telephone book?"

Critical choices are made in quiet rooms by people with imagination before a single frame of film is exposed to light.

Ethan is faster at typing than his older brother, probably because he once worked as a statistical typist at Macy's, banging numbers into rows and columns. So when the Coens are inventing a new world, Ethan pounds away at the keyboard. But he doesn't do it alone. Ethan and Joel write together. Unlike many writing partners, they don't divvy up scenes and then come back together and edit each other's work. Instead, The Brothers agree on a premise or imagine a character with a plan or a problem, and then, together, they compose the scene on the page. Sometimes, they pretend they are the characters, and they imbue them with life. Film editor Michael R. Miller witnessed this firsthand when the pair took over a corner of his editing booth one night.

"Joel was lying on the floor smoking cigarettes and Ethan was smoking a cigarette and pacing, and they started going back and forth with what sounded like the ravings of two lunatics," Miller said. "But it was the beginning of the 'We Ate Crawdads' scene from *Raising Arizona*. It seemed like that was their writing process, to act these crazy things out for each other, which Ethan would then write down."

For the Coens, speech is key to unlocking a unique cinematic universe. "Whatever the movie, [language] is how you work your way into the story," Ethan said. "Writing it, you want to make it a specific world, and a big part of that is how the characters talk. . . . In a way, it's what it's all about. Take that away and then the characters are just communicating plot points or defining themselves as the hero or the bad guy, you know?"

In addition to writing, directing, and editing the films, The Boys—or sometimes just Ethan—zipped off tongue-in-cheek introductions to their published screenplays. *Blood Simple, Raising Arizona, The Hudsucker Proxy, Fargo,* and *Collected Screenplays 1* contain witty—and sometimes sophomoric—riffs on the movie business and storytelling. In the preface to *Blood Simple,* The Boys bitch about how college students and film nerds ask them about shooting ratio (the feet of film shot compared to the actual feet of film that appear in the final print).

"For some reason the question fascinates people the world over, while other pointlessly precise questions are never asked," they wrote. "No one asks about our teamster ratio, for instance, which compares the total number of teamsters employed on the picture to the number of teamsters who worked. Nor does anyone ask about paper ratio, which compares the total number of pages of notes and drafts to the hundred or so pages of finished screenplay manuscript."

This commentary hints at the Coens' frustration with the public's lack of interest in the craft. They point out that rewriting isn't "cheating." As evidence, they share a supposed first draft of *Macbeth*: "It is a tale told by an idiot / Full of sound and fury / And all manner of things." A second draft also falls short: "It is a tale told by an idiot / Full of sound and fury / Nor meaneth it a thing." A third draft is worse still.

The preface concludes with Ethan and Joel pretending to give up the goods on writing: "The rule is, you quit rewriting when your manuscript starts to bore you. Only the amateur, who has boundless energy and who lacks the imagination to quit, ever works beyond that point."

Coen screenplays are filled with short, vivid sentences that describe the action or scenery. Sentences pop with action verbs and colorful descriptions. From *The Hudsucker Proxy*: "He takes loping dwarfstrides down the aisle." And: "The elevator screams into overdrive." Often, words not spoken by characters evoke not just visuals but sounds, like these excerpts from *Fargo*: "The phone pops out of her hands, jangles across the tile floor, smashes against the door and then bounces away, its cord having been ripped free." And this: "Norm snores away like the great American buzz-saw." The Coens also dig inventing words or inserting slang into their work, even if it's never spoken. In *Barton Fink*, a hellish fire at film's end "races along the wall-sweat goopus." (The "goopus" is the thick pus that oozes out between the faded wallpaper in Barton's flat.) In *Fargo*, a police car's flashing lights are "gumballs." The punchy sentences and evocative word choices are hallmarks of Dashiell Hammett, Raymond Carver, and other noir novelists of the twentieth century.

"We've always tried to emulate the sources of genre movies rather than the movies themselves," Joel said. "For instance, *Blood Simple* grew out of the fact that we started reading James M. Cain's novels in 1979 and liked the hard-boiled style."

The pair nabbed several plot points from Cain's *The Postman Always Rings Twice* (1934) for *Blood Simple*, their first feature. Both stories chronicle bitter workers falling hard for the boss's wife, then whacking the boss. In *Postman*, a drifter plots a murder with the boss's sultry wife. In *Blood Simple*, a detective hired to snoop on the cheating wife shoots the boss, but it's the bitter employee who kills him. And in an obvious homage to Cain, the antagonist bosses in both stories are Greek business owners—in

Blood Simple, Julian Marty owns Marty's Bar, and in *Postman*, Nick Papadakis owns the Twin Oaks Tavern, "a roadside sandwich joint, like a million others in California," writes Cain. In the first few pages of the *Blood Simple* screenplay, Marty clues us in on his ethnicity: "You know in Greece they cut off the head of the messenger who brought the bad news." In *Postman*, Papadakis is referred to as "the Greek" in the bitter employee's first-person narration. Both Greeks end up dead: Papadakis in a bloody car crash and Marty in a shallow grave, buried alive.

Like a lot of noir protagonists, Julian Marty mistakenly thinks he's smarter than those around him. In *Blood Simple*, Marty hires a private detective to track his cheating wife, played by a nymph-like Frances McDormand, making her film debut. When he asks the detective to kill her, Marty gets double-crossed and shot in his office, left bleeding next to a pile of rotting fish. That night, Ray, the wife's boyfriend, stumbles upon Marty's body, which appears dead, but isn't. Ray finds his lover's gun at the scene and assumes she's killed Marty. So he heaves Marty into the trunk of his car and drives out to the Texas prairie in the middle of the night. Once they arrive at the barren countryside that will soon be Marty's grave site, Marty comes to life, barely, and tries to crawl to safety along a deserted road. Now the task of burying a dead body has suddenly become the kidnapping of a living man. Ray grapples with what to do next: should he drive to the hospital and get Marty medical assistance, or should he finish the job he believes his girlfriend started and kill Marty under the light of a Lone Star moon?

In typical, twisted Coensian fashion, Ray takes the deadly option. He digs a shallow grave, drags Marty into it, and methodically shovels dirt over Marty's still-living body. As Marty struggles to breathe, Ray tosses more dirt on his face. The shoveling, hesitant at first, quickens as Ray realizes the faster this goes the better it is for everyone involved. Marty will die quicker. Ray will be done with this horrific task sooner. So he piles on the dirt and piles on the dirt. We see Marty gasping, dirt pouring into what was once his piehole and is now his dirt hole. Then Ray finishes the job in a terrifically cinematic way. He lifts the shovel high and hammers it into the dirt covering Marty's head.

That's the first kidnapping, of sorts, in a Coen Brothers story. There will be many more.

After *Blood Simple*, The Brothers made *Raising Arizona*, a 1987 romp starring Nicolas Cage and Holly Hunter as two bumbling but big-hearted people. Cage plays H. I. McDunnough, a hapless criminal. Hunter plays Ed, a cop. In the movie's opening scene, Ed is booking H. I. for an unknown crime. As he flirts with her, calling her a "little desert flower," she bosses him around, instructing him to "turn to the right" so that she can capture his mug shots. She also lets it slip that Ed is short for Edwinna. He says, "Call me Hi." That romantic spark blossoms into love when H. I. is released from prison. They get married, but they can't have babies. They realize life in their shitty little trailer home is mighty lonely without children. So they scheme to steal a child from one Nathan Arizona Sr., a rich sumbitch whose wife just gave birth to quintuplets. Hi and Ed's reasoning: they've got five, we don't have any, life ain't fair, so we'll just take one of theirs. And they do. What follows is one mighty fine kidnapping tale. H. I. climbs a ladder, sneaks into the babies' room, and grabs a towheaded boy in a white diaper. A few moments later, he returns to Ed, who's waiting in the car, hands her the stolen child, and mumbles, "He's awful damn good. I think I got the best one." Next comes a series of funny and harrowing adventures as H. I., Ed, and the baby attempt to evade capture by the police, ex-con friends of H. I.'s who want in on the reward money, and a bearded, cigar-chomping, tattooed man riding a chopper.

Next in the Coens' oeuvre came *Miller's Crossing*, *Barton Fink*, and *The Hudsucker Proxy*. Not a single kidnapping story in the bunch. But the Coens had written *The Big Lebowski*—complete with alleged kidnapping—before they made *Fargo*. They'd intended to get *Lebowski* on film before *Fargo*, but Jeff Bridges, the actor Joel and Ethan wanted for the role of the aimless slacker known as The Dude (or Duderino if you're not into the whole brevity thing), was busy working on another film. So *Fargo* moved up in the queue.

Kidnapping, and The Dude's confusion regarding the abduction of a rich man's wife, pushed the Raymond Chandler–like *Lebowski* plot along. Like Chandler's Philip Marlowe, The Dude was the detective, trying to figure out what was happening while randomly getting beat up in the process. At times, we see The Dude's brain working in very Dude-like slow motion, as when he's in the rear of a black limousine with the other Lebowski—the one whose wife has been kidnapped, supposedly by nihilists—and he says, "There's a lot of angles. Lots of ins and outs, man."

The advantages of kidnapping plots are their numerous angles, their ins and outs, their alternating perspectives from people with competing interests. Once the victim has been snatched, the kidnapper wants the money, but the family may want to negotiate a lower price, and may or may not want the cops involved. The twist in both *The Big Lebowski* and *Fargo* is that the husband is the instigator. In *Lebowski*, the seemingly rich Jeffrey Lebowski hires the bowling- and White Russian–obsessed Jeffrey Lebowski to deliver the ransom money to the kidnappers. But we later learn there was no kidnapping, and the suitcase full of ransom money was filled with something else, stacks of paper maybe. The seemingly rich Lebowski is a fraud. In *Fargo*, the husband, also desperate for cash, puts his wife's precious life in the hands of criminals with guns and an idle wood chipper up north by the lake.

"We've always been interested in kidnapping," Joel told *Premiere* magazine, shortly before *Fargo* debuted in theaters. "We wanted to try something based on a real story, and tell it in a way that was very pared down."

◈◦◈

At the beginning of a writing project, the Coens typically work quickly, then ease off to grapple with a screenplay's structure. As Ethan told Goldman, "because we're doing our own thing, we can get stuck and literally grind to a halt and put it aside for a year even." That's how *Barton Fink* was born. The Boys were at an impasse with *Miller's Crossing*, unsure of how to finish that complex gangster tale. So instead of wallowing in writer's block, they wrote a screenplay about a screenwriter suffering from it. Most movies about writers—particularly successful writers—feature a scene showing the writer dashing off page after page of a manuscript, often underscored by jaunty or soaring music synched to the clacking of typewriter keys or the snap of a return carriage. Pages are stacked next to the writer. End of scene. Voilà! A novel!

Barton Fink is the dark side of that illusion. The title character (played by John Turturro) is a screenwriter living in a shitty Los Angeles hotel room with paper-thin walls. He spends most of his day *not* writing a wrestling picture the studio has assigned him. Instead, Fink daydreams about a girl at a beach and slips his feet in and out of shoes while tapping out tentative sentences. When he does write, Fink is awful: "We can faintly hear the cry of the fishmongers." While pacing the floor in the shithole with peeling wallpaper (oozing "goopus"), he's befriended by a serial killer disguised as an amiable insurance salesman (John Goodman). The movie ends when the serial killer shotguns a pair of cops, sets the hotel on fire, and screams at Fink—and the world—"I'll show you the life of the mind!"

Writer's block. It's a bitch.

So is life for most Coen characters. They die after being sliced in the neck, buried alive in a shallow grave, clobbered in the head, zapped by an air gun, thunked with an ax, or executed in the woods. Those lucky enough to survive may get kicked in the balls or have an ear chewed off. But the grisly deaths and gross injuries don't fully explain the sense of foreboding that hangs over numerous Joel and Ethan creations. In *Barton Fink, No Country for Old Men, A Serious Man,* and *The Man Who Wasn't There*, characters mope through life with faint hope of a happier tomorrow. Fink lives in Los Angeles but rarely sees the sun. The men battling Anton Chigurh in *No Country* seem resigned to defeat. The serious man in *A Serious Man* is seriously fucked—his wife leaves him, the rabbi won't make time for him, he's wrongly accused of unethical behavior at work, and he can't get it up for the hottie next door.

This Coensian darkness is best embodied in the black-and-white bleakness of Billy Bob Thornton as Ed Crane in *The Man Who Wasn't There*. Through a haze of cigarette smoke, we watch him shuffle through life in a barbershop and a bad marriage. We see him snip hair, endure another barber's inane small talk, and settle. His wife, Doris (Frances McDormand), enjoys silk underwear and perfume. From inside their dark bungalow in a small California town, he watches her flirt with a bigger man more alive with possibility. And what's worse, he doesn't protest. When she bathes, he stands with his back to her. She asks him to shave her legs. He complies. There's no hint of joy or sizzle between them. One afternoon, McDormand boozes herself into oblivion at a family picnic, then slumps over, asleep on a bed. The image of his besotted wife prompts this from

Thornton, who tells us—in a resigned voice-over—how the pair met on a double date. "It was only a couple weeks later she suggested we get married. I said, 'Don't you want to get to know me more?'

"She said, 'Why? Does it get better?'"

✧✦✧

Unlike *Miller's Crossing, Barton Fink, The Man Who Wasn't There, No County for Old Men,* and *A Serious Man, Fargo* doesn't wallow in darkness. In between shocking moments of violence, there are slivers of kindness. And in the end, there's hope.

Fargo begins with the claim of truth, that the story happened in 1987, that it will be told exactly as it happened to honor the dead. We watch the husband huddle with the bad guys in the bar, and then it's off to the suburbs, the car dealership, the break-in, and soon, the triple homicide. So far, so Coensian. But when we meet Brainerd police chief Marge Gunderson (McDormand), the earth shifts. She's a confident cop who stumbles through deep snow to do her duty, which is to figure out who killed a cop and two innocent bystanders on a lonely, country highway. When Marge, who is visibly pregnant, leans on her knees and stares at the ground, her deputy asks, "You see something down there, Chief?" Marge's deadpan response is one of the movie's funniest: "No, I just think I'm gonna barf." That and other moments in McDormand's first lengthy scene in the film touched Goldman's heart.

"When I saw *Fargo* the first time, after that scene I felt a sense of peace," Goldman wrote. "I have seen everything the Coens have done, and I know they are perverse. But I could not conceive that even the Coens could kill Marge. (My god, Frances McDormand is married to Joel. No way he offs his wife.) Which means I have faith I can give her my heart."

Other moviegoers must have felt the same way; Marge does touch our hearts. So does Norm, her husband, in a clunkier way. He's a quiet, dreamy fella. And look how much he loves her. He makes her eggs. Fetches Arby's for lunch. I bet he'll be a good father to their child. John Carroll Lynch, the actor who portrayed Norm, told me he thought the Marge–Norm love affair was rare in a Joel and Ethan script.

"The warmth of that relationship, the genuineness and love and non-ironic affection that they have for each other is the only relationship like that that I can think of in a Coen Brothers movie," Lynch said. "I guess the closest one would be *Raising Arizona*. The two of them have real love for each other, and it's also, in some ways, around pregnancy and around a baby."

When Marge crawls into bed with Norm, viewers get a break from kidnapping, murder, and bloodied snow. They're at home, and everything is going to be just fine.

"Both Marge and Norm gave the audience a safe haven, and often Joel and Ethan don't give audiences that in their movies," McDormand said. "[The couple is] this amazing unit. This idea that they have a great relationship is no mystery. There is an amazing sense of how well it works. You can laugh at the Midwest and think of it as simplistic, but there are couples out there that are like that."

The Coens' first stab at writing *Fargo* didn't amount to much more than sixty pages, ending at the scene where Shep Proudfoot pummels Carl Showalter for getting him in trouble with the cops. "We got stuck two-thirds of the way through writing this script," Ethan said. "We would fire up the computer for weeks, months, and the last typed line would still be 'Interior. Shep's Apartment. Carl is humping the escort.' For months we couldn't figure out what happens next?"

Interior. Shep's Apartment. Carl is humping the escort.

"It's true," Joel said. "We spent at least two or three depressing months turning the computer on and looking at that line."

Ethan laughed at the memory because the solution was so straightforward.

"That's child's play," he said. "Shep . . . would come in and beat the shit [out] of Steve Buscemi. For some reason, we didn't see it. So we started working on something else." That something else turned out to be *O Brother, Where Art Thou?* After working awhile with that script, they turned back to *Fargo*, decided Shep would indeed beat the shit out of Carl, and scenes started rolling again.

After the Coens revealed the horror of the wood chipper in the climax, the next several scenes wrapped up the story: Marge wonders how anyone could pulverize another human on such a beautiful day, Jerry gets

Shep Proudfoot's apartment—the setting of the Coens' bout with writers' block. (Photo by Lauri Gaffin)

nabbed at a drab motel outside of Bismarck, North Dakota, and then we're alone with Marge and Norm in their bedroom, wondering how their lives will change once the daughter- or son-of-a-Gunderson arrives in two months.

End of story? Not really.

Like mechanics troubled by the sound of a sputtering V8 engine, Joel and Ethan overhauled *Fargo* until it purred. In fairness, *Fargo* never leaked oil, but it did require tinkering to reach its full potential.

During my research for this book, I found a draft of the *Fargo* script at the University of California, Los Angeles. The special collections section of its library holds an ocean of film material, including oral histories of actors, personal papers, picture stills, lobby cards, publicity ephemera, film scores, and scripts. Inside box 1160, there's an undated version of *Fargo*.

This script—let's call it the UCLA draft—is an early draft. I know that because I found three other versions: 1994 casting script, 1995 shooting script, and the 1996 published script. The 1994 and 1995 scripts are archived at the Writers Guild Foundation Shavelson-Webb Library and the Margaret Herrick Library at the Academy of Motion Picture Arts and Sciences, both in Los Angeles. The 1994 and 1995 versions are only available for reading inside the library. Visitors can't make copies or click photos, but they can take notes. The UCLA script is available for purchase, and hell yes, I bought a copy.

The UCLA draft begins and ends like the filmed, edited, and scored movie. On the first page, the Coens assert the story is true, then over the next ninety-five pages, we meet the main characters; witness the kidnapping, the murder, and the investigation; and finally read how Marge solves the crimes. Jerry Lundegaard, Carl Showalter, Gaear Grimsrud, Marge Gunderson, Norm Gunderson, just about everybody we see in the 1996 movie are in this early draft. But what we don't get is a multidimensional Marge. She's sweet, she's smart, but something about her doesn't feel whole.

"I've always told them they write great women, but that there's always something missing from them," McDormand said. "They fall just short."

Joel and Ethan must have felt it too.

In this earliest known version of the screenplay, there's no phone call from high school friend Mike Yanagita while Marge is in bed with her husband, there's no secret meetup with Yanagita, and there's no revelation from a female friend that Yanagita lied about his wife's death from leukemia.

"She fought real hard, Marge," Yanagita (played by Stephen Park) tells Marge in the 1996 movie.

William H. Macy, who played Jerry Lundegaard, told me he was confused at first by that scene, which was added to the 1994 casting script. "Being a writer myself and dealing with a lot of scripts for the last thirty or forty years, the whole subplot of the Asian guy who takes her out to lunch and then hits on her—on one level you could look at that scene and say, 'That has nothing to do with the plot. I wonder why that was in?' It's a time-out. It's a sidebar. It does not move the plot forward at all.

"And yet, on another level, how brave of those guys to leave it in because it did on a different level, on a subconscious level, move the plot. It showed how Marge's world was getting so bizarre for her that things felt out of sync. She was more and more perplexed by the things she was seeing around her. In a weird way, I felt that scene belonged, but I guess if you're going to get Aristotelian about it, you would say, 'Perhaps that scene should have been cut,'" Macy said.

Weaving in Yanagita gives us a glimpse of Marge's life before she married Norm. At the hotel bar, she's married-but-single, enjoying the attention of a man but keeping him at a distance. She arrives wearing a frilly dress. Other than in her bedroom at home, it's the only time we see Marge in something other than a brown police officer's uniform. Yanagita also gives Marge insight into human deception. After her rendezvous with Yanagita, Marge chats on the phone with a friend. She tells the friend how sad it is that Yanagita's wife died. The friend gives Marge the real story. Yanagita never married. That woman he says was his wife? He stalked her. Yanagita is a desperate loser living in his parents' house. After this, we see Marge driving her prowler to the Hardee's drive-thru, then thoughtfully eating a breakfast sausage sandwich before returning to question Lundegaard at the car dealership.

In short, Yanagita adds emotional depth to Marge's otherwise placid existence. "She has an inner life that is not immediately evident but which keeps revealing itself," McDormand said. "As normal as she seems, there's something about her that people want to know more about because they don't fully understand her."

Marge doesn't fall short.

❧

Before they added Yanagita in later drafts, the Coens were stuck on what to do with Detective Sibert.

Described in the script as a "large black woman," Sibert is a Minneapolis cop who investigates homicides. Just as with Yanagita, Marge has a pair of phone calls with or about Sibert and one in-person interaction. She talks to Sibert from the pay phone inside the Radisson and calls her when Lundegaard flees the interview at the car dealership. "What the heck— I can't—I can't see his darn license," reads the UCLA script. "Well it's prob'ly his own car—he's drivin' a royal blue late-model Delta 88 . . . Yah,

Frances McDormand in makeup before her scene with Stephen Park as Mike Yanagita in a hotel bar. (Photo by Stephen Park)

he was real darn agitated . . . Oh for Pete's sake." (In the movie, Marge simply makes a phone call and says, "Detective Sibert please.")

After a brief detour, the UCLA script cuts to Marge walking inside a police station with a "toplit modern institutional hallway" wearing a parka that "goes SHWEEK-SHWEEK-SHWEEK as she walks." When Marge first sees Detective Sibert, Sibert is sharing a "loud laugh" with another officer. Then Sibert updates Marge on the case. The cops are searching for Lundegaard and aim to arrest Shep Proudfoot for assault. After Sibert makes a nod to Marge's pregnancy ("When're you due?"), the conversation turns to children. Marge asks if Sibert has kids; Sibert shows her a photo of Janet and Morgan, ages nine and three. Then Marge asks, "Where'd you get him that parka?"

SIBERT: "Right here Dayton's."
MARGE: "He's adorable."

SIBERT: "You can get those, you know. I believe they still sell those."
MARGE: "Oh yah?"

The scene is flat.

Unlike the Yanagita scene, the scene with Sibert advances the plot, but it's dull, filled with paint-by-numbers information. There's no shared history between Sibert and Marge. There's no tension. There's no spark of danger or wonder. It's just one self-satisfied mother sharing parenting tips with a mom-in-the-making. As Macy points out, what happens in the Yanagita scene chugs the film forward, but it happens inside Marge's head. Yanagita's duplicity about working for Honeywell ("Yah, if you're an engineer, yah, you could do a lot worse") and his imagined wife's death ignites a spark inside the small-town detective. *If Yanagita lied about his job and wife,* Marge wonders, *who else might be lying?*

Still, the Coens kept Sibert in the script through two subsequent re-writes: the 1994 casting script and the 1995 shooting script. (In the 1994 casting script, the Sibert–Gunderson encounter shifts from an office to a cafeteria. The spelling of her name varies from time to time as well; sometimes "Sibert" becomes "Siebert.")

The Boys hired Isabell Monk O'Connor to play Detective Sibert. "I believe I got the role because my classmate, Frances McDormand, wanted to have me do a part with her since I lived in Minneapolis at the time and they were shooting here," O'Connor told me.

O'Connor and McDormand had met at Yale School of Drama. O'Connor, a native of Maryland, graduated in 1981, one year ahead of the future Academy Award winner. "The girls hung out together, and that's how we got to be friendly," O'Connor said. "Franny just has a great, big old heart. She's just good, good people."

Before *Fargo*, O'Connor had small roles in a pair of Minnesota-made movies: *Grumpy Old Men* and *Untamed Heart*. She was also a member of the Guthrie Theater in Minneapolis, appearing in *Death of a Salesman*, *Medea*, *Uncle Vanya*, and many other productions. In 1990, she won an Obie Award for her portrayal of Gloucester in *Mabou Mines Lear*, a flip-the-script interpretation of *King Lear* by New York–based experimental theater company

Mabou Mines. Frank Rich of the *New York Times* called O'Connor's performance "dignified and passionate."

Five years after winning an Obie, O'Connor reunited with McDormand in Minneapolis. The Coens filmed the scene featuring the two female cops at the University of Minnesota, but when Joel and Ethan returned to New York to edit *Fargo*, they sliced out the only African American in the film.

The movie's sole Native American doesn't fare much better.

After serving time at Stillwater prison, Shep Proudfoot (Steve Reevis) lands a job as a mechanic at the car dealership where Lundegaard works. He's given Lundegaard the name of Carl Showalter, one of the prospective kidnappers, although he doesn't "vouch" for the other one. A stoic man with black hair pulled into a ponytail, Proudfoot wears blue coveralls with his first name embroidered on a patch. Chief Gunderson interrogates Proudfoot in a wood-paneled office off the shop floor, peppering him with questions about the triple homicide up north. The Boys give Proudfoot just four words of dialogue in the scene: "Nope." "Yup." "Nope." "So."

I didn't get a chance to talk to Reevis about his portrayal of the defiant Proudfoot. Born in Browning, Montana, on the Blackfeet Reservation in 1962, Reevis died in 2017. According to IMDb, he graduated from Haskell Indian Junior College in Lawrence, Kansas, then moved to Los Angeles in the late 1980s. He received an award from First Americans in the Arts in 1996 for his roles in *Fargo* and *Crazy Horse*, a made-for-television movie.

The Coens chose Reevis over several Minnesota-based Native American actors, but they didn't love everything about his performance. His natural voice wasn't deep or menacing. And the Coens wanted deep *and* menacing.

So they asked a white guy named Bruce Bohne to step in. A member of the acting ensemble at the Guthrie, Bohne played Deputy Lou, the not-so-bright cop who stands by the road while Chief Gunderson investigates the murders. During rehearsals, Reevis wasn't at the table read, so Bohne picked up his part. He remembers doing that for other actors who weren't present for the seated rehearsal. Later, the Coens approached Bohne about taking on an additional, uncredited role.

"They came to me and said that [Reevis] looked fantastic, but when they got down to the editing and sound, his voice didn't sound right to them," Bohne told me. "His voice didn't sound like it matched his big, fearsome character. So they said, 'Would you do that accent, that voice that you did at the table read?' I said, 'Sure, that sounds like fun.' It was my first looping job ever."

Bohne had spent time with Native folks living near the US and Canadian border. "Previously, I had been dating a woman up on the Nett Lake Indian Reservation, so I was familiar with their accents and rhythms, so reading Shep Proudfoot, I just talked like the people up on the reservation talked. They don't move their lips too much, and it resonates in the nose. Again, the Coen Brothers were just laughing about that, and I think that's why it turned out ultimately that they asked me to do his voice."

The UCLA script includes a scene, later cut from the movie, between Chief Marge Gunderson and one of her officers, Gary Olson.

> GARY: "So the Minneapolis PD says Shep kind of isn't saying who called him?"
>
> MARGE: "Kind of?"
>
> GARY: "They say he kind of doesn't talk at all. Not whole sentences and stuff."
>
> MARGE: "What do you mean? Is he a dumbbell?"

In subsequent revisions, Joel and Ethan smoothed off the edges. Instead of painting Gary and Marge as racists, the final draft gives Marge wiggle room. In the movie when Gary tells her Shep Proudfoot is a name, Marge simply says, "Uh-huh." It reads as distracted, not judgmental.

The UCLA script also included a Native American dream sequence wedged between scenes showing Carl pounding on a television with a fuzzy signal and Marge and Norm slipping under the covers for a pleasant sleep.

"FADE DOWN FROM WHITE But still white," the Coens wrote. "A native American in a war bonnet glides into frame and travels optically across it, his image slowly rotating as he does a war dance, his tomahawk raised high. The THUMP-thump-thump-thump is war drums, and we also hear a distant chant."

That image is followed by smoke curling up the poles of a tepee, an arm pointing a gun toward viewers, a silhouette of a man collapsing, then a pair of figures in a hotel room. "One is taller, one shorter. Facing them, and us, are two backlit women, each holding a sheet stretched in front of her, upon which her naked form is projected. The women dance sinuously in time with the thumping of toms. The war-bonneted Indian once again travels through frame."

As I read this passage two decades after the film's release, my head shook with disbelief. The trope of the war-mongering Native American is just too much. The Coens wisely axed it, but seemingly not out of any sense of moral righteousness.

During a 2009 conversation with film critic Elvis Mitchell onstage at Minneapolis's Walker Art Center, Mitchell told the Coens that race in their movies is more about comic tension than preachiness.

"Oh geez," Ethan said. "I don't even know that we deal with it."

Joel jumped in to defend their writing, saying they create stories featuring characters in specific places with specific problems. "Constructing a story that's supposed to be a comment about race, per se," Joel said, "that's something that wouldn't be interesting to us, that the story is geared towards that."

Added Ethan, "We just kind of don't give a shit about people's sensitivities. You know what I mean?"

Scenes showcasing the winter bleakness of *Fargo* are also missing from the UCLA draft. In this earliest version, there's no Jerry freaking out with the ice scraper or Mr. Mohra telling the cop about the guy going crazy up there at the lake. Both were added in 1994, giving viewers an indelible sense of Minnesota as a bone-chilling place in winter.

Still, this early version is crammed with local references. Jerry hooks up with the kidnappers at a fictional bar called the Jolly Troll Tavern (not the King of Clubs), named after a real-life suburban cafeteria of the Coens' youth that offered Scandinavian smorgasbord. The lead kidnapper is given a variation on the name of a former Minnesota governor, Carl Rolvaag. (He becomes Carl Showalter.) The father-in-law watches the "Norstars," Minnesota's beloved National Hockey League franchise that departed to Dallas in 1993. (In the film, he's watching the University of Minnesota Gophers hockey team.) Minneapolis television newscasters Dave Moore and Bill Carlson appear in this early draft, as does Rudy Perpich, another former governor. None survived the movie's final cut.

By November 2, 1994, the script was getting closer to what the Coens would shoot when principal photography began two and a half months later. With the addition of the Yanagita and Mohra scenes, and a stolen television scene later cut from the movie, the screenplay had grown to 104 pages from the 95 pages of the UCLA draft.

(The stolen television scene featured Grimsrud removing a Sony Trinitron from his ex-girlfriend's home. As he unplugs the machine and hauls it out to the car, she yells at him, with a weeping three-year-old at her side: "Put that down! Where's my checks?! You're behind two checks, you sonofabitch! Put that down! You fuckeen asshole. Put that down!" The scene ends with a plea to the father's conscience: "You selfish fuckeen asshole! What is Kyle supposed to watch? Your own flesh and blood!")

In the days just before the script was submitted to the Writers Guild of America library, a Coen colleague—line producer John Cameron—hopped a Northwest Airlines flight from Los Angeles to meet with Minnesota Film Board staffers in Minneapolis. A breathless film board memo, dated October 24, 1994, detailed Cameron's impending arrival, noting the made-in-Minnesota movie would feature "a woman sherriff [sic] in a small town," to be filmed beginning on "Jan 23 95 through February" featuring the following locations: "car dealership, cabin in woods." Over the next couple of months, the Coens completed preproduction, which included location scouting, set design, securing a production office in St. Paul's Midway neighborhood, and quietly, behind the scenes, editing and rewriting parts of the screenplay.

By January 20, 1995, the script had reached 113 pages. Days later, principal photography began.

Project Title: *Fargo*

Company: Coen Bros.
Dist. / Network: Working Title Films

Name, Title: John Cameron, Line Producer
Address:
City: _____ **State** _____ **Zip** _____

Phone 1 212.666.2404   **Fax** 212.749.1582 FAX

Phone 2 _____   **Fed Ex** _____

CONTACT #2
Name 2 [   ]

Address 2
City 2 [   ]
State 2 [   ] Zip [   ]

MFB PROJECT MANAGER

Type: ☒ Feature ☐ TV: Segment ☐ Industrial/Corporate ☐ Short Film ☐ Local
☐ TV: Movie ☐ TV: Special ☐ Music Video ☐ National ☐ International
☐ TV: Series ☐ Commercial ☐ Documentary ☐ Regional

Status Hot   **Info Sent** ☐ MPG   ☐ Location Folders: Specific ☐ Computer lists ☐ Other
Priority [2]   ☐ Location Folders: Generic ☐ Crew/Contact Lists ☐ Tourism Info

Locations needed: car dealership, cabin in woods

Schedule: shoot to start on Jan 23 '95 through February

SCOUT Dates? 10/25/94 - 10/28/94
Comps ☒ Hotel ☒ Vehicle ☒ Northwest ☐ Meals
Hotel Holiday Inn Metrodome
Total room nights 3
days in vehicle 3

Total Budget $6 _____ **MN Budget** _____

The Story Action Needed

10/26/94 RA/KP met with John Cameron, very early in process (he hasn't even had time to break down scipt for locations etc) he'll be here through Friday; wants to see hotels etc.
10/24/94, 5:39:59 PM Bob Graf got a call from Gilly, they want to meet withhim; they also called Julie Hartley;
10/24/94 coming tomorrow afternoon, wants to talk crew, etc. will give us the secret of the story then!!, thru lv Friday - LAX;
10/4/94 9/22 issue of Reporter page 28, a note saying that they are "talking about directing" this picture, not sure if it is the same one;
8/26/94 tip from Jule Jappe, heard that they were looking at Fargo (maybe written for Fargo)

Personnel:
Writer _____
Director _____
Producers John Cameron
Executive Producer _____
Line Producer / UPM Gilly Ruben
Designer/Art Director _____
Loc. Manager _____
Production Exec. _____
Others _____
Stars _____

10/26/94

Production request form from the Minnesota Film Board, October 26, 1994

When *Fargo* was published in 1996, Ethan's introduction grappled with the philosophical concept of truth. He begins by relating a story of how "a large Negress" tried to steal his grandmother's wallet from her New York City apartment. The woman had entered on a pretense, and when his grandmother's back was turned, the intruder reached into a purse for the wallet. Grandmother caught her in the act, the pair struggled, and the wallet was dropped.

"Grandma told the story of the large Negress many times and we never tired of it—the innocent ringing of the doorbell, the meeting, the startling character reversal, then the drama of the slapfight," Ethan wrote.

Ethan remembers the story vividly, its details evolving, becoming more outrageous with each telling during their childhood. It wasn't until he was older that he began to wonder about its veracity. Why did the woman ascend twelve floors to Grandma's apartment when there were plenty of opportunities for theft on lower floors? How did the woman flee?

The essay continues for a couple more pages, ruminating on truth, storytelling, and the inevitable merging of the two. "People crawl across this thin crust to arrive at some improbable place where they meet other crawling people," he wrote. "They do various improbable things with and to each other, and later tell stories about the things they did, stories having greater and lesser fidelity to truth."

The essay ends with the references to Ford, Hardee's, and Siberia, followed by a confession.

"It aims to be both homey and exotic," Ethan wrote. "And pretends to be true."

chapter 2

This Is a True Story

The Five Words That Changed Fargo

"Pilot Denies Disposing of His Wife in Chipper."

—*New York Times*

"This is a true story."

—*Fargo*

Pretends to be true or is true?

The Coens have always wanted it both ways. When writing screenplay introductions, speaking to reporters, or chatting off the record with actors, *Fargo* was fiction. But when selling the movie to audiences and critics, the kidnap-murder tale wasn't simply a story.

It actually happened.

THIS IS A TRUE STORY.

Those words, in bold, capital letters, begin Joel and Ethan's sixth film. Then: "The events depicted in this film took place in Minnesota in 1987. At the request of the survivors, the names have been changed. Out of respect for the dead, the rest has been told exactly as it occurred."

When a director begins with the written word, it's more than a scene setter. The written word is a signal to the audience. *Pay attention. This is important.*

Alfred Hitchcock opened *Psycho* with a sweeping shot of a desert metropolis followed by these words:

PHOENIX, ARIZONA

After a quick fade, we see more downtown office buildings, then:

FRIDAY, DECEMBER THE ELEVENTH

Just before Hitchcock's creepy camera famously ducks under an open window of a hotel room occupied by Janet Leigh and her lover, we are confronted by this incredible specificity:

TWO FORTY-THREE P.M.

Hitchcock wants us to remember the place, day of the week, date, and time. A little later, when Leigh pockets a sleazy oilman's big wad of cash, we know her boss won't learn about the missing money until the bank opens on Monday. Then when she decides to return the cash—along with the $500 she spent on a car—we breathe a sigh of relief. After a shower and a good night's sleep at the Bates Motel, she can return to Phoenix and make things right.

A little over a decade after the release of Hitchcock's classic thriller, Kim Henkel and Tobe Hooper, the writers of *The Texas Chain Saw Massacre*, begin their film with words. Against a dark screen, they warn viewers about a "tragedy" that claimed the lives of five people. "It is all the more tragic in that they were young," the written, on-screen introduction continues. "But, had they lived very, very long lives, they could not have expected, nor would they have wished to see as much of the mad and macabre as they were to see that day. For them an idyllic summer afternoon drive became a nightmare."

Then, without claiming veracity, but certainly implying it, Henkel and Hooper refer to the deaths as "one of the most bizarre crimes in the annals of American history." Now they've got my attention. "The Texas Chain Saw Massacre." The screen returns to darkness, followed by a specific date: "August 18, 1973." As the screen turns dark yet again, we hear the sounds of a shovel digging up dirt.

Fargo's beginning is more succinct: forty-three words compared to 114 for *The Texas Chain Saw Massacre*. However, the key elements are the same. Both picture openings include a date, an explicit or implicit claim to truth, and language suggesting filmmaker research. In *Chain Saw Massacre*, one imagines Henkel and Hooper combing through FBI records, trying to determine Leatherface's rightful place in the pantheon of serial killers. In *Fargo*, the Coens suggest they've actually spoken to family members of those killed: "At the request of survivors . . ."

When *Fargo* was released, Ethan and Joel stayed on script. During interviews with reporters, The Brothers stuck with the assertion that the movie was based on a true crime. In an interview with *Premiere* magazine, a reporter asked, "How close was the script to the actual event?"

Joel's answer: "Pretty close."

On television, the Coens made a similar claim. As they sat across a table from Charlie Rose on PBS, the host began the give-and-take with a straightforward query. "Here is my first question," asked Rose, throwing his hands in the air and enunciating the following words slowly. "This movie was . . . not based . . . on . . ."

The producers cut to a two-shot of Ethan and Joel. Ethan, wearing a long sleeve, gray shirt, smirks at Rose. Joel, wearing a black suit without a tie and looking like a second-rate Las Vegas magician, appears poker-faced. Ethan waits for Rose to finish the question, but it's clear he knows exactly where Rose is headed. The camera stays on Ethan and Joel as Rose wraps up his query.

CHARLIE ROSE: ". . . an . . . actual . . . crime."

ETHAN COEN: "Who says?"

CHARLIE ROSE: "Was it?"

ETHAN COEN: "Yeah."

Frances McDormand, who is off camera, can be heard laughing faintly.

CHARLIE ROSE: "This story is completely based on a real event."

At this point, Ethan leans back in his chair and then moves forward to explain. Before he has a chance to begin, Joel interrupts with a definitive answer.

"Yeah, the story is," Joel says.

Then he adds, "We weren't interested in making a documentary. The characters are really inventions based on an outline of events. So we invented the characters, and they're really our creation and the creation of the actors who played the parts."

So let's recap.

Regarding the truthiness of *Fargo*, we have a "pretty close," a "yes," and a "yes" with quibbles. The quibbles are clear. Joel is telling us the Lundegaards, Gustafsons, Gundersons, Showalter, Grimsrud, and Proudfoot are fictional characters based on *an outline of events*—that is, real people doing real things. What are those events? And why did the Coens tapdance so vigorously to convince us that somewhere, in the snowy Great Plains, there was a horrific husband who hired men to do unspeakable things to his wife?

❖

On the morning of Wednesday, March 6, 1963, an intruder murdered Carol Thompson in her St. Paul home. She'd been home alone, wearing just a nightgown, when a man confronted her upstairs and knocked her unconscious with a rubber hose. As the man rifled through her dresser drawers, Carol woke up, grabbed a mop, and started hitting him. She hurried downstairs and tried to rush out the front door, but a chain latch prevented a quick escape. Her assailant hit her with the butt of a gun, then grabbed a knife and stabbed her in the neck. Carol managed to open the door and rush outside, the metal blade protruding from her neck. As she made her way down an alley, she touched a nearby garage, leaving bloodstains on the painted wood. She stopped at a neighbor's house four doors away, banged, and waited. When her neighbor opened the door, Carol was covered in blood, unrecognizable, and babbling.

Three hours later, the mother of four was dead.

"It scared the hell out of everybody," William Swanson, author of *Dial M: The Murder of Carol Thompson*, told me. "This is not where these kinds of crimes happen. It was brutal beyond imagination."

Carol Thompson's death shook the Twin Cities to the core. Thompson lived in "fashionable" Highland Park, a safe, quiet area full of middle-class homes. She was married, deeply involved in her children's lives, church, the community. She was just like the rest of us.

Innocent. Decent. Hardworking.

What the heck had happened?

Carol Thompson had married the wrong man. She had judged Tilmer Eugene Thompson, whom everyone called T. Eugene, a loving man. He was the father of their children, Margaret, Amy, Patty, and Jeff, who were six to thirteen years old at the time of her death. A respected attorney by day, T. Eugene was a philanderer by night, often meeting up with a younger woman at a local motel. When his lover threatened to cut off the affair, saying she wanted someone who might make a life with her, T. Eugene asked for time to make things right. Just give me eleven months, he told her. Then he purchased massive life insurance policies and arranged for Carol's murder. Eventually, he found a man who agreed to execute his plan, which encompassed hiding in the basement, thwacking Carol with a rubber hose, then drowning her in the bathtub to make the death appear accidental. T. Eugene promised to leave a side door unlocked and water in the tub. He also moved a bedroom telephone to another room and took the family dog, a dachshund named Schatzie, to the veterinarian for donation to another family.

The problem with T. Eugene's scheme, as with the plans of so many criminals, was that the guy he hired didn't follow orders. ("This is a no rough stuff type of deal," Jerry Lundegaard of *Fargo* told two thugs over longnecks at a dingy bar. The bad boys ignored Jerry's orders, turning the next several days into an incredibly violent, rough stuff type of deal.) Instead of executing T. Eugene's plan, the original hired thug hired a second thug, a roofing contractor named Dick W. C. Anderson. Instead of drowning Carol in the bathtub after hitting her in the head, Anderson rifled through her things looking for stuff to steal, which gave her time to wake up and run for her life.

At the time of the murder, eight-year-old Joel and five-year-old Ethan lived about fifteen miles west of the red brick Thompson home on Hillcrest Avenue. For ten months, the news of Carol Thompson's bloody demise, the arrest of her husband, and the lengthy trial that followed dominated local news. Headlines like "Thompson Murder Story Woven with Details of Bumbling, Greed" filled newspapers. The *Saturday Evening Post*, a respected national news weekly, sent a reporter to the Twin Cities to write a five-page story titled: "Why Was Carol Killed?" The subhead: "At first it looked like the act of a maniac. But then came rumors of a fortune involved. And one man told a chilling story soon to unfold in court." Photos accompanying the article show Carol's husband sporting a buzz cut with a slight grin on his face, holding a photo of his dead wife; the bloodied garage; the murder suspect working at home.

At T. Eugene Thompson's trial, lawyers tussled over jury selection and points of law. The prosecutor described Carol as "a warm friend, a gracious hostess, and a sought-after guest" who was active in her children's lives, serving as a leader in Girl Scout and Brownie troops. He also spoke, in exhaustive detail, about the many life insurance policies, totaling $1,055,000, the defendant had amassed in the months leading up to Carol's death. In the end, the jury convicted Thompson. The trial and conviction of T. Eugene Thompson was covered in newspapers across the nation, interrupted only by the assassination of President John F. Kennedy in Dallas two weeks prior to the verdict.

In 2015, Thompson died of natural causes. The *New York Times* deemed him worthy of an obituary. Its headline: "T. Eugene Thompson Dies at 88; Crime Stunned St. Paul." Before publication, a *Times* reporter rang up Joel Coen and asked if the sensational murder served as an inspiration for *Fargo*.

"It's completely made up," Joel told the reporter. "Or, as we like to say, the only true thing about it is that it's a story."

⋈

During filming, the Coens also debunked the truthfulness of *Fargo*. After all, the actors had read the script and were curious about the movie's opening printed words, appearing on the screen for the audience to absorb. One day, William H. Macy got up the nerve to ask the Coens about it. "Tell me a little bit about the actual case." *No, it's just made up*, he was told. The actor clarified his question, asking, "No, the story that it's based on." *It's not based on any story. We just made it up.* "Guys, it says at the beginning of the script 'based on a true story.'"

THE BOYS: "Well, it's not."

MACY: "You can't do that."

THE BOYS: "Why not?"

MACY: "Because you're saying something that's not true."

THE BOYS: "The whole movie is not true. We made it all up. It's a movie. It's not true."

MACY: "Okay. Okay."

It wasn't the first time Joel and Ethan toyed with their audience, like a cat tapping a mouse between its claws before biting the head off its prey. In the introduction to *The Hudsucker Proxy* screenplay, for example, a fictional film studies professor from the University of Iowa interviews Hollywood mogul and *Hudsucker* producer Joel Silver for *Cine Quarterly*. Silver claims that Ethan asked to star in the movie, going so far as to shoot a screen test. When asked about its quality, Silver termed it "goddamned embarrassing . . . it was like the early days of talkies. Ethan is lumbering around on this pathetic little set they've mocked up, with his flat Midwestern voice, chopping the air with his hands, these stiff gestures, I mean, Richard Nixon doing a love scene. Stiffo."

The entire exchange is completely made up, of course, and I get the sense this is Ethan poking fun at himself for his on-screen performance in *Henry Kissinger: Man on the Go* or *Lumberjacks at Play*. If so, good on him.

For *Collected Screenplays 1*, the Coens claimed the book's introduction was written by Roderick Jaynes, the person credited with editing Joel and Ethan's first six films. Jaynes is a pseudonym, another Coensian prank. Joel and Ethan edit their own films, only occasionally hiring outsiders to help (mostly when there's a looming deadline). When *Blood Simple* was released in 1984, the Coens didn't want to appear to have done everything themselves, so they invented the name Roderick Jaynes and gave him credit as film editor. (It wasn't until *Fargo* was nominated for a film editing Oscar that the secret was revealed.)

In the introduction to *Collected Screenplays 1*, the Coens present Jaynes as a stuffy Englishman, writing from his home in Haywards Heath, Sussex, sipping tea and complaining about screenplays as an art form. "The utility or interest of a motion picture script seems nil," Jaynes writes. "It is not a literary artifact, not having been written for publication and therefore never attracting the grade of author who would merit it. Scenarists are inevitably amateurs, boobies, and hacks. Their scripts are invariably shoddily bound and shot right through with errors of spelling and punctuation—not to speak of the lapses of taste. At best the scriptwriter is a student of writing rather than a writer *per se*; he is like a child scraping away at his scales on the violin."

Instead, Jaynes argues, it is the film editor who deserves praise. "It is the organization of moving images that is the very art of cinema, and true authorship resides in the hand that wields not the pen, but the razor," he writes.

Ah Jaynes, slurp some more Earl Grey and stare out the window at the English countryside, you tottering fool.

⟡

The Carol Thompson murder case has several similarities to the tale depicted in *Fargo*. Both involve lying, scheming businessmen hiring ruffians to kill or kidnap their wives. T. Eugene outsources Carol's murder to a felon, who instead of perpetrating the crime himself, finds someone else to do it—similar to Shep Proudfoot, the *Fargo* mechanic, recommending one kidnapper, who in turn brings in an unvouched-for accomplice. In both cases, the man who wasn't directly hired by the husband botches the job. In the Thompson case, the knife-in-the-neck completely undermined T. Eugene's plan for a death meant to look accidental. In *Fargo*, the Swedish kidnapper murders the wife at the cabin in the woods, despite Lundegaard's insistence on no rough stuff, ultimately leading to the collapse of his plan. And finally, both assaults occur in midmorning, after a hardworking wife and mother has cared for her husband and children, only to be attacked by evil intruders hired by her husband.

Details from a second sensational crime may have also found their way into *Fargo*. In July 1972, when Ethan and Joel were in their mid- to late teens, a thin, white-haired woman named Virginia Piper was kidnapped by armed gunmen in Orono, Minnesota, a rich suburb about thirteen miles west of the Coen home. It was a Thursday—the day the cleaning ladies tidied up the Piper home—and Virginia was outside working in the garden. Gardening kept her busy while the hired help vacuumed and the like. Suddenly, one of the cleaners rushed outside and shouted, "Oh, those men!"

Virginia, whom friends called Ginny, went inside and encountered a pair of masked men pointing guns at her. They asked about a safe. Ginny said the family didn't have one. They asked about jewelry. "You may have three of my pieces that are upstairs," she replied. "That's all I have."

"Where's your old man?"

"He's not here," she said. "He's at the office." Ginny's husband was Harry C. Piper, CEO of a prominent Minneapolis investment firm, Piper Jaffray.

"Okay, Mrs. Piper, you're coming with us."

The men tied up the cleaning ladies inside the Piper home. Then one of them poked a gun into Ginny's back, placed a pillowcase over her head, and shoved her in the back seat of a car. The two assailants jumped in the front seat and headed north, not stopping for several hours. Thus began Ginny's three-day ordeal as a kidnap victim.

Unlike Jean Lundegaard, Ginny lived. These cutthroats didn't botch the jewel they'd snatched from a garden on the banks of Lake Minnetonka. One of the men huddled with the blindfolded Ginny at Jay Cooke State Park, near Duluth. Dressed in slacks and a blazer, Ginny shivered through the night. So did her assailant.

"We just sort of sat there for two days," Piper recalled. "One of the kidnappers was in my attendance all that time. I was handcuffed the entire time."

Meanwhile, the other kidnapper demanded $1 million in twenty-dollar bills from Harry Piper. Piper had called the FBI, but he also followed the kidnappers' instructions. He drove to a hole-in-the-wall Minneapolis bar and left the fifty thousand twenties in a 110-pound duffel bag in his car. As Piper walked inside to make a call from the bar's pay phone, one of the kidnappers—or an accomplice—removed the bag full of cash from Piper's car.

After getting the money, the criminals held up their end of the deal. They alerted authorities to the whereabouts of Ginny Piper, still handcuffed to a tree at the state park near Lake Superior. Ginny expected police to arrive shortly after dawn the next day, but hours and hours passed. She remained alone, the handcuffs digging into her wrists.

"I figured nobody would ever find me again," she said.

Finally, off in the distance she heard what she thought was the sound of a car door slamming. "I yelled, 'Help!' and it was the FBI," she said. "And five of them came running through the underbrush. I've never been so glad to see people as I was to see them."

The crime generated big headlines in an era when headlines still mattered. So did two subsequent trials, when the men accused of the kidnapping were tried, but not convicted, of forcing a housewife into a car at gunpoint and taking her off to a secluded location.

It's hard to imagine that Joel and Ethan didn't hear about Ginny Piper's abduction through the media and remember cinematic details like the covering of the victim's head with a pillowcase, shoving the innocent housewife into the rear of a car, and whisking her away to a wooded area, where one of the kidnappers stayed with the victim through a cold night in northern Minnesota. Similar details found their way into the *Fargo* screenplay and the abduction of Jean Lundegaard by Gaear Grimsrud and Carl Showalter. "From the back seat we hear whimpering," the Coens wrote. "Grimsrud twists to look. Jean lies bound and curled on the back seat underneath a tarpaulin."

⋇

To Joel and Ethan, it didn't matter if *Fargo* was true or not. What matters is they told us it was true. And that assertion of truth, articulated in the film's first moments and defended in interviews with reporters and public appearances, made *Fargo* a turning point.

Whereas *Blood Simple, Raising Arizona, Miller's Crossing*, and *The Hudsucker Proxy* were self-consciously noir, comedy, gangster, and mid-century screwball comedy films, respectively, *Fargo* was a crime drama with quirky detours and an unconventional climax. Its protagonist didn't appear until thirty-three minutes into the film.

Instead of showing the other kids in the sandbox the cool filmmaking techniques the Coens had mastered, *Fargo* turned its back on Hollywood's past to tell a story about a small group of people in an odd, cold place, speaking in a way never heard before in American cinema. To do this, The Brothers nearly stopped moving the camera for the first time in their professional lives.

"We wanted to make it much more observational than, say, *Barton Fink* or *The Hudsucker Proxy*," said cinematographer Roger Deakins. "The camerawork is much more restrained, really. There's not a lot of fast tracks and flowery camerawork and camera moves." For a while, the Coens flirted with the notion of not moving the camera *at all*. Then, Ethan said, they came to the realization "that 'purist' attitude was pretty stupid."

(I haven't met either Coen, but I like Ethan best because he often says honest stuff like this. He's also funnier, more off the cuff and less cerebral than his older brother. Not only was he willing to don a tutu in a remake of *Lassie Come Home* called *Ed, a Dog*, he also lied to Princeton University. According to *Playboy*, he took a leave of absence during his undergraduate years, then reapplied, but was tardy filling out the paperwork. Ethan's excuse? His arm got "blown off in a hunting accident." Princeton sent him to a therapist before allowing him to enroll again.)

The Brothers eventually dropped the camera-never-moves idea, choosing "to move the camera sometimes, but in such a way that the viewer does not notice it," Joel said. "We didn't want to make the camera movement dramatic like we'd done in the past because we did not want to emphasize the action, make it seem either dramatic or irrational."

This observational style is on display early in the film, when the Lundegaard family is seen eating dinner in their suburban Minneapolis home. The actors are William H. Macy as Jerry; Kristin Rudrüd as his wife, Jean; Harve Presnell as Wade Gustafson, the father-in-law; and Tony Denman as Scotty, the teenage son. The camera is placed on a staircase, its wood banister slanting across a small portion of the left side of the screen. In most films, this would be an establishing shot, one that lets the audience know where the scene is taking place. Depending on the movie, it might last about three or four seconds. But not this shot. This shot of the Lundegaards eating dinner is held for twelve seconds. In a movie, twelve seconds with no camera movement and very little action or dialogue is an eternity. Here's what we see in those twelve seconds: Macy sits slightly hunched and nearly motionless. Rudrüd, wearing a pink sweater, faces her on-screen father, wired into his words and the feelings of everyone around her. Presnell is erect, stern, his back to the camera. Denman rocks back and forth impatiently in his chair. Because the camera is perched on the second or third step of the staircase, we are looking down on the family. The angle and the long, still shot encourage us to observe the everyday details of Lundegaard life: the tiny house plants next to the sofa, the ketchup bottle on the table, the patio door, and most of all, the "Home Sweet Home" embroidery on the wall behind the actors.

"You're just outside of the conversation a little bit," Deakins said. "The photography and image doesn't draw attention to itself, and you're just immersed." Whereas *Hudsucker* employs a self-conscious visual style, *Fargo* has a "slightly observational feel to it," he added.

This continues throughout the movie. In the scene between Mike Yanagita and Marge Gunderson at the hotel bar, the conversation is shot over each actor's shoulder, as if we, the viewers, are in the next booth,

Roger Deakins, *Fargo* cinematographer, taking a walk in the woods during a break in filming. (Photo by Lauri Gaffin)

eavesdropping. The stillness throughout *Fargo* is a dramatic change from earlier Coen Brothers films. In the screenplay for *Blood Simple*, The Boys were explicit about how the camera should move and the kind of shot (wide, close-up, extreme close-up, point-of-view) they envisioned for each moment. The first twenty pages of the published screenplay include specific references to camera movements such as pullbacks, tracking, tracking forward, match cuts, reverse angles, tilt downs, characters entering frames, and characters speaking off-screen. Write Joel and Ethan: "The camera is tracking forward, past Marty, to frame on the window." And: "At the cut the music and all the other bar noise drops out. We hear only the rhythmic whir of the fan. We tilt down from the ceiling fan to frame Marty, tilted back in his desk chair, staring at the fan."

This specificity yields spectacular results. *Blood Simple* is a taut thriller with camera movements that add to the drama, including a purposely shaky tracking forward shot early in the film. It occurs near the end of an attempted rape scene. Marty has snuck into Ray's bungalow, hid, and surprised a still-in-her-nightgown Abby (McDormand). From behind, he grips her mouth with one beefy hand while grabbing her waist with the other hand. As he pushes her through a flimsy screen door, Marty whispers, "Let's do it outside . . . in nature." As he moves her out of the house, the Coens switch perspectives. We're on the sidewalk in front of the bungalow and running fast toward the pair at a low angle. It's as if the filmmakers tied a camera to a dog's back and ordered it to run. What they really did was bolt a camera to a block of wood, attach metal grips to each end, and tell a couple of crew members to hang on to each end and hustle toward the actors. Joel learned this trick while working on Sam Raimi's *The Evil Dead*, a horror movie featuring a man with a chain saw and a shotgun blasting hellish figures to damnation. In *Blood Simple*, the shaky cam is four seconds of terror as we wonder whether Abby will escape the horrifying hold of her rapist husband. As the shaky cam nears the pair, there's a quick over-the-shoulder cut, then we're back to a close-up of husband and wife fighting. Still in his grip, Abby snaps her husband's index finger like a pencil—we hear it crack—she pauses, and as he winds up to smack her, she kicks him in the balls. He places his hands on his knees and vomits, defeated.

The action sequences in *Fargo* lack the camera wizardry of *Blood Simple*, yet they aren't any less thrilling. During the tense, parking ramp confrontation between Carl Showalter and Wade Gustafson, in which they bicker over the exchange of cash and Wade's daughter, the Coens embrace a more staid approach to the camerawork. At the beginning of the sequence, they employ subtle zooms as each character delivers lines. But once we're in about waist-high, it's just a simple back-and-forth.

"Where's my damn daughter? No Jean, no money."

Cut.

"Drop that fucking money."

Cut.

"No Jean, no money."

Cut.

"Is this a fucking joke here?"

Pulls gun. Shoots.

The no-frills cinematography choices are easy to miss on first viewing, but when contrasted with the Coens' earlier work, the camera movement is much more restrained and contributes to a sense of truthfulness. The assertion of truth in the film's opening doesn't just influence cinematography choices; it also allows more freedom in the storytelling, especially the climax.

"The fact-based nature of the film liberated the storytelling," Joel said. "If an audience believes that something's based on a real event, it gives you permission to do things they might otherwise not accept: you can have a murder film that doesn't necessarily lead up to a clever action sequence, and the audience will still go with you. Whereas if they went in expecting a thriller, they'd feel cheated."

⋇

Now *that* is true.

Fargo lacks a stunning climax. There is no knife-through-the-hand (*Blood Simple*), fireplace-shovel-to-the-head (*Miller's Crossing*), or serial killer with a shotgun stomping down a flaming hallway (*Barton Fink*). There is simply a pregnant police chief shooting a suspect in the calf on a frozen lake. Oh sure, there's the surprising appearance of a man's leg being fed into a wood chipper. There is that. But compared to most kidnapping-for-hire thrillers, *Fargo* is understated, philosophical, even hopeful. As Marge drives to the county jail with her catch handcuffed in the rear of the prowler, she grapples with the mess she's untangled. The lovely score has faded. We're alone with Marge (McDormand) and Grimsrud (Peter Stormare). She ticks off the murders he's committed. He fails to respond.

"There's more to life than a little money, you know," she says.

No music swells. We're alone with her words.

"Don't you know that?"

Pause.

"And here ya are."

Pause.

"And it's a beautiful day."

Of course, the scene that precedes this quiet exchange is one of the most gruesome—and memorable—scenes in the entire film: the wood chipper. It is a shocking and stunning moment, but unlike a typical movie climax, it doesn't explain anything for the viewer. We don't know why the quiet, murderous Swede chopped up his victims like firewood and stuffed them in the grinder. Marge is left searching for answers as she drives Grimsrud to the police station. Still, the movie's most violent, most outrageous scene is also one that lends credence to claims of *Fargo* as true story.

In interviews about *Fargo*, Peter Stormare was anything but mum on the topic of the film's veracity. "It is a true story, but it might not have happened," he said. "[The Coens] have taken their years of growing up in Minnesota, maybe stories they heard later on when they moved to New York, and put it all together like one event, like an autobiography. I asked about the wood chipper, and they said, 'Actually, there was a killing with a wood chipper.' It's bizarre. Then I got information that there had been about sixty-three. So there is a Marge somewhere out there."

Had Joel and Ethan taken Stormare's body count of sixty-three for inspiration, their movie might have been titled *Minnesota Wood Chipper Massacre*. But the chipper isn't an instrument of death, wielded by a murderous monster in the woods, splattering blood on the lonely countryside.

It's a body disposal tool, designed to reduce limbs to red-tinged dust—
and shock the audience. And although the Coens are known to reveal
their ghastly imaginations at times, they're kind enough to shield us from
the darkest details of this body disposal. Would a torso fit in the chipper?
What about a head? Neck first or hair first?

Too gruesome?

Not for Richard B. Crafts. In 1986, the Eastern Airlines pilot murdered
his wife, Helle Crafts, then sliced her up with a chain saw and fed her re-
mains into a rented wood chipper. She also worked for Eastern, as a flight
attendant. Just a decade earlier, he'd spotted her at work. They'd flirted
inside jets and airports, fell for each other, and finally committed to a life
together in Newtown, Connecticut. Born Helle Lorck Nielsen in the Copenhagen suburb of Charlottenlund, Helle changed her name to Crafts when
the couple married in 1979. In the months before her death, Helle sus-
pected Richard of cheating on her with other flight attendants. So she
hired a private detective. After friends became concerned in late 1986 that
they hadn't seen or heard from Helle for several weeks, Richard said she
had returned to Denmark to visit relatives. Local police bought Richard's
story, but the private detective didn't. He contacted state police, who
searched Crafts's car and discovered tooth and hair fragments belonging
to Helle. Although her body was never found, that forensic evidence was
enough to convict Crafts of murder. Prosecutors didn't just rely on scien-
tific analysis of tiny body fragments to convince the jury of the pilot's
guilt; they also felt the need to prove the power of the chipper.

"Perhaps the goriest detail has been the prosecution's move to be allowed
to play a videotape in court that shows a dead pig being cut up by a wood
chipper," according to a *New York Times* article from May 1988. "The tape
is intended to show the machine's destructive power." Inevitably, most
newspaper headlines about the crime featured its two most unusual elements: the profession of the accused and the body-disposal mechanism.

"Pilot Denies Disposing of His Wife in Chipper" and "Pilot Convicted of
Killing Wife in Wood-Chipper Murder Trial" read a pair of Associated Press
headlines from the period. Both stories appeared in the *New York Times*,
available for thirty-five cents in the city Joel and Ethan then called home.

Tony Denman, the actor who played Scotty Lundegaard, the teenager whose mother is snatched away from him, hadn't seen a Coen Brothers movie before appearing in one. When he watched the story of his fictional mother's kidnapping and murder at a Los Angeles screening, he wasn't even old enough to drive. When I interviewed Denman, he was a grown man with two children. At the time, Denman's oldest was a twelve-year-old boy, whom he'd shielded from a full *Fargo* viewing.

He didn't want to scar the child.

"I think it changes you," he said of the film. "You lose a little bit of innocence."

chapter 3

I'll Shoot Your Dog

Fargo *Auditions*

"I was nothing if not bold."

—WILLIAM H. MACY

"It's really a buyer's market."

—ETHAN COEN

For actors, auditions are sink-or-swim, performance-based job interviews. For directors, auditions offer a glimpse into the future. While the men and women reciting lines aren't in costume or makeup, each is attempting to elevate a screenplay from page to life. The actor has memorized the scene to be performed, has pondered the character's dilemma or motivation in that particular moment in the script, and has practiced the scene multiple times—perhaps dozens of times—with other actors, friends, anyone willing to watch. An unblinking camera records every twitch, sniffle, tilted eyebrow, and half smile. The room is uninviting, gloomy. Most likely, the walls are white, the carpets gray, the chairs uncomfortable.

William H. Macy hates auditioning. "It's the most inhumane thing I've ever seen," he said. "It is dehumanizing. It's more frightening than anything you've ever experienced."

And yet, for the role of Jerry Lundegaard, the lying car salesman with a nightmarish plan to get ahead, Macy fought like hell to go through several dehumanizing, frightening experiences—er, acting auditions—with the Coen Brothers.

"I was called in to read for the young cop," Macy told me. He performed. The Boys liked what they saw. "I think Ethan said, 'That's real good. You wanna read Jerry?' And I said, 'Oh boy, do I ever.' So I went back out in the hall and I worked on it a little bit. And I went inside the room and read for Joel and Ethan. They said, 'That's real good. You want to go home and work on it and come back tomorrow?' And I said, 'Yes, I do.' So I went home, called every actor I knew. They did turns, and I learned the whole script and went back in and read again."

After the second audition, the Coens told Macy, "That's real good. We'll let you know."

Meanwhile, another actor was tempting the Coens with solid auditions for leading man. Minnesota native Bill Schoppert had coproduced and starred in *The Personals*, a 1982 Minnesota-made movie about singles looking for love through ads in weekly newspapers. Like Macy, he was a doe-eyed, plain, middle-aged man. Before his first Jerry Lundegaard audition, Schoppert received two telephone calls at his Minneapolis apartment. One was from a fellow actor who lived in Los Angeles. "Bill, the Coen Brothers have this new film they're going to be making," he said. "And there's a part in there that's just perfect for you." The other call came from casting specialist Jane Drake Brody, a woman who'd worked with the Coens on *Miller's Crossing* and *The Hudsucker Proxy*. She rang up Schoppert, told him the same thing, then added, "You gotta be in it."

So Schoppert auditioned. Then he auditioned again. Then again. And again. In the business, a return audition is known as a callback. He'd received three callbacks, which is a mostly positive sign. It shows the moviemakers are intrigued, but it might also indicate they're having trouble making a decision. Schoppert really wanted the role. He knew it could be the one to catapult his career from the snowy Midwest to sunny Los Angeles. Yet, he still had to eat and pay the rent. He did this by working as an emcee at corporate meetings, which required him to get on an airplane, fly to another city, take the stage, and rev up a bunch of suits in town for a conference. One Friday in 1994, Schoppert was preparing to do just that, for a gig in Florida. Then the phone rang. It was Carol, his representative at Moore, a local talent agency.

"Bill, the Coen Brothers want to see you again." She told Schoppert his fourth callback was scheduled for the following day. The day he was supposed to fly coach to Florida.

"Geez, Carol. I've already had three callbacks," he replied. "They've seen me. What more do they need to see? I can't make this callback. I think they've seen enough of me."

Carol put her foot down. "They've been to New York. They've been to LA. Right now you're the only person they are considering for this part. So I think you better show up."

Schoppert conceded.

He phoned his corporate client, informed them he'd be a little late for rehearsal the next day, and booked another flight, which he paid for with his own money.

For the fifth time, Schoppert slipped into the role of Jerry Lundegaard. The portion of the script he'd been shown—and the one he performed— is Jerry alone, in the kitchen of his suburban home, preparing to call his father-in-law. Jerry has arrived home to discover the successful completion of the kidnapping he planned with a pair of felons. Doors are torn off hinges. Shattered glass is sprinkled on the floor. And here's Jerry, rehearsing his sorrow and panic, before dialing the victim's father.

"I wish they had me reading a different scene," Schoppert told me. "It was bad news on the phone. I do remember that. Maybe they chose it because it was a little more difficult, this scene."

Macy, meanwhile, didn't wait for the phone to ring.

"I found out that they were auditioning in New York," he said. "So I got my Lutheran ass on an airplane and flew to New York and crashed the audition. And I said, 'I want to audition again. I'm worried you're going to make a mistake on this thing and cast somebody else.'"

Macy loves to tell this story. And because he's an actor, he tells it well. When he told it to me for a public radio documentary I was making about the cultural impact of the film on Minnesota and North Dakota, he paused at just the right places, said "that's real good" in an understated, possibly midwestern way, to indicate Joel or Ethan said those words. It was captivating.

William H. Macy.
(Photo by James Bridges)

The one thing he didn't tell me is how he threatened to kill Ethan's pet if he didn't get the job. Macy did mention it to another interviewer, though. "No seriously," Macy claims he told Ethan. "I'll shoot your dog if you don't give me this role."

I can imagine Ethan cackling and a half smile crossing Joel's face.

"I was making a joke," Macy added. "Luckily, it landed."

So did his audition. Up to that point, Macy's film credits were sparse, but he'd had many television roles, appearing on episodes of *Law & Order*, *L.A. Law*, and *Spenser: For Hire*, on an episode of *ABC Afterschool Specials*, and in a recurring role on the hospital drama *ER*.

When it came time to choose between Bill Schoppert and Bill Macy, the Coens chose the Bill who'd traveled across the country, who'd insisted on another audition, and who may have threatened physical violence against one of the directors' pets. Joel and Ethan chose Bill—known to moviegoers as William H.—Macy for the role of Jerry Lundegaard.

"He really showed he wanted the part," Schoppert said of Macy. "Well, he deserved to get it. It never occurred to me to do that."

That's partly because Schoppert rarely had to audition to nab roles. The phone rang, Schoppert answered, and the person on the other end usually offered him a job. "That's what happened with *The Personals*," he said. "That happened to me over and over again. The phone rings. Then I have work. My career has been charmed in that I have not had to do a lot of auditioning. But it's also been cursed in that I did not have to do a lot of auditioning. I did not get very good at doing the auditioning. It is different. You walk in there and you have to be that person immediately. You have to turn it on right away."

More than two decades later, the other Bill is at peace with fate. "My life has turned out just fine," Schoppert said. While Macy was portraying desperation on camera for the Coens, Schoppert was wooing the woman who would soon become his wife. The couple married in the summer of 1995, just months after principal photography on *Fargo* ended. "I have sometimes wondered how much my life would have changed," he said. "What might have been and what was and is. I have no regrets about that."

❖❖

For *Fargo*, three actors were spared the pains of multiple auditions. The roles of funny-looking guy Carl Showalter, hotcakes-obsessed Gaear Grimsrud, and police chief Marge Gunderson were written with Steve Buscemi, Peter Stormare, and Frances McDormand in mind.

Buscemi, who was pushing forty years old when *Fargo* was filmed, had small roles in earlier films by the Minnesota brothers: *Miller's Crossing* (Mink), *Barton Fink* (Chet), and *The Hudsucker Proxy* (Beatnik Barman). Clearly, the Coens saw potential in the diminutive actor. "It was a nice opportunity as far as Steve's character is concerned," Joel said. "To give Steve a part that was more substantial than what we had given him in the past."

His biggest role before *Fargo* was as Mr. Pink in 1992's *Reservoir Dogs*, a bloodstained heist film. Like the other baddies assembled to rob a jewelry store, he was given an alias based on a color. Other guys got dubbed Mr.

Steve Buscemi.
(Photo by James Bridges)

White, Mr. Orange, Mr. Blonde, Mr. Brown, Mr. Blue. But Buscemi? He got stuck with pink.

"Why am I Mr. Pink?" Buscemi's character complains. "Why can't we pick our own colors?"

He loses that battle, but at least his character lives. In *Fargo*, Buscemi's Carl Showalter gets thwacked with an ax before being pulverized in a wood chipper. Buscemi's characters ended up dead so often in the decade after *Fargo* that the *New York Times* wrote about it, headlining the story, "They Keep Killing Steve Buscemi, But He's Not Complaining."

Born in Brooklyn, Buscemi studied acting at the Lee Strasberg Theatre & Film Institute in New York. Like a lot of actors, he couldn't pay the rent. Instead of waiting tables, he worked as a New York City firefighter at Engine Company 55. But he didn't tell his colleagues about his dream of appearing in movies. "I didn't tell anybody in the firehouse I had any aspirations of being anything," Buscemi said. "I was just the quietest guy in the firehouse."

Buscemi's partner in crime in *Fargo*, Peter Stormare, was a virtual unknown in America when the Coens made *Fargo*. Born in Sweden, Rolf Peter Ingvar Storm changed his name to Stormare after discovering another actor had the same last name. He attracted Ethan Coen's attention in 1988, when Stormare was starring in *Hamlet* at the Brooklyn Academy of Music, just across the bridge from Manhattan, where Ethan lived. Produced by the Royal Dramatic Theatre and Sweden's National Theatre and directed by the cinematic genius Ingmar Bergman, this *Hamlet* was unconventional. The sets and costumes were a striking mix of red, white, and black. Ophelia, instead of appearing in only a few scenes, never left the stage. Bergman also rearranged Shakespeare's words, famously moving Hamlet's "to be or not to be" soliloquy to a new place in the play.

Stormare had appeared in a production of Bergman's *King Lear* in 1984. With *Hamlet*, many critics opined that the aging director saw a bit of himself in Stormare. "He's a very, very modern young actor," Ingmar Bergman said. "He's extremely talented in ways that are right . . . anarchistic, aggressive to our profession." The production generated a lot of attention, including an article in *New York* magazine that featured a photo of Stormare with sunglasses perched on his nose and a smirk on his face. He's leaning against a skull—a memorable prop to theatergoers familiar with the classic play. The cheeky headline: "Taking Hamlet by Stormare."

Those New York appearances sparked an opportunity for the Swedish actor. "It sold out because it was a Bergman thing," Stormare said. "Ethan saw the production and [he] said, 'We're going to do a movie called *Miller's Crossing*, and we want you in it. We're going to write a special part for you called Swede.' I went back home to the National Theatre and went up to the boss of the theater and said, 'I have three weeks in New Orleans with the Coen Brothers for *Miller's Crossing*. Here's the script. It's Hollywood, man!' He said, 'Peter, shut up! You ain't going to Hollywood!'"

Five years later, Stormare had a second theatrical encounter with the Coens when he appeared in *The Swan* opposite Frances McDormand at the Joseph Papp Public Theater in Lower Manhattan. Written by Elizabeth Egloff, *The Swan* tells the story of Swan, a confused man-bird trapped

Peter Stormare.
(Photo by James Bridges)

inside the house of Dora, a nurse who sleeps on the sofa in a white slip. As Swan, the winged Stormare gnaws on pizza slices and pecks at the skin on his arm. He also eviscerates a neighbor's pet rabbit and swoops spiders off the floor and pops them into his beak. The Swan has no spoken lines for the first third of the play. When he finally speaks, he jabbers nonsensically.

Dora, played by McDormand, attempts to civilize Swan by teaching him checkers and dressing him in her ex-husband's clothes.

"I had long hair that was bleached," Stormare remembers. "I was blessed to have Frances McDormand onstage doing the play with me, and thank god her husband, Joel Coen, came with Ethan to see the play. They said, 'That's the Swede again.'

"After a couple of months they came around again and said, 'We have another part. Are you going to turn us down or can we send you a script?'"

That script was, of course, *Fargo*.

Among the lines the Coens had drafted for Stormare: "Unguent . . . I need unguent." And: "Where is Pancakes Hause?" And: "We stop at Pancakes Hause."

Stormare's first reaction: "Where the hell is the part? There are no lines at all. He hardly spoke." Indeed, during the kidnappers' long drive from Fargo to Minneapolis, Showalter pleads with Grimsrud: "Would it kill you to say something?"

Frances McDormand, on the other hand, had plenty of lines in *Fargo*. But before she had met, let alone married, Joel, she too had to audition for the Coens.

In 1982, the Coens were in New York auditioning actors for *Blood Simple*, a thriller set on the Texas plains. Like Joel and Ethan, Frances McDormand was young, wildly ambitious, and an unknown, cinematic outsider. She was living in a cheap flat in Queens with another unknown actor—Holly Hunter. McDormand auditioned for the role of Abby, the secretive wife of a bar owner in this film by a couple of unknown brothers from Minnesota. The Boys had auditioned other actors, including Hunter, but hadn't found the person who could truly inhabit this more-nuanced-than-one-might-expect character.

To portray Abby, an actor needed to convey a complex web of intelligence, motivation, and emotion. Abby is unknowing, but she's not naive. Abby isn't particularly bright, but neither are the men around her. Abby appears fragile, but she possesses a hidden determination and a strong will to survive.

After seeing her audition for Abby, the Coens asked McDormand to return the following day. In sharp contrast to Macy, who pleaded for another audition and flew across time zones in order to land a role in a Coen Brothers film, McDormand simply told Joel and Ethan she had other plans. It turned out her boyfriend at the time, also an actor, had a tiny role in a soap opera, and she'd promised to be there.

I'm busy, she told them.

Some directors wouldn't have bothered to follow up, figuring an actor not willing to accommodate during casting might turn out to be difficult

Frances McDormand.
(Photo by James Bridges)

during filming. But the Coens saw it differently. "We really liked that," Joel said. "It was so guileless—just what we wanted for Abby."

Hiring McDormand for the role of Abby changed their lives. Joel and Frances fell in love and later married. The resulting film, with graceful cinematography by Barry Sonnenfeld, surprised and delighted audiences for many reasons, including McDormand's portrayal of a woman being chased by a crazed, gun-toting private investigator in a yellow leisure suit.

❖❖

So what's it like to be inside a room with actors auditioning for Joel and Ethan?

Jane Drake Brody, a Chicago-based acting coach and casting specialist, had been there twice already by the time she was helping to cast *Fargo*. She worked for The Boys on *Miller's Crossing* and *The Hudsucker Proxy*. When she first met the Coens, the pair reminded her of bookish graduate students, not bossy film directors. Especially when one of them offered her a cup of joe.

"I've never had a director in my life ask me if they could make me coffee," Brody said. "It was unbelievable they would do that. Usually the casting director not only provides a menu of actors, but also sets up snacks and goodies."

During preproduction for *Miller's Crossing*, the trio settled in, watching actors take a whack at roles as Irish hit men or Italian toughs in the gangster drama. Several hours later, they broke for lunch. After Joel and Ethan departed, Brody got a glimpse of their creative process by peeking at what they'd written during that morning's auditions. "Their notes were like, 'Meh.' Or 'Squirrel cheeks!' Or 'Huh?' There was no discernible, intellectual way for me to know who they liked."

For the next film, Brody was with the Coens in Chicago, helping sift through actors for *The Hudsucker Proxy*. That's when she learned that their sixth film would be set in her hometown, along the I-394 and I-494 highway ribbons full of car dealerships and nearby snowy plains. "They knew I was from Minnesota," said Brody, who grew up a few blocks from Lake Harriet in Minneapolis. She urged the Coens to let her return to the Twin Cities, a place she knew was rich in acting talent. She'd led classes there and watched actors work at the Guthrie Theater, the Children's Theatre Company, and the Jungle Theater.

"Let me do the Minnesota casting," she told the Coens. "I can cast a lot from up there."

Brody got the job and a very specific set of recommendations for the kinds of actors they wanted in front of the camera.

"One of their instructions to me was, 'We only want to see blond people.' That was one of their big instructions," she said. "I didn't follow it completely, but I followed it a lot. And boy, there were some actors in Minnesota who were madder than hell at me that I couldn't see [them audition]. I knew they were not in the picture that the Coen Brothers had in their head. They were too othered. They were not Scandihoovians."

As writer-directors of captivating scripts, the Coens can afford to be choosy. They know there are more talented actors than there are well-written parts. "It's a buyer's market," Ethan said.

A green hotel door separates actors waiting for a shot at cinematic fame from those currently under the microscope. Inside the drab yellow hotel room sits Brody, reading glasses dangling from a chain around her neck. On the table in front of her are sides, the script pages from which hopefuls will perform for her, and a video camera on a tripod.

The first person on the tape, a dark-haired woman, isn't sure how to begin. "The agent was suggesting there should be a little bit of an accent," she says, her voice trailing off.

"Suggesting?" Brody replies. "They should have been demanding."

"Right. But how thick?"

"We've got to have a recognizable accent," Brody says. "I think it's best to err on the side of thick because people are not quite doing that or they think they are thick and they're not thick at all."

As instructed by Brody, the woman begins reading the lines for the parts of both Hooker #1 and Hooker #2. After a single read, Brody dismisses her with a terse "Thank you."

Then Brody flicks off the camera and when she flicks it back on, another actor appears, staring blankly and waiting for instructions. At that moment, she states the actor's name and the role she hopes to nab. Sometimes the actor isn't sure whether to look at Brody or the camera. *Look at me*, Brody says. Sometimes the actor is apologetic about not having memorized the script. Brody dismisses such concerns. "I hate memorized reads," she says, not explaining why.

Through the clips of dozens of hopefuls trying out for a variety of roles, a pattern emerges. Show promise, and Brody asks for additional reads, often offering suggestions about how to emphasize certain lines. If the second and third attempts go well, she promises an audition with her boss, casting director John S. Lyons. Succeed in front of Lyons, and it's on to an audition with Joel and Ethan. For now, neither Lyons nor the Coens are present. Brody is on this talent quest alone.

Those without promise are dismissed quickly. Sometimes, even those who show promise have to suffer through a lecture from Brody. After one actor reading for Hooker #1 and #2 delivers a performance worthy of a return audition, Brody cautions her against wearing too much jewelry to the next audition.

"I don't want you coming in with this," Brody says, gesturing to the actor's face and pointing at her gaudy, leaf-shaped gold earrings.

"You want me to get rid of it?"

"I'm going to call you back," Brody says. "I don't want that."

"Thank god," the young woman says, tugging at the jewelry.

"I think you should wear something very simple," Brody says. "You can leave your hair like that or any way you want. It doesn't matter to me."

"She came right out and told me blue eye shadow," the actor says, likely referring to an agent.

"I know she did," Brody whispers. "She's trying. She's trying really hard. Most casting directors, I think, she might be right because most of them are pretty goddamn stupid."

The actor laughs.

"There's no way you can hide your eyes and your bone structure, which is what I'm looking at," Brody adds, returning to a normal tone of voice. "You can't hide that. We are either going to go with it or not. Whether you have blue eye shadow on doesn't make one bit of difference."

With that, Brody returns to the business at hand. "Now I have callbacks," she says, looking at a calendar. "Would you like to come this afternoon?"

With that, the *Fargo* audition videos flicker from a hotel room with a green door to a conference room with white walls. And there's Larissa Kokernot, the actor who eventually lands the role of Hooker #1, alone at a table, the script in front of her. She's wearing a fuchsia blouse and matching lipstick. Blonde bangs droop over her forehead. When Brody introduces her off camera, she smiles broadly, glances down at the table, and whispers, "Awesome."

Without comment, Brody launches into the scene, reading Chief Gunderson's lines. With each question about where she's from, what the suspects looked like, Kokernot pauses, thinking, before answering. At the end of the brief scene, Brody praises her, then pauses the tape, presumably offering tips that go unrecorded. On the second read, Kokernot considers her replies to Chief Gunderson's queries even more.

"Good," Brody says. "One more take, and we'll be where we want to be. Do the least necessary to communicate. Just that. Do the least necessary."

On the third read, Brody interrupts Kokernot when the actor reads the line, "They said they were going to the Twin Cities."

Brody's note: "That's where you're pushing it."

Kokernot tries it again, this time more matter-of-factly.

Brody's reaction to this third attempt also goes unrecorded.

More and more actors appear on the audition video, trying out for the roles of Jerry, Jean, or Scotty Lundegaard. They also read for Wade Gustafson, Stan Grossman, Glen Yanagita (later changed to Mike Yanagita), Shep Proudfoot, Irate Customer, The Girl at the Carlton (later changed to Escort), and of course, Hooker #1 and Hooker #2.

Some of the reads are startlingly lame. There's a mumbling Shep Proudfoot, a flat Jerry Lundegaard, and an actor who lays on the Minnesota accent so thick it sounds like he's performing an Ole and Lena joke.

Others are inspired.

John Carroll Lynch, the actor who landed the role of Norm, Marge Gunderson's stay-at-home husband, stands out. What little hair Lynch had in 1995 was dark, not the blond the directors demanded. But on a bald man with just a tuft of hair around the bottom of his skull, its color didn't matter much. Lynch could act. And because he worked at the prestigious Guthrie Theater for eight years leading up to *Fargo*, he understood local culture.

"When I was at the Guthrie," Lynch told me, "one of the lines we'd always use about doing comedies for Minnesota audiences was 'Oh, geez. That comedy was so funny, I almost laughed out loud. I could barely contain myself.'"

From 1987 to 1995, Lynch appeared in forty productions at the Guthrie. In *Frankenstein—Playing with Fire*, a Barbara Field adaptation of the Mary Shelley novel, Lynch portrayed the Creature. A *Frankenstein* production photo shows a bare-chested Lynch looming over an operating table with the good doctor at his side.

Lynch, who looks more like a bus driver than a leading man, also appeared in dramas like *Uncle Vanya*, *Death of a Salesman*, and *Richard III*, as well as lighter fare like *The Front Page* and *Measure for Measure*. Like nearly every other actor in town, he was excited about auditioning for a movie role. And he figured his deep experience and his body type gave him a chance to land the role of Norm.

Seven and a half minutes of Lynch's encounter with Brody is recorded on the tape. He's wearing a comfy, white shirt with big breast pockets. As he interacts with Brody-as-Marge, he pretends to shake a small box of night crawlers during the lunch scene at the Brainerd police station, chats with her about duck paintings, and discusses the impending birth of their child.

"Hiya, Norm, how's the painting going?" Brody asks.

"Ah, not bad," Lynch replies, leaning back in his chair.

A few seconds later, Brody asks him again. And he offers a different take on the line, this time slightly more upbeat. When he bitches about the Hautmans entering the duck painting contest again this year, Brody stops him.

"I wouldn't complain there," she says, switching back to her role as casting specialist.

On his next attempt, he delivers the line more nonchalantly, more Minnesotan.

Brody is smitten. She offers a quick compliment, then digs in with more specific notes. "Don't reveal," she tells him. "You know in stage acting, you want to reveal."

Lynch leans in, agreeing and interrupting. "You don't want to broadcast," he says. "That's the difference, the difference I'm just beginning to realize. I haven't done a whole lot of film work."

Their exchange continues.

BRODY: "One of the things you should think about is when people watch a film, it's different than watching a stage. People watching a stage are always aware of people around them. Whereas in film, people become the character."

LYNCH: "It's an individual response. You're watching it alone."

BRODY: "You're completely alone and kind of in an altered state. The audience becomes the character and does the actions for him or her. So the more you do for me, the less involved I am."

LYNCH: "That makes sense."

BRODY: "If you look at the pages you're on, [the audience has] already met you. You need to do very little reveal. It's an odd thing. It shouldn't be less or small."

The audition ends with another read of the movie's final scene: Marge and Norm in bed, talking about the results of the duck stamp competition and the future.

"Two more months," Brody says, off camera.

Lynch inhales ever so slightly, looks off in the distance, and replies: "Two more months."

Brody recommended Lynch to the casting director and the Coens. Before auditioning for Joel and Ethan, Lynch continued to practice, often with Brenda Wehle, a Minneapolis actor who later became his wife.

"Do you know what you should do?" Wehle told him. "Do you know how sometimes you wake up and you've got a throat full of phlegm and you hock that up? You should do that right before you say, 'I'll fix ya some eggs.' You should do that."

Lynch loved the idea. "It was like yes, I really should. I really should do that."

So during the audition, as he's mimicking the sleepy Norm rising slowly from bed, just before he utters the line "I'll fix ya some eggs," Lynch engages in a full-throated, spit-filled, deeply audible clearing of the esophagus.

"Ethan laughs easily, and Joel is a little more stoic, a little more inside himself," Lynch said. "When I did that, both of their heads jerked, and Ethan had to not laugh because they were taping the audition, but afterwards he laughed and said, 'That was good.'"

Brody remembers Lynch's reads vividly. "He was astonishingly good. He, I never forgot, ever," she said, pausing with an actor's emphasis. "He was number one from the start for that role. His size was important. [The actor portraying Norm] had to be a big lunk. He had to be sweeter, more tender than she. I knew we had to have a sensitive soul inside a body that didn't really look like that. I don't know if I knew that before we read him or after we read him. Often, a good actor will tell you what you need through the audition. They add to the creativity. He was such a skillful actor, you knew he could hold a scene."

Lynch has gone on to prove it, starring opposite Michael Keaton in *The Founder* and sharing the screen with Angela Bassett, Jessica Lange, and Kathy Bates in *American Horror Story*. Lynch played Twisty the Clown, a deformed killer who had been dropped on his head as a child.

⋄⟨⋄

While the Coens landed quickly on Lynch as Norm Gunderson, they couldn't make up their minds about who to cast as Scotty Lundegaard, the teenage son of a suburban car salesman and his carrot-chopping wife. In the movie, we see Scotty in three scenes: eating cereal and staring at a television while his mother harangues him; anxiously leaning back in his chair at the dinner table, rocking back and forth like a caged animal; and hugging a pillow after his mother's disappearance.

One of the actors Brody watched audition for the role was Tony Denman, a local who lived in suburban Chaska, Minnesota, about a mile from Prince's Paisley Park studio. "We'd kind of make fun of [Prince] because he would dress incognito and drive around in his purple Prowler and go to McDonald's and get chicken nuggets," Denman told me. "We were all like, 'All right, Prince, dude, we know it's you,' but we played along with Prince. There's not many other people that are five-foot-two dressed in a fake old man's wig and mustache driving a purple Prowler around Chanhassen."

Despite not being old enough to drive, Denman had a deep acting résumé filled with television commercials, plays, and movies (*Little Big League* and *Angus*) to his credit. In 1989, a full six years before he auditioned for *Fargo*, Denman appeared in *December Mornings*, a play about Truman Capote's childhood. Peter Vaughan reviewed the History Theatre production for the *Star Tribune* and called Denman's acting "one of the finest performances by a child I have ever seen locally. He gives Buddy a knowing spark and is exceedingly convincing in his affection for his older friend."

Denman's mother was excited by the prospect of Tony appearing in a Joel and Ethan movie. "I remember auditioning for it and my mom is going, 'Oh wow, it's a Coen Brothers movie!' I'm going, 'Oh wow! Who are the Coen Brothers?'" Denman said. "I don't think I had been allowed to watch any of their films up to that point."

Brody liked Denman immediately. "He was just comfortable," she said. "He could do his work. He was truthful. He wasn't older than he was. He wasn't younger than he was. He wasn't putting on anything. He was giving me a simple reading that was truthful from his perspective as this fourteen-year-old boy."

At his brief audition for Brody, the self-assured Denman waits for her to introduce him, turns to the camera, nods, and looks back at her. While chomping on a wad of gum, he ignores Brody's lecture until he has to drop the f-bomb. He drops it naturally, full of righteousness and conviction. At the end of the less than one minute captured on tape, Brody says, "Good. Very good."

At that, Denman's gaze returns to the camera.

The Coens weren't convinced. The problem: Tony's hair was a dark, thick mop of black hair, not blond. "I send the tape of Tony," Brody remembers. "We don't want him. We don't want him. They read every kid in LA. They can't find one. I say to the The Boys,"—and at this point her voice raises an octave for emphasis—"'We could dye it. We could dye his hair and his eyebrows blond.'"

They still weren't convinced.

So on Sunday, January 22, 1995, after weeks of searching for Scotty, and a single day before shooting was scheduled to begin, the search continued. Brody watched as hundreds of Minnesota boys tromped into Gangelhoff Center at Concordia University in St. Paul, hoping for their big break. One day earlier, the *Star Tribune* had published a tiny article at the bottom of page 9E about the search for a boy to play Scotty Lundegaard. Appearing under advice columns by Ann Landers ("Man with lousy sex life should learn to woo his wife") and Dear Abby ("Neighbor kids should pay for broken garage window"), the story invited pretty much anyone to show up at the arena.

"Boy's role to be filled locally in Minnesota-filmed 'Fargo'" read the headline. The story called *Fargo* "a turn-of-the-century crime drama" (ha!) and said its creators were "looking for a blond boy between 10 and 14. No previous acting experience is necessary, but the maximum height is 5-foot-3."

To say Brody wasn't looking forward to the come-one-come-all audition, which is known as an open call, is an understatement. "Sheer hell" is her term for such events. "An open call means you advertise on the radio, on the television, in the newspapers, that you'll see anybody who wants to be in a movie between the ages of twelve and fourteen," Brody said. "You get people who are eighteen saying, 'I can play it.' You get mothers bringing in children. It's just so awful. It doesn't bring out the best in humanity."

Added Brody, "I read thousands of kids. Every kid in Minnesota who has ever been on TV, a stage, in a film. I read all of them. Oh my God. What a mess that was."

From a director's perspective, casting is crucial. It's one of many key decisions about how a movie will look. And coming off *The Hudsucker Proxy*, the Coens were likely exceedingly picky. Brody told me that the studio had pushed an actor on The Boys they didn't want for one of the starring roles. Although Brody wouldn't name names, film critic Adam Nayman, author of *The Coen Brothers: This Book Really Ties the Films Together*, claims the Coens didn't much want either Tim Robbins or Paul Newman in the movie. Instead, they preferred Tom Cruise and Clint Eastwood in the roles of doofus hick and sly businessman. They'd also recently delayed production of *The Big Lebowski* because Jeff Bridges and John Goodman were busy working on other projects. So yes, casting is crucial.

After the open call, the Coens made a decision. Hire Tony Denman to play Scotty Lundegaard. Two decades later, Brody laughs at the memory. Her boss, the national casting director, told her the news, saying, "We're going to use Tony."

For his part, Denman waited and waited before finally receiving word he'd secured the role. "You know, I just remember thinking, 'Oh yes, I get to miss school!'" he said. "It was the most important thing that was going through my mind at that point."

Denman also joked about why the Coens hired him, speculating that it was *because* of his hair, not *in spite* of his hair. "Probably because I could make that Bill Macy pompadour hair," he said. "Who knows?"

chapter 4

Dancing in Your Mouth

Dialect and Preproduction

"I would have to say, they introduced me to a musical score."

—ELIZABETH HIMELSTEIN

"Everybody in Minnesota talks so stupid, don't they?"

—TONY DENMAN

Michael Rapaport chewed out the front-desk staff, claiming they'd mis-spelled his surname. Carrie Fisher flashed room service a glimpse of her snatch. Matt Dillon trashed his suite. Jack Lemmon fretted about the hotel's mattress.

In the 1990s, Hollywood came to Minnesota, filming sixty-five movies in a place unaccustomed to pampering stars. Still, Devie Hagen, senior sales manager of the chic Marquette Hotel for much of the decade, tried. From big productions like *Grumpy Old Men* and *The Mighty Ducks* to inde-pendent efforts like *Mallrats, Beautiful Girls,* and *Fargo,* visiting cast and crew often bunked at the Marquette. One of Minneapolis's most expensive hotels, it opened as the Marquette Inn in 1973, one year after construction was completed on the IDS Center. Designed by architect Philip Johnson, the glass modernist skyscraper soars nearly eight hundred feet above the prairie. The Marquette Hotel is ensconced in an adjoining eighteen-story replica of the taller building. At the time, the hotel was owned by Hilton International, which also operated Chicago's Drake Hotel, Windows on the World in New York City, Ojai Valley Inn near Los Angeles, and the

Kahala Hotel and Resort in Hawaii. On April 7, 1994, President Bill Clinton stayed at the Marquette, then led a rally the following day at the IDS Crystal Court.

Not every guest was a pop star or politician. The Marquette also wooed visitors with "sunset dinner packages" for couples in search of romance. The 1991 promotion offered visitors a deluxe room for $149 per night, which included free parking and "succulent cuisine" at Windows on Minnesota, a restaurant with "magnificent full-length windows." Movie productions often paid less on a per-night basis than locals or business travelers, but their lengthy stays helped fill the hotel's 285 rooms. Those responsible for operating cameras and microphones, building sets, putting on actors' makeup, sewing costumes, and the like rarely caused trouble; mostly they just wanted to find a place to eat and somewhere to do laundry on weekends. It was the marquee actors—or those who considered themselves marquee—who ruffled feathers and, on occasion, charmed staff.

Before beginning work on 1995's *Grumpier Old Men*, two-time Academy Award–winner Lemmon inspected the Marquette, with his wife in tow. He measured the depth of the king-size mattress with his hands and wondered whether it would be sufficiently comfortable. That worried Hagen. Experience told her that if a guest complained before check-in, more complaints would follow during the stay. "Perhaps you'd be happier somewhere else," Hagen suggested.

Walter Matthau, who starred opposite Lemmon in the *Grumpy* movies, also stayed at the Marquette, and he charmed Hagen. Matthau, an Oscar winner himself, chatted often with Hagen, invading her personal space with his weathered face.

"He looks you right in the eye, like an inch from your nose," she told me. "He would go on and on, telling stories about other Hagens he knew, commenting on the furniture, cracking jokes. All I could see besides his eyes was the hair coming out of his ears."

Added Hagen, "Walter was my most favorite. So down-to-earth and just kind to everybody. He never complained."

In stark contrast to Matthau, Matt Dillon was nightmare. He stayed at the Marquette during filming for *Beautiful Girls*, a 1996 Miramax release.

"He had crap all over the place," Hagen said. "He would yell and scream at the staff. He would bring in different girls all the time, not that we cared about that. But there were cigarette burns on the furniture. He just trashed the room really bad."

After the Marquette booted Dillon, maids brought her a trash bag full of stuff he'd left behind. "One of the things in there was an invite to the Academy Awards," she said. "I can't stand to watch him in anything now."

On November 4, 1994, Hagen began wooing *Fargo* to stay at the Marquette. In a one-page letter oozing with enthusiasm, she wrote: "Yehhhh-hhhhhhhhhhhhhhhhhhhhhhhhhhhhhhhhhhhhhhhhhhhhhhhhhhhhh!!!!!!!!!!!!!!!!!!!!! This is a great partnership—once you get into Minneapolis and get checked into your room, you'll know what I mean. The hotel is just buzzing about the arrival of your group."

When Joel and Ethan Coen returned to their hometown later that month to begin preproduction on *Fargo*, Hagen didn't know what to expect. Often mid-level talent caused the biggest headaches, and Hagen didn't think the Coens were that big of a deal. The Brothers were coming off the biggest flop of their career to that point: *The Hudsucker Proxy*, a paean to Hollywood's screwball comedy. Unlike earlier films—or *Fargo*—*Hudsucker* was a money pit. The Brothers spent $30 million of studio cash on grandiose sets designed to replicate the art deco interiors of a New York skyscraper, special effects showing a fat, cigar-chomping corporate boss plummeting to his death from said skyscraper, and Tim Robbins's hair gel. Didn't see it? Few did. *Hudsucker* earned back less than one-tenth of its cost at the US box office. Joel joked he was relieved the studio hadn't repossessed his brother's car.

Now here they were, a short drive from their childhood home at a pivotal time in their lives. Both were on the precipice of middle age—a frightening time in an ambitious filmmaker's life. Both were recently married and soon to become fathers. Joel, a lanky man who wore his shaggy black hair in a ponytail, had just turned forty-one. He and McDormand shared a New York City apartment and had parenting on their minds. The couple was in the process of adopting an infant son from Paraguay, whom they would name Pedro McDormand Coen. Not only that, the pair was also working together again in a very big way. McDormand had the starring role in *Fargo* as Marge Gunderson. Ethan, at thirty-eight, sported big, bushy hair and thick, round glasses, and had recently quit smoking. Ethan was also married, to Tricia Cooke, a film editor. Within a few months, Cooke would give birth to the couple's first child, Buster.

Once inside the Marquette, Joel and Ethan didn't fuss about mattresses or burn holes into furniture or flash hotel staff. "They were very quiet," Hagen said. "They were just part of the landscape. You didn't know who they were. I'd see them walking through the skyway." Workers at Minnesota's first Starbucks, located on the skyway level of the IDS Center, recall the Coens frequently sitting at a window table, sipping coffee and watching people hustle to and fro.

McDormand projects a similar, just-one-of-us vibe. In 2017, she refused to wear makeup for a *New York Times Magazine* cover shoot. An accompanying article noted that when asked for selfies, McDormand routinely declines, insisting fans lock eyes with her in search of a more intimate human connection.

"I don't think of myself as a movie star and I can pretty easily convince other people that I'm not a movie star," she once told a reporter. "I love it, and this happens rarely, but I'm at the grocery store or I'm on the subway and someone says, 'What are you doing here?' and I say 'I'm going to work' or 'I'm buying my groceries, for god's sake. What do you mean what am I doing here?'"

Added McDormand, "I am an ordinary person. And when I fart in a minute, you'll know I am."

Hagen doesn't recall getting that kind of whiff from the movie star. She simply remembers McDormand as a kind, personable woman who happened to be an actor. That doesn't mean McDormand was sleeping on a cot in the storage closet. *Fargo*'s leading actor and her husband camped out in Room 1668, an executive-level suite with a walk-in steam bath, comfy bathrobes (a hotel rarity in the mid-nineties), in-room breakfast service, and free cocktails on weekday evenings. A staffer in the film's production office arranged for the suite, making this annotation in the margin of a notebook: "Want it for Fran."

Ethan Coen, Stephen Park, Frances McDormand, Joel Coen, and dialect coach
Elizabeth Himelstein. (Photo courtesy of Stephen Park)

The Coens and McDormand arrived at the Marquette in time to re-
hearse the script with several cast members, including William H. Macy,
Kristin Rudrüd, John Carroll Lynch, Steve Buscemi, Peter Stormare, and
Bruce Bohne. Joining them was Elizabeth Himelstein, a dialect coach from
Fort Wayne, Indiana. Before being tapped for *Fargo*, Himelstein possessed
just a handful of credits, working on *Cry-Baby*, *True Colors*, and *Carlito's
Way*, among a couple others. So when the Coens called, she was pumped.

"You just cannot imagine how excited I was to get the job to work with
The Brothers," she told me.

Himelstein didn't set out to be a dialect coach. While she was studying at the Juilliard School in New York, a teacher pulled her aside and
said, "I think you would make an amazing voice and speech coach." That
teacher was Edith Skinner, a legendary drama professor who wrote *Speak
with Distinction: The Classic Skinner Method to Speech on the Stage*, a book
first published in 1942 that is full of warm-up, articulation, and elocution

exercises for actors. As a radio reporter, I'm tempted to repeat these Skinner-suggested word pairings before stepping in front of a microphone again: "kinky cookie . . . giggle gaggle (don't swallow) . . . lilli lolli lilli lolli . . . Culligan and calla lilly . . . Topeka Bodega Topeka Bodega Topeka Bodega."

Skinner didn't take any of this lightly. "Through voice and speech, more than any other qualities the actor lays bare before an audience the soul of the character impersonated," she wrote. "Since the words express the meaning of what the actor says and the tone of voice reveals feelings about what is said, the actor's vehicle for carrying words—the voice—must be flexible. It must communicate the nuances of the most hidden emotions being portrayed in the most effective and convincing way this is possible."

After graduation, Himelstein studied under the Polish director Jerzy Grotowski. "I started to really work on my voice then in Poland," she told me. "By the time I was finished with the workshop and with studying, I decided that what I really wanted to do was teach voice and speech to actors."

By the time she was twenty-four, Himelstein was teaching at Purchase College, State University of New York, and she soon landed a job at Carnegie Mellon University in Pittsburgh.

"Edith Skinner, I have no idea what she saw in me," Himelstein said. "I thought that I was average and embarrassed and not very good at all, but she was wonderful, and she really inspired me. I think also I love teaching and I love actors and I love the process so much, and I think that what she saw in me was a teacher."

Himelstein gravitated to sound and coaching actors on how to perfect local dialects. In recent years, she's coached San Francisco–born Liev Schreiber on the nuances of a South Boston accent for the Showtime series *Ray Donovan*. She's also trained Margot Robbie, a native of Australia, for the role of Tonya Harding in the biopic *I, Tonya*, and the Scottish actor Ewan McGregor on the third season of *Fargo*, the FX show.

"I think that fifty percent of it is doing the great research and finding the wonderful sound samples and making sure that you have all the notes of the dialect and that you know how to break it down," Himelstein said. "The other fifty percent of it is being a kind, supportive, inspiring teacher and just being able to work with each individual person in their own way, whichever way the actor works best."

Most of the time, Himelstein's work isn't noticeable to audiences. "Usually the work that I do is to help actors either disguise their own accent or create an accent that is so neutral that nobody is thinking about it," she said. "In fact, if nobody mentions it, then I've done a great job."

Himelstein's assignment on *Fargo* was to teach actors how to perform an obscure, local dialect that had never been portrayed in major American cinema. Dialect coaches do this by finding locals, recording them, then sharing the recordings with actors. For *Fargo*, the Coens were a step ahead of the coach they hired.

"Ethan had tapes that he had already put together, fantastic tapes," Himelstein said. "He said, 'Here are the tapes that I want you to listen to.' They just knew intuitively how they wanted it to sound."

⋈

When The Brothers wanted someone to drive around Minnesota and record people speaking in the local dialect, Ethan called an old friend. Many years earlier, Ethan had shared a suite with William Preston Robertson and a few other boys at Simon's Rock, a boarding school for rich kids located in Massachusetts. Ethan and Robertson connected through their goofy senses of humor, and they stayed in touch.

During postproduction on *Blood Simple*, the Coens turned to Robertson and other friends for help on their low-budget film. They asked Robertson, a gregarious man then working as a writer in Minneapolis, to impersonate the voice of a radio preacher during the protagonist's dark drive through the West Texas plains.

"Now in Matthew Chapter Six, Verse Eighteen," the *Blood Simple* minister tells listeners, "the Lord out and tells us that these are the signs by which we shall know that He is at our door." The Coens believed Robertson would deliver a fire-and-brimstone Elmer Gantry–style preacher, but Robertson had other ideas. His fictional evangelist delivering apocalyptic warnings was speaking to radio listeners from a one-room, concrete bunker in a nasal drawl. "There are many good people disagree with me, but it's my belief that this Antichrist is alive today and livin' somewhere in Europe, in that ten-nation alliance I spoke of, bein' groomed for his task—"

The Boys liked what they heard and layered it under images of headlights and blacktop. They didn't pay Robertson, but they gave him a humorous credit: Rev. William Preston Robertson, radio evangelist. Soon Robertson added other postproduction credits to his résumé: mimicking the sound of a panting German shepherd in *Blood Simple*, an FBI agent and other off-screen voices in *Raising Arizona*, crying jags and death gurgles in *Miller's Crossing*, and most notably, the disturbing weeping-laughing of a killer in *Barton Fink*. As Fink frets over sentences in his bleak hotel room, he hears a man whimpering on the other side of the thin wall. He phones room service and complains.

In the screenplay, the sound is described as "weary, solitary, mirthless" and "end-of-the-tether." It was supposed to bubble up from John Goodman, the actor who portrayed serial killer Charlie Meadows, but he couldn't muster it. The Boys remembered their friend and asked, *Can you do this?*

Sure, Robertson said.

"Apparently, John Goodman hasn't done a whole lot of weeping-laughing in his life," Robertson told me.

As an emotion, weeping-laughing rattles the soul because it goes beyond sadness to a place of darkness where few find hope. "It's unnerving," Robertson said. "You can't tell if it's laughing. You can't tell if it's weeping. I'm a depressive personality. I come from a long line of crazy southerners. I know exactly what [they were] talking about."

In preparation for *Fargo*, instead of having Robertson make sounds, the Coens asked him to record the sounds of Minnesotans talking. They didn't explain exactly what they looking for. They didn't have to; the Coens and Robertson shared similar sensibilities. Not long after The Boys made their request, Robertson had recorded several heavily accented Minnesotans: a Hopkins barber, a friend's father, an office assistant in a medical facility, and Pat Forciea, an Iron Range political insider who later served time in federal prison for embezzlement.

With the cassette recorder's red light on, Robertson asked each subject about their lives, jobs, and hobbies. The questions varied slightly. But one query remained the same: *Do you vacation anywhere in the state?*

"Because I knew they would always say, 'I got a little cabin up dere on de lake,'" Robertson laughed, remembering the setup and enjoying the answer again. "Every one of them would say that. They either rented it or they owned it. It became, to the Coens, a laugh line anytime in an interview when I asked. They would just burst out laughing. They knew I was doing it willfully. They knew that I knew what the answer was going to be. And *they* knew what the answer was going to be."

One of the Coens' favorites was Patty, an office assistant at the Veterans Administration hospital in Minneapolis, where Robertson's wife worked as a physician. Patty didn't just speak in a Minnesota accent. She exuded the personality and spirit the Coens were trying to capture in the movie. They were really excited about her.

I asked Robertson what the process was like with the Coens.

ME: "How would you describe the qualities that it turns out they were looking for?"

Robertson laughed nervously. "Fuck you, man."

I laughed, knowing that to answer the question he'd need to define Minnesota-ness.

ROBERTSON: "You're putting me in an awkward position."

I waited.

Then I waited some more.

Finally, he answered.

"Chipper, friendly, yet oddly tight-lipped," he said. "It's the 'Well, that's different' mentality when they're encountering something really socially odd. Rather than saying that's appalling, Minnesotans will say, 'That's different.' It's the fierce holding on to the belief that life could be normal. You know? It's the hallmark of the Minnesota cultural personality."

⋈

In the *Fargo* script, Joel and Ethan incorporated Minnesota slang and pronunciations, often changing the spelling of words so actors could mimic the sounds on the page. "Believe me" became "bleeme." "Groceries" became "growsheries." "Hundred" became "hunnert." And "interested" became "innarested." The Brothers also peppered the dialogue with local phrases like "end a story," meaning "I don't want to talk about it anymore," and "doing pretty good," meaning "life is hell here in the winter, but I haven't slipped on the ice and cracked a hip." And, of course, "yes" became "yah." In the published screenplay, which includes a few scenes cut from the movie, I counted 179 yahs, mostly uttered by Jerry Lundegaard.

I turned to Himelstein for details on perfecting my Minnesota accent, which I gotta say, was already pretty good. "It's really dancing in your mouth," Himelstein said. "You've got to place everything correctly. So in other words, if we were going to do one of the very first sounds, which is the front vowel EEE, tip of the tongue is behind the lower front teeth, lips are smiling—EEE. So it's very pure."

When pronouncing the words "keep," "seep," and "geez," it's critical to elongate the EEE sound, she told me.

"Another very strong one is that O," she added. "Keep the tip of the tongue behind the lower front teeth, lips are rounded—keep them rounded, keep them rounded—Oooh, Oooh."

"Ooooh," I said to Himelstein, as if I were an actor.

"Right, very pure," she said, reassuring me. And there were more sentences with the OOO sound. "Ooooh nooo, Ooooh nooo. Yes, it's ooover. What am I supposed to dooo."

Minneapolis actor Bruce Bohne didn't need Himelstein's help to nail the accent for the relatively few lines of dialogue spoken by his character, Deputy Lou. He picked it up through marriage. His wife was from Chisholm, on Minnesota's Iron Range, and his sister's husband was from Cook, which is even farther north. "I had spent a lot of time hearing those rhythms and pronunciations," Bohne told me. "So as soon as [the casting director] said, 'This is the accent that we're looking for,' I didn't even have to think about it. It came so naturally to read the lines like Lou."

That expertise with the dialect propelled Bohne to the front of the line during casting. "I think I had one audition and then a callback before I actually met The Brothers and read for them in person. They laughed the whole way through my audition. I was pretty sure they were laughing for the right reasons."

His secret to nailing the accent goes beyond pronunciation to also include rhythm. "Well, it's a kind of a 'ba dump ba dump ba dump,'" he told me. "It's very Scandinavian, but they definitely do have a cadence to their speech."

And an understated way of reacting to significant events, like news of a family member catching a big break in his career. After learning that he got the part, Bohne huddled with his family for the weekend. During a walk in the woods on a crisp autumn afternoon with his brother-in-law from Cook, Bohne told him about landing the Deputy Lou role in *Fargo*.

"Getting cast in this movie is a huge deal," Bohne said. "A lot of it is thanks to your family because I've heard the way you, your mom, your dad, everybody in your family speaks a certain way. It really helped me nail it."

Silence. Then a little more silence.

Then this from the brother-in-law: "Oh yah?"

By November 14, 1994, the Coens had created an official business entity—Fargo Pictures—and they soon rented office space in St. Paul. Staffers transformed a squat, concrete bunker at 2313 Wycliff Avenue into a maze of offices, a makeshift screening room, and a big, empty space to build sets and film the occasional scene or an insert. They rented desks, tables, chairs, typewriters, telephones. A kitschy green-and-black, loon-themed wallpaper lent the lobby a midwestern flair.

John Cameron, the line producer, was in charge of money. On the Coens' previous film, *The Hudsucker Proxy*, he worked as assistant director. But for *Fargo*, he wanted to try something new. As line producer, his first job was to negotiate a budget with PolyGram Filmed Entertainment and Working Title Films. That is a tricky dance. Directors want as much money as possible, and funders want to hand over only what is absolutely necessary.

Ethan and Joel Coen with *Fargo* line producer John Cameron. (Photo courtesy of John Cameron)

"What filmmakers always want is more time, enough time to make the film to their satisfaction," Cameron told me. "The pressure of the money is you have to do it in less time because this is the amount of money this material is deemed worth by the financier." After some negotiation, they settled on $6.85 million, which wasn't a "micro" budget film, but it wasn't a "studio level" budget movie either.

"We thought, we're going to make it really cheaply and nobody will get hurt," Joel said.

Added Ethan, "You have to be aware and not kid yourself about what you're doing and ask yourself whether it will justify the cost of what it will realistically take to make the movie."

With the budget set, various creative leads were soon turning to Joel and Ethan for direction. During a scouting trip to a Radisson Hotel one day, production designer Rick Heinrichs spotted a lifeless hallway and asked if something like that might be right for the movie. The Coens' response: No.

"All it is is a corridor," Heinrichs protested, "with a couch and a painting on the wall."

"Well," Joel replied, "maybe if there was no painting it would be all right."

The Brothers basically wanted their top designer to use as little of his talents as possible. "We want the most banal, soul-crushing kind of architecture and landscape," Joel recalled. "And no set design, please."

Still, they had to fill their sets with objects. For that, Joel and Ethan turned to Lauri Gaffin, the set decorator for *Fargo*. "The Coen Brothers were very specific in terms of wanting it to look very normal, nothing too outrageous like their other films," Gaffin said. "It's meant to have an everyday ordinariness to it."

Gaffin, who once studied with conceptual artist John Baldessari, spent days looking for stuff the Lundegaards and Gundersons might display on a kitchen counter, office shelf, bedroom wall, nightstand, dresser, or television console. She imagined Jean Lundegaard as a collector of porcelain pigs, Jerry Lundegaard as a golfer, and Marge Gunderson as the proud owner of tiny Paul Bunyan and Babe the Blue Ox figurines.

"I would come up with ideas and say, 'Do you like this idea?' and I would show [the Coens] pictures," she said. "I photographed everything I was going to buy because it was a small enough movie."

Since the budget was limited, Gaffin shopped at thrift stores. Most of the stuff she found was tattered, definitely secondhand. One exception was a portly pig cookie jar. In the movie, it's positioned near a Trimline phone in the kitchen, and you can see it in scenes when Jean or Jerry is talking on the phone. The pig is on its haunches, eyes closed, with its meaty paws resting happily on a big belly, allowing its owner to drop delicious cookies inside. It really is quite the find.

Mary Zophres, the film's costume designer, was also busy buying stuff or, occasionally, having stuff made. The garish top Marge Gunderson wears to her date with Mike Yanagita at the hotel bar? A local seamstress sewed that. The boots worn by Grimsrud in the wood chipper scene? Zophres paid nearly $100. I didn't see the receipt, nor did the Coens. But the price is visible on the Swede's sole after he gets shot by Marge:

99.99. The Coens left the handwritten price tag in the movie. During a cast and crew screening, Zophres saw it and was mortified. The Coens howled.

The actors also peppered Joel and Ethan with questions, including about the vague title of the film. "I asked Ethan why they called it *Fargo*," Macy told me. "And he said they didn't think anybody would go see a movie called Brainerd."

They told everyone that. It's a genius line. But it doesn't describe why North Dakota's biggest city got the nod.

"There's something about the name or the word 'Fargo,'" said Tony Denman, the actor who played Macy's son. "What is that? What's that about? It's also just got this bland quality to it as well. It's just funny sounding. It's got this odd ring to it, all around. They're clever calling it that when most of the movie doesn't take place there. It throws people off. That's what the Coens like to do, put people on a back foot and make people think about it."

Added Denman, "A lot of times they just do it because they like messing with people."

Don "Bix" Skahill was one of the early office hires. He'd worked as an office production assistant on other movies, but quit the business to attend graduate school. The opportunity to work with the Coens lured him back. In the early days, Skahill was trying to understand Joel and Ethan's communication style.

"You've seen their body language, right?" Skahill said. "Joel lets Ethan do all the talking. They start with obtuse, and they get weirder from there. It's word jazz. They're messing with us, but you shouldn't put that in the book because it will ruin the illusion. People read the stuff they're saying very seriously. They're just goofing around. Ninety-nine percent of what they're saying is goof. . . . To sit there and watch them talk to each other is creepy. There's these weird long pauses. Then one of them says, 'Well, we could . . .' [and] the other one will go, 'Rent it.' Then they go off in a new direction. You can't follow it."

Added Skahill, "I'm not even sure there's two of them."

❄︎

As principal photography neared, actors began rehearsing in earnest and discussing characters.

One day at the Marquette, McDormand asked Bohne out for drinks. "Since you're my deputy and I'm your boss, we're partners basically, so we should get together and talk about it," McDormand said.

Bohne liked the idea.

So the pair met at the MARQ VII, the hotel bar. "We ended up sitting there for a good couple of hours and knocked back plenty of drinks," Bohne recalled to me, "and talked about everything under the sun except for the movie, except for the script, except for our scenes, except for our characters. We didn't touch on any of that.

"Suddenly we both looked at each other and she said, 'Maybe that's enough drinks.'"

Bohne said to her, "We didn't really get to talk about our characters or our scenes."

"Yah, but you know what?" McDormand replied. "I have a feeling we know each other as well as Lou and Margie know each other after just sitting down here talking, so we should be fine."

Bohne's response more than two decades later: "And we were."

McDormand also met with Larissa Kokernot, who played Hooker #1, before filming began. Kokernot appears in two scenes. In one, she's riding Steve Buscemi, aka "the little fella," in a dimly lit hotel room. In the other, Kokernot and Hooker #2 (Melissa Peterman) are being quizzed by Chief Gunderson about their clients. Kokernot, like Bohne, is a native Minnesotan.

One day, before shooting began, Kokernot's phone rang. It was the film's dialect coach. "I got a call from Liz Himelstein saying basically that, in talking to Joel Coen, he had said that I had the sound that they wanted for Frances," Kokernot said. "He was like, 'That's the sound we want for her character.'"

Then Himelstein popped the question: "Will you come and hang out with us? We'll have some lunch, and we'll just talk."

During her audition, Kokernot had not only performed the Minnesota/North Dakota accent flawlessly, she also nodded her head vigorously. She hadn't thought about it. She just did it. The Boys giggled, eventually casting her as Hooker #1, and soon she found herself in McDormand's suite at the Marquette.

"I remember there were floor-to-ceiling windows," Kokernot told me. "They had a living area separate from the bedroom. It was the fanciest hotel room I had ever been in. It was just really nice."

When Kokernot arrived, the trio began talking. McDormand had only one stipulation for their lunchtime meeting. "If you could do the whole thing in a Minnesota accent, that would be great," the future Chief Gunderson told the future Hooker #1.

So she did. For the next several hours, Kokernot chatted with McDormand about acting, Minnesota, and other stuff. And about the accent, of course. "We talked a little bit about if I had any wisdom about the dialect," Kokernot said. "I told them about the nodding thing, and I told them about the 'Oooohs' and the nasality of it. You want people to agree with you, that's where a lot of the gestural things go with it and the 'yahs.'"

By the "nodding thing," Kokernot is referring to people who nod their heads during conversations. A frequent up-and-down nod of the head lets the other person in the conversation know you agree with them, or if you don't agree with them, that at least you empathize with them. It's something people in small towns in the northern Great Plains do a bunch. Kokernot remembers first hearing about it during a Nordic legacy class at Brown University, where she majored in theater arts. And she must have repeated the physical gesture during her audition for the Coens, because when she finished, they mentioned it.

McDormand adopted it too, especially near the end of the scene in which she questions Kokernot and Peterman at a grungy strip club. As the hookers rattle off a series of clueless clues about the johns who'd hired them ("Like I say, he was funny lookin', more than most people even"), Gunderson offers slight nods, then more vigorous head nods at the end of the conversation.

In thinking about her character, McDormand wanted Chief Gunderson's pronunciation of words, her phrasing, and her physical demeanor to be specific to the region.

"Marge was the most pronounced accent," she said. "Generations of her family came from there, so she wore it as a badge of authenticity. I was trying to make it authentic. I worked with . . . Himelstein, who is great because she doesn't just work with the technique of a dialect, she works with the character of a dialect. We really worked on how it could come out of me through the script and then become Marge Gunderson."

But McDormand's on-screen nemesis, Macy, wasn't sold on the long EEEs and rounded OOOs. "Thank you so much for teaching this," Macy told Himelstein. "This is fun. I really like it, but I'm not going to do it like that because I need for my character to be real and I'm not going to use these sounds as much."

By "real," Macy meant more subtle, not soooooo Far-gooooo.

"You do whatever you need to do," Himelstein told Macy. "I'm just introducing you to the sounds and, of course, it's up to you."

Later, Himelstein told me that dialect can't lead an actor's performance; rather, it has to follow other choices. "The actor has to make all of the decisions as to how he or she is going to play this role, and then the dialect will support that," she said.

Macy's acting choices are based on lessons he learned from David Mamet, writer of the Pulitzer Prize–winning play *Glengarry Glen Ross*, many other plays, and the films *The Untouchables*, *Wag the Dog*, *Hoffa*, and *The Verdict*.

In 1971–72, Macy enrolled in Mamet's acting class at Goddard College in Plainfield, Vermont. Mamet was strict with his charges. Late-arriving students were refused entrance or charged one dollar for every minute of tardiness. After collecting the money, Mamet put a match to it so students could see his aim wasn't to profit, but rather to demonstrate dedication to theater as a sacred endeavor. Macy thrived under Mamet's tutelage. The pair became friends. Later, both ended up in Chicago, which is where Mamet cast Macy in *Squirrels* at the St. Nicholas Theatre Company and, most importantly, in *American Buffalo* at the Goodman Theatre Stage Two. Mamet wrote and directed both productions.

In *American Buffalo*, three men conspire to steal a rare coin from a yuppie who'd just purchased it from a junk shop. Macy played Bobby, a sycophantic gofer who works for the junk shop dealer. He was the guy who got coffee and came back with reports about what people in the neighborhood were gossiping about. In the end, Bobby was also duplicitous.

Mamet plays mimic everyday speech patterns, even when characters say goodbye, as in this snippet from *American Buffalo*.

TEACH: I'll see you later, Bobby.
BOB: I'll see you, Donny.
DON: I'll see you later, Bob.
BOB: I'll come back later.
DON: Okay.
Bob *starts to exit*.
TEACH: See you.

"Sometimes you get this stylized thing in Mamet plays, this repetition of words," Joel said. "Even though we were attempting to capture a naturalistic speech pattern for that region, it's reminiscent of something as stylized as Mamet. You just don't want to tip it so far over that it seems artificial or an exaggeration."

Gary Houston, who played opposite Macy in *Fargo* as the disgruntled customer who didn't want to pay for TruCoat, witnessed Macy's *American Buffalo* performance. "Wide-eyed, flat-voiced and utterly without guile, [Macy's] naïveté came across cleanly and effortlessly in the play," Houston wrote in a review for the *Chicago Tribune*. "His rat-a-tat-tat retorts were lightning quick without seeming quick-witted. He was nightly awarded laughs the laughers themselves could not explain."

"Bobby was definitely my first break," Macy recalled of his role in *American Buffalo*. "I felt as if I was really coming into my own."

After a brief Chicago run, *American Buffalo* premiered on Broadway and later became a film starring Dustin Hoffman. Macy wasn't cast in the New York play or the film adaptation, which may explain his hunger for winning auditions like the one for *Fargo*. Still, the lessons of Mamet lingered. For the roles he landed, Macy embraced Mamet's philosophy of acting, which is best articulated in *True and False: Heresy and Common Sense for the Actor.* In the 1997 book, Mamet dismisses the idea that actors need to "become" their characters. "The phrase, in fact, has no meaning," Mamet wrote. "There is no character. There are only lines upon a page. They are lines of dialogue meant to be said by the actor. When he or she says them simply, in an attempt to achieve an object more or less like that suggested by the author, the audience sees an illusion of a character upon the stage."

In an attempt to achieve an object.

Meaning, the actor should do what we all do in life: try to get something from other people. To please the boss, we get the report done early. To get a friend to loan us that cabin up north, we do *her* a favor. This happens all the time, and most of us don't even think about it. It's just how life is. Mamet's suggestion that actors work to get things their characters want is a philosophy in opposition to what many people assume actors do.

"He or she is as free of the necessity of 'feeling' as the magician is free of the necessity of actually summoning supernormal powers," Mamet wrote. "The magician creates an illusion in the mind of the audience. So does the actor."

Macy blurbed the book, writing a glowing paragraph for the dust jacket: "No one has defined the actor's job better than Mamet. So much of the acting we see these days is, in my opinion, emotional glop. The actors are not really acting the story, they are acting what the story means. When all is said and done, it's just indicating. And as Mamet so outrageously and compellingly shows us, the future belongs to those actors who don't indicate at all, ever."

So when Macy told Himelstein he wanted his car salesman to be "real" and not so dialect-focused, his training under Mamet was likely driving his decision. After all, just a year earlier he'd appeared in *Oleanna*, a film written and directed by Mamet.

Then, one day at the Marquette, everything changed.

Himelstein and Macy were riding in the hotel elevator, and a couple of local women jumped on and started talking about the weather, a favorite topic of Minnesota conversations, especially in winter.

"Oh yah, it's real cold out dere."

"Oooh, I know, I know!"

A moment passed.

"See you later."

"You betcha."

The women exited the elevator. The doors closed. Then Macy turned to Himelstein and summed up his change of heart in five straightforward, almost Mamet-like words.

"I'm doing it. I'm in."

FARGO-ESE

A—Of

Better'n—Better than

Bleeme—Believe me

Could do a lot worse—Minnesotans expect things to turn sour at any moment, so "could do a lot worse" means the person is doing okay.

Darn tootin'—Yes; that's right. Often used to affirm another person's statement: "You're darn tootin.'"

Deal—Situation

Dint—Didn't; did not

Doin' pretty good—See "Could do a lot worse."

Doon—Doing

End a story—End of story; "I don't want to talk about it anymore."

Fer—For

From up—From up north; Chief Gunderson is "from up" Brainerd way.

Funny-looking—Not from around here; possibly Jewish

Geez—Wow!

Growsheries—Groceries

Heck—Hell; shit; fuck

Her—It; "Thanks for calling her in."

Hiya—Hello

Hunnert—One hundred

Innapendently—Independently

Innarested—Interested

It's pretty good—Great!

Jif—Short for "jiffy," meaning "one moment."

Munce—Months

Not too bad—Good

Okey-dokey—Okay then

Outfit—Company

Prowler—Police car

Real good now—Okay

Real good then—Okay

Sump'n—Something

Ta—To

That's the deal—That's the bottom line

Unguent—Salve

Unnerstand—Understand

Vouch—Recommend

Whyncha—Why don't you

Wuddya think—What do you think

Ya—You

Yah—Yes

Yer—Your

chapter 5

Unblemished White

Shooting Begins

"If I could, I'd have Hooker #2 vanity license plates."

—MELISSA PETERMAN

"All movie sets are plagued by weather, budget, and ego—but beyond that, the shoot went wonderfully well."

—WILLIAM GOLDMAN, *Which Lie Did I Tell?*

When Frances McDormand read *Fargo*, she wasn't smitten.

"I was like okay, Marge, a midwestern cop," McDormand said. "It was not that interesting at first for me."

In the eleven years between the release of *Blood Simple* and the beginning of principal photography on *Fargo*, her husband and brother-in-law hadn't given her much to chew on. The Coens had cast her as a swinger's wife in *Raising Arizona*, a mousy secretary in *Miller's Crossing,* and an actor in *Barton Fink*. The *Miller's Crossing* and *Barton Fink* roles were barely noticeable: in the gangster pic, she didn't speak, and in the story of the writer with writer's block, she wasn't seen.

During that time, television provided some opportunities. In 1985, McDormand appeared in six episodes of *Hill Street Blues* as an assistant district attorney with a drug addiction. Two years later, she appeared in ten episodes of *Leg Work*, a one-season-and-done girl power drama about a female district attorney. McDormand played the best friend. She also showed up in an episode of *Spenser: For Hire*, which I didn't bother to watch. (I'll only go so far in the name of research.)

For meatier roles, McDormand turned away from the camera to the stage, starring in Anton Chekhov's *Three Sisters*, Arthur Miller's *All My Sons*, and Wendy Wasserstein's *The Sisters Rosensweig*. Hollywood wasn't a total wasteland—she'd acted in *Mississippi Burning* and *Almost Famous*— but she craved deeper, more nuanced parts.

"At the time I thought a psychopath, a killer, a whore, something with a little more meat to it," she said.

Instead, here she was in Minnesota portraying a mostly chipper, pregnant cop. A happily married, singsong, small-town chief of police who loved roast beef sandwiches.

Her character was in the last trimester of pregnancy, about to become a mother for the first time. McDormand was about to become a mother too. But unlike Police Chief Marge Gunderson, she was adopting a child, not birthing one. So Mary Zophres, the film's costume designer, created a pregnancy undergarment for the actor.

"It was a beautiful thing," McDormand said. "I zipped right into it. It was like a whole onesie. It had the boobs and the stomach and the padding, and it was full of birdseed so that it had a little more weight to it."

McDormand also wore a wig of wavy, blonde hair, which Zophres hated. It was a cheap, store-bought wig due to budget, but something about it worked. Small-town women in Minnesota and North Dakota wore their hair just like that in the eighties. To prepare, McDormand spent time with a pregnant St. Paul police officer who taught the actor how to hold a gun and described how the baby kicked every time the officer fired her weapon.

"She said the baby would kind of jump up in her belly," McDormand said.

The first several days of shooting *Fargo* occurred inside a suburban Minneapolis automobile showroom, Wally McCarthy's Olds, located on a busy stretch of Penn Avenue in Richfield. McDormand made her debut as Chief Gunderson, strapped into the birdseed-filled onesie, draped in a beige cop uniform, wearing a wig, and chirping at William H. Macy as Jerry Lundegaard, who was seated behind a salesman's desk making awkward jokes about Babe the Blue Ox.

Still, McDormand felt unsure about her role as Marge.

"It was that moment of transition that I was having trouble with," she said. "I kept losing the accent and the speech patterns, and Joel kept saying, 'You're losing Marge. You're losing Marge.'"

Added McDormand, "I think I kept losing her because I felt too much like myself."

JANUARY 22–25, 1995

If those early days as Jerry Lundegaard were tense for Macy, he didn't reveal it.

On the first day of principal photography, Macy woke up an hour before sunrise at the Marquette Hotel, then was escorted to the car dealership for a 7 AM makeup call. Forty-five minutes later, he was on the showroom floor, ready to meet his first customer, wearing a gray suit, white shirt, and gray tie.

Macy's first filmed scene as Jerry involved chatting up a customer before being called away for a phone call. It's a blip that appears near the middle of the movie, but it was the first time Macy had the opportunity to slip into his role. As a fat man inspects a car, Macy slouches, shoves his hands in his pants pockets, and makes a lame effort at conniving a sale out of the Minnesotan in a thick, winter parka.

The customer spends the scene ignoring Macy. He walks past him, peers inside the Olds, settles into the driver's seat, and stares straight ahead. Macy's character, defeated, makes only a passing effort at selling him TruCoat, an unnecessary sealant designed to make salesmen and the dealership a few extra bucks. When the man refuses, Macy shrugs. "Yeah, you don't need that."

It's the only half-ass thing Jerry does in the entire movie.

During the four days of filming at Wally McCarthy's Olds—renamed Gustafson Olds for the film—he's fleecing customers, doodling on a golf-themed notepad, misleading an accountant at GMAC Financing, lying to Gunderson when she comes in asking pesky questions, and trying to find Shep Proudfoot, the dour mechanic.

"I completely understood his point of view," Macy said about Lundegaard. "I completely knew why he was doing what he was doing, and in that weird way that actors can do it, I thought he was noble. . . . I know he's one of the greatest fools in American letters, but the way that I decided to play it was that it was a man fighting for his family and he was willing to do just about anything to ensure the safety and comfort and the future of his family. If the father-in-law was going to be intractable, I would have to go outside the normal rules of engagement to win, and it just spiraled out of control."

Inside his glass cage at Gustafson Olds, Macy clenched his jaw, twirled a thumb, jammed his hands into his slacks, and, if the truth was too painful, evaded eye contact with others. He weaseled, charmed, and befriended. He did all of this without really thinking. He simply imagined what Jerry Lundegaard wanted from the people in his life.

"I'm the sort of actor—I break down the script for objectives, for intentions, scene by scene what the character wants," Macy said. "That tends to be my preparation. I didn't think there was any need for a physicalizing. I've always believed that the imaginary circumstances will speak to you, and however it comes out is just fine."

Early in the movie, Macy's Lundegaard endures the wrath of a customer who just wants to pay for his car and drive it home. Lundegaard and the man have already agreed on a price, but unbeknownst to the customer, the salesman has added the unnecessary TruCoat and charged him for it. (One crew member claimed something similar happened to Joel when he purchased a Mazda Miata.) As the man chews out Lundegaard for charging him for something he didn't want, didn't order, and is determined not to pay for, the car salesman takes it all in, tilting his head down slightly, slowly twirling a thumb.

Gary Houston, a Chicago journalist and actor, played Bucky, the irate customer. His actual movie credit is "Irate Customer," though at the end of the scene, when he calls Lundegaard a liar—and worse—his wife ("Irate Customer's Wife") whispers his name.

"Bucky, please," she says, as he blurts out the f-bomb.

Macy and Houston knew each other from Chicago theater circles. One night in Minneapolis, after shooting wrapped, the pair grabbed dinner.

Macy picked at his chicken, bummed a cigarette, and reminisced about the old days. At the end of the evening, Macy opened a fortune cookie: "Don't be hasty: Prosperity will knock on your door soon."

Two decades after *Fargo*'s release, I asked Macy to evaluate his performance.

"How long did it take me to nail it, or how well do I think I nailed it?" he asked.

"How well did you nail it," I said.

"Oh, pretty good," he replied. "I think I did pretty well. I haven't seen the film in a while, but the last time I saw it, it was close. It wasn't dead on. If I could do the role again, I think I would work a little harder, but it was pretty close."

Jane Drake Brody, the film's local casting director and an acting coach, believes Macy nailed it.

"He begins not terribly panicked and by the last scene he is out of his mind with hysterical panic," Brody told me. "He begins with a small problem he thinks he can handle if he gets money. Little by little as the film goes on, he becomes more and more desperately panicked, more and more incapable of doing what he needs to be doing. And each time finding it harder and harder to get what he wants. It's a comic trope that he plays so brilliantly. Even when shooting out of sequence, he needs to knows where he is at that time. He's got to know where he is and what he needs to bring at that moment."

While waiting to bring just the right amount of tension to each scene filmed inside Jerry's office, Macy often lingered while crew members fiddled with lights.

"For whatever reason, I stayed there and I was doodling on a pad," Macy said, referring to a white golf-themed notepad he'd filled with an intricate series of circles and straight lines. "Ethan came over and said, 'What are you writing?' It was just designs and it had gotten quite complex because directors of photography are famous for saying, 'I need two minutes,' and twenty-five minutes later, you're still sitting there. It had gotten quite complicated and Ethan said, 'Joel, look at this.' Joel said,

'Let's change the shot.' They pulled the camera around and they shot my doodles and they put it into the scene."

Added Macy, "They thought that spoke volumes."

To the Coens, the suburban car dealership was the perfect setting for the fictional Gustafson Olds.

"They fell in love with the place," said Anne Healy, a location scout who worked on *Fargo* and 2009's *A Serious Man*.

The dealership had everything Joel and Ethan needed: a mechanic's bay, a paneled back room, a showroom floor, and a corner office with a picture window where Macy spent most of his time. The set decorator, Lauri Gaffin, found cheap trophies and silly golf sculptures to line Lundegaard's shelves and clutter a nearby windowsill. The salesman's window gave viewers a hint at life beyond the car dealership's walls. That was a big draw for Joel and Ethan.

Joel Coen provides instruction as Frances McDormand looks on during principal photography at Wally McCarthy's Olds, playing the role of Gustafson Olds in the film. (Photo by James Bridges)

"They are really entertained with what's outside a window," Healy told me. "They wanted to see bleak highway traffic, perpetual motion, a depressing no-man's-land."

With blurry streaks of minivans, cars, pickups, and semis whizzing by on Penn Avenue South through the window, they got it. Inside the dealership, Ethan favored comfortable, long sleeve T-shirts or a gray hoodie. Joel was often seen wearing a dark green fleece jacket and stonewashed jeans with a newspaper tucked in a rear pocket. The *Star Tribune*, the state's largest newspaper, published a daily weather column written by Ken Barlow, a local television meteorologist. As principal photography began, the weatherman delivered bad news.

"No doubt about it, this has been one of the mildest winters in years," Barlow wrote. "Quiet weather will continue right through the week with no major storms in sight."

Added Barlow, "Snow lovers must keep in mind that most of our snow falls in March."

Those words offered little solace. Joel and Ethan needed snow now, in January.

In an early draft of *Fargo*, the Coens made no fewer than fifty-one references to "snow" or phrases containing "snow," including "snowswept," "snowfields," "snow swirls," and my personal favorite, "snow clods," referring to those dirty chunks of frozen snow that get wedged underneath cars or shoved to the side of the road by snowplows. (My wife loves kicking them off the car's underbelly with her boots.) They also made twenty references to "white," such as "granular white," "unblemished white," "everywhere white," and "surrounded by white," most of the time describing the color of snow, but at other times making more metaphorical references.

Among the many mentions of snow: Jerry's meeting with the kidnappers was supposed to be at a bar in a "snowswept parking lot of a one-story brick building." When the kidnappers are rolling down a rural highway, chatting about pancakes and hookers, Joel and Ethan wanted that scene's opening shot to show "a black line [curling] through the white. Twisting perspective shows that it is an aerial shot of a two-lane highway, bordered by snowfields. The highway carries one moving car." And when Jerry comes home to discover the kidnappers have abducted his wife, he "looks at the open window, through which snow still sifts in, shuts it."

Historically, Minnesota and the Dakotas get plenty of snow.

The Children's Blizzard of January 1888 killed at least 250 people on the Great Plains, including a group of South Dakota kids trapped outside while trekking from school to home. On Armistice Day 1940, sixty-mile-per-hour winds whipped snow across Minnesota, freezing hunters to death and causing two Twin Cities men to collapse and die from exhaustion. In 1975, also in January, thirty-five Minnesotans perished in yet another snow-storm, leading many locals to dub it the "Storm of the Century."

When I was a teenager in North Dakota, blinding snow forced me to bunk at a girlfriend's house, miles from my hometown. Her parents shrugged, handed me a blanket, and pointed to the living room sofa. As an adult, three other blizzards halted travel attempts across the vast rectangular state, including one flat-out cancellation of a Greyhound bus due to pick me up at a bowling alley in Dickinson, which sent me across the street to an unheated room at a motel misleadingly named the Oasis. In 1991, as I took my six-year-old and four-year-old sons trick-or-treating, something other than candy began collecting in their bags. Thick flakes twisted in the wind, covering the ground in white and coating tiny Snickers bars and multicolored M&M's. Over the next three days, the "Gods of Winter" dumped twenty-eight inches of snow on the Twin Cities. That October 31–November 2 storm became known as "the Halloween Blizzard." Some Minnesotans who lived through it, and even some who didn't, proudly wear T-shirts proclaiming "I Survived the Halloween Blizzard."

But during the nine weeks the Coens spent filming *Fargo* in January, February, and March 1995, capturing snow on film would prove to be surprisingly difficult.

JANUARY 26, 1995

Most exotic dancers and sex workers have stage names; they don't want customers knowing their real ones. So they lie, telling the men who pay them that their names are Dezire, Bunny, or Bubbles. Or maybe Sierra Mist.

Larissa Kokernot had the opposite problem. The Coens didn't bother giving her character an actual name. She was just Hooker #1, the blonde girl on the left side of the screen with the world's most unfortunate perm. So Kokernot, who was twenty-four at the time and a Brown University graduate, christened her character "Becky." Becky, because in addition to rocking a cheesy sweater, Kokernot was wearing a necklace in the shape of the second letter of the alphabet.

"The costume was truly genius," Kokernot told me. "That sweater with the two cats looking at the moon was originally up to my neck. [The costume designer] cut out the neck and made it into a boatneck and then she gave me a little silver chain that had a 'B' on it."

Generally speaking, I don't stream movies or buy Blu-rays or DVDs. I'd rather watch a movie in a dark theater with people I don't know. But after Kokernot told me she was also wearing an "awful stonewashed jean miniskirt," "horrible pink tights," and "scrunchy boots" in the scene, I pulled out my copy of *Fargo* and paused it on the establishing shot of Kokernot, Melissa Peterman (Hooker #2), and McDormand sitting at a high-top table in a bar. It's a long shot. On the right side of the screen are a trio of stripper poles. And on the left is Kokernot and her miniskirt, tights, and scrunchy boots.

"It was the perfect Minnesota eighties costume," she added. "It was everything I needed. I didn't need anything else for the character."

Those stripper poles and high-top tables were inside the Loch Ness Lounge, a strip bar in Houlton, Wisconsin, just across the St. Croix River from Stillwater, Minnesota. But wait a minute, you might be asking, what about the shot of the Lakeside Club, a dumpy, blue-and-white concrete bunker, that appears on-screen just moments earlier? Movie pros call that "faking it on the outside." This happens when a director shoots the interior and exterior at different locations. In this case, the Coens craved a seedy interior. The Loch Ness wasn't just a bar with nude dancers and neon beer signs. It was a bar with nude dancers and neon beer signs that encouraged its patrons to don miners' helmets, complete with headlamps.

On the morning of January 26, Kokernot and Peterman arrived at 6:30 AM. "They sent us to the makeup truck and got us all dolled up, both

Melissa and I, so we look like we're going out for the night," Kokernot said. "Big huge hair and lots of makeup and the whole thing."

When they walked into the bar, Joel and Ethan were waiting. Joel had his dark hair pulled back in a ponytail. Ethan wore an *Army of Darkness* long sleeve T-shirt tucked into a pair of jeans. Grain Belt and Michelob signs glowed in the background.

"Joel takes one look at us and says, 'Oh no, this isn't the night of, this is the morning after,'" Kokernot said. "They're not going out to turn tricks. This is them just having woken up and put on their clothes. So they sent us back to the makeup truck."

Inside the truck, a crew member grabbed a makeup wipe and scrubbed Kokernot's face clean. Blush, mascara, eye shadow—it all disappeared. Gazing at herself in the mirror, the actor thought she'd never looked worse in her life. But when she returned to the set, Joel loved it.

"Perfect," he said.

After *Fargo* wrapped, McDormand offered Kokernot help getting movie roles. *Move to one of the coasts and I'll see what I can do*, she told her. Kokernot chose Los Angeles, but opted for theater, where she worked mostly as a director. She doesn't regret the choice, but sometimes her ego wishes a different version of Larissa Kokernot had been captured for cinematic immortality.

"I still have a picture somewhere of 'the night of,' and you could see why somebody would want to pay to have sex with me," she said. "But when you look at 'the morning after' . . ."

Kokernot's voice trails off.

"You have to put your ego away because that was what they wanted."

Peterman's "morning after" look wasn't as tragic. As Hooker #2, she sported an off-the-shoulder sweater exposing a pink tank top and a fuchsia bra strap. Her blonde hair retains its side part, and her lips maintain a hint of pink gloss. Like Kokernot, she christened her character with a name: Chevrolet.

"Her mom thinks it's French," she says, pronouncing the American car with a faux Parisian accent. Peterman doesn't believe Chevrolet is hooking every night. She mostly works at her father's hardware store and turns tricks for a little extra spending money.

"You know, fishing licenses are expensive," Peterman told me, joking about her character's secret backstory. "She's been caught by the game warden. They're out to get her. She's gotta get her cash."

Like Kokernot, Peterman moved to Los Angeles after her memorable role as Hooker #2. ("Go Bears!") She focused on acting in film and television. Among her biggest successes: playing the floozy Barbra Jean Booker Hart in *Reba*, a television series starring country music sensation Reba McEntire.

To nab the roles of Hooker #1 and Hooker #2, Kokernot and Peterman each auditioned many times with other women. "I had been kept around for many hours," Kokernot said. "They had other people reading for other roles, but they just kept holding onto me and having me read with another woman each time, and then they would say, 'Hey, can you stick around a little longer?'

"Finally, Melissa and I were in there and we read through it and they laughed through the entire thing. They had laughed some before, but this was the first time they had really laughed. They were like, 'You guys are so funny!' I remember saying to them, 'You guys wrote it! We're just doing what you wrote!' It was a nice moment and feeling to be acknowledged, but [I] also felt stunned that they thought somehow we were responsible."

Why did it work? Like all great comedy duos—even ones that flicker on-screen only briefly—one played it straight while the other played it funny.

"Melissa is one of the funniest people I've ever met," Kokernot said. "I think what worked is that I was in there with somebody who was truly funny. I was the straight person, a little more deadpan, but somehow, that combination just worked."

Kokernot credits Peterman with the impromptu vamping that leads into the scene. As we see the establishing shot of the Lakeside Club, followed by the interior shot of the Loch Ness with stripper poles in the foreground, we hear them chat about enrolling, then failing to graduate from community college.

"I went to Normandale for about a year and a half."

"Yeah, that's where we met."

"But I dropped out though."

"Yeah, she dropped."

"Yeah."

Those words aren't in the script. They're not sparkling bits of dialogue, but the patter establishes a pattern of unhelpful chatter that McDormand as Chief Gunderson tries to untangle. We see McDormand's head bob slightly left, then slightly right as she listens to Becky and Chevrolet. Then, Peterman utters one of the better lines in the scene, also one of her own creation that wasn't in the Coens' script. When Gunderson asks them where they are from, Chevrolet responds that she went to high school in White Bear Lake, pauses, then inserts a silly "Go Bears!" with a half-hearted fist in the air.

When I talked to Peterman about her tiny but cheery and ridiculous role in *Fargo*, she seemed more interested in discussing the importance of collaboration among actors.

"A lot of actors want to be the best and funniest," Peterman said. "They want it to be about them every second. But most scenes are not about one person. If another actor gets a laugh, [a selfish actor] encourages the director to cut that line. They don't want to give another actor a moment. They would rather have it all to them. But most acting is a team sport. If everyone is good in a scene, the scene looks a million times better. You don't want to be the best person in a scene because then there's something wrong with the scene."

As an example, Peterman points to McDormand as an actor dedicated to sharing the spotlight. She used the word "generous" to describe McDormand's style. So did Bohne, who played Deputy Lou. By generous, both Peterman and Bohne suggest how McDormand, and actors like her, engage with others, but don't try to usurp them just to get bigger laughs, more empathy, or more attention.

"And they give you room," Peterman said. "If people are enjoying it, they don't immediately jump their line. They give you space and time to shine. They want it to be a collaborative thing. They're open to making sure the scene is served before they are."

As the Loch Ness scene plays out, Kokernot struggles to describe how her greasy sex partner (Steve Buscemi) looked, finally settling on "funny looking." Peterman is equally clueless, telling McDormand her client (Peter Stormare) looked like the Marlboro Man, maybe because he smoked a lot of cigarettes. McDormand, as the investigator searching for clues to the biggest crime her town has ever seen, looks on dumbfounded, lips pursed. Finally, Kokernot's Hooker #1, who has been nodding, and gently rocking her upper body, as Hooker #2 tells her side of the story, offers a useful tip.

"Hey, they said they were going to the Twin Cities."

Cut to McDormand, who appears deep in thought.

Cut back to the hookers, who are always seen as a pair, and Hooker #1 says, "Is that useful to ya?"

McDormand replies, "You betcha. Yah."

Then the Coens cut back to Kokernot and Peterman, and we see them in full bobblehead mode. The upper bodies and blonde heads of Hooker #1 and Hooker #2 move up and down three times, fully in sync. That's followed by a quick cut to McDormand, who is seen nodding twice on the same beat. The effect is like a punctuation mark on the scene.

A glorious, head-nodding exclamation point.

JANUARY 27, 1995

Radissons are pretty good hotels. But sometimes, a Holiday Inn will suffice.

The Coens shot snippets of four scenes featuring Frances McDormand at the Holiday Inn Minneapolis West on the I-394 strip. On another day of shooting at the Holiday Inn, Stephen Park portraying Mike Yanagita tells McDormand during their midday rendezvous, "Yah, you know, it's a Radisson. So it's pretty good."

On this day, McDormand was filmed greeting hotel staff in the lobby, placing a telephone call from a pay phone, chatting on the phone with her ice-fishing husband (a scene snipped from the final cut), and packing clothes in her suitcase while dissecting her encounter with Mike Yanagita at the hotel bar.

JANUARY 29, 1995

After a day off on Saturday, January 28, the *Fargo* crew took over Edina City Hall the following day, transforming it into the Brainerd Police Department. The scene begins with Chief Gunderson striding through glass doors and passing a row of coworkers answering phones and typing. She turns to one of the women and says, "Two more of those Skin So Softs." (I always loved that little throwaway line because, like Margie, my skin gets so dry in the winter.)

In addition to McDormand as Chief Gunderson, the actors in this scene are John Carroll Lynch (Norm Gunderson) and Bruce Bohne (Deputy Lou). Gunderson has just returned from investigating the triple homicide with Deputy Lou. Before arriving at the station, she picked up night crawlers for her husband, who enjoys dipping his fishing line through a hole in the ice for walleye. He's thinking of her too. The big lug picked up roast beef sandwiches and french fries from Arby's for a lunch date with his wife.

Before principal photography began, McDormand and Lynch met for lunch at Kramarczuk's, a Polish deli in Northeast Minneapolis. They ate sandwiches and discussed their fictional movie marriage. It's something actors do to add nuance to performances. How did Marge and Norm become *those* people?

As they ate, McDormand and Lynch decided Lynch's character—a stay-at-home husband—was an ex-cop who quit the force in favor of a quieter life of painting. So in early takes, when Bohne bounds into the room to announce a lead in the case, Lynch turns his head and pays attention.

"I'm listening to her talk about the case with [Deputy] Lou, and Joel and Ethan come over and go, 'You don't really care about any of that,'" Lynch said. "I was like, 'Really, because we had talked about maybe he had been on the force.'"

"No, that's not right."

"Oh, okay."

"He doesn't really care."

"Oh, okay."

Added Lynch, "It was really clear that that's what they wanted. They wanted him disinterested in her work. I didn't understand why that was, but okay, I'll play that. I can play that. So I'm playing that, and then I see the film and I realize that one of the things that Norm does for her is give her safe haven. She comes home from these terrible things and she knows she's in a safe place and she never, ever, ever, ever, ever has to talk about it."

For Bohne, the biggest worry was the sound of his own voice. He'd been working as an understudy on *Macbeth*, which was being performed at Minneapolis's Guthrie Theater. In the days leading up to the filming of Bohne's first *Fargo* scene, the actor playing Macbeth fell ill. So Bohne was thrust onstage, playing the lead role of one of the most tragic figures in the Shakespearean canon—which was fine, he said; he could do that. But projecting his voice as the murderous *Macbeth* to an audience of about a thousand people every night and twice each weekend day, *that* was a strain.

"My voice was blasted," Bohne said. "I knew everything about Macbeth except for how much vocal energy it takes. By the time I had done six shows in a row, I didn't have a voice. I was terrified that I was going to get to the set and they were going to say, 'Bruce, now that you don't have a voice, we're going to have to recast the role of Lou.' Somehow I got through it. I didn't really notice that I didn't have a voice, but it was terrifying."

Food also played a supporting role that day inside Edina City Hall. Marge gets excited when she sees Norm has brought her Arby's. She returns the favor with a box of night crawlers. The Coens make a joke out of the juxtaposition, cutting to an insert of the squiggly worms right as she says, "Oh, yah, looks pretty good" in reference to the Arby's lunch.

During the filming, McDormand and Lynch are snarfing Arby's, not pretending to snarf Arby's. We watch Lynch and McDormand dig into their roast beef sandwiches and discuss Norm's progress on his duck stamp painting, both of them talking with their mouths full. In most movies, you rarely see actors actually chewing and swallowing food. They order food. The food arrives. They talk to other actors while food waits, uneaten, in front of them. But rarely do they actually put food in their mouth and masticate. Not so for John Carroll Lynch.

"A lot of times you'll see actors and they'll have one piece of lettuce on a fork and you never actually see them eat it," Lynch said. "That always feels untruthful to me. I've always felt like, if I'm going to eat in a scene, I'm going to eat," he said. "Especially as Norm. I didn't know enough to know that was going to be a problem."

But it was.

"I think I had about fifteen Arby's sandwiches that day," he added. "I didn't eat full ones, but enough."

JANUARY 30, 1995

A day after eating Arby's at the police station, McDormand and Lynch shoveled more food into their maws at Tinucci's Restaurant in Newport. Twenty-two patrons, two busboys, and a meat carver were also on hand to provide atmosphere at the fictional all-you-can-eat, cafeteria-style restaurant portrayed in the picture.

In the opening shot, the camera lingers over vats of steaming meat: chicken and dumplings, chicken fricassee, fried torsk, boiled torsk, and Swedish meatballs. We hear a Muzak version of "Do You Know the Way to San Jose" as McDormand scoops up mounds of fricassee layered in a goopy, creamy sauce onto her plate. She scoots past the fried torsk, pauses to consider the boiled torsk, then dives into the meatballs with the plastic tongs.

She is, after all, eating for two.

The setting was inspired by the Jolly Troll, an ersatz Scandinavian cafeteria in Golden Valley. The Coens and other local kids dug the Troll because it was all-you-can-eat and because the restaurant didn't serve up just giant dollops of food but also fun. The Jolly Troll lived up to its name by featuring mechanical, white-bearded little trolls doing various troll-like chores.

Ray A. Anderson and his wife, Alice Anderson, opened the Jolly Troll in 1964. Newspaper ads encouraged Mother's Day and Thanksgiving visits, highlighting a price of $2.95 per person, with children under age ten paying just twenty-five cents per year. The concept was so popular, the Andersons expanded the Troll to other cities, including Des Moines, Eau Claire, Rockford, Tulsa, Oakland, and Seattle.

By the time Joel and Ethan returned in 1995, the Golden Valley Troll was gone. But the restaurant was still on their minds. In an early draft of the script, they dubbed the bar where Jerry meets the kidnappers at the beginning of the film "Jolly Troll Tavern" and imagined as its sign a neon troll lofting a champagne glass.

"Unfortunately, there are sort of aspects of, you know, the city that has disappeared since we grew up there," Ethan said. "It used to be there were any number of Swedish smorgasbords . . . but we couldn't find a single one when we went back to shoot there."

JANUARY 31, 1995

As the winter days ticked by, Minneapolis roads stayed dry.

On January 31, nine days after principal photography began, meteorologist Ken Barlow wrote about the weird weather in the *Star Tribune*. "This is the last day of what will go down in the record books as one of the warmest Januarys in several years," he noted. "Many days were more than 10 degrees above the average. There has been a lack of snow, and for many it has been a disappointing month."

Meanwhile, the Coens and crew were inside the Chanhassen Dinner Theatre to shoot a sequence that was making Michelle Hutchison nervous. Her role as an escort called for nudity. She understood that. The character had no name in the script, just "Escort." Hutchison's agent told her not to ask for more information about the nudity. If she asked for more information, like how much or what kind, Hutchison was warned, the Coens might think she was nervous about baring it all. So just don't ask.

When Hutchison, an Ohio native who moved to Minneapolis as a kid, arrived at the location, she still hadn't learned anything about what part of her body would be exposed for the camera. What she did know was this: the Chanhassen Dinner Theatre was a stand-in for the Carlton Celebrity Room, a Las Vegas–style lounge in the Minneapolis suburbs. The 2,200-seat

venue, which opened in 1979, hosted A-list country artists like Loretta
Lynn and Johnny Cash, funk and R&B legends like James Brown and Ray
Charles, pioneering rockers from Chuck Berry to Jerry Lee Lewis, and a
host of big-name comedians like Rodney Dangerfield and George Carlin,
not to mention a lengthy roster of B-listers and Vegas regulars; the act that
the escort and her date, Carl Showalter, watched in *Fargo*, José Feliciano,
also performed at the real-life Carlton Celebrity Room. The venue was
bulldozed in 1987 to make way for the Mall of America.

Beyond the location of her first scene, Hutchison also knew she'd be
on a "date" with Buscemi's character, Carl Showalter. They'd make small
talk, then escape to Shep Proudfoot's dumpy apartment to get it on. The
Celebrity Room scene was to be filmed first, but Hutchison couldn't get
her mind off the later scene. In a cramped fitting room, Hutchison lis-
tened as Mary Zophres, the film's costume designer, showed her the outfit she'd be wearing inside the dinner theater. Finally, Hutchison blurted
out, "But what about the nudity?"

Zophres replied, "Nobody has talked to you about this yet?"

"Nobody has talked to me about this yet," Hutchison said. "I've asked
everybody, but nobody will tell me."

"Don't worry about it, Michelle," Zophres said. "Let's go in. The Boys
are in the sound studio. We'll go talk to them about it."

They walked to a nearby room, where Ethan and Joel were working.
When Hutchison entered, The Boys greeted her with a "Heeeey, Michelle.
How ya doing?" When she tells the story, Hutchison drags out the "how
ya doing" like a stringy dope-smoker.

"They're such hippies," she said. "They're very laid back."

In the screenplay, the sex scene is just five words: "Carl is humping the
escort."

The description lacked specificity about the actors' positions or what
the escort would be wearing. "I want to know more," Hutchison said.
"How nude will I be?"

"You don't know?"

"No, I don't."

The Coens broke it down for Hutchison, frame by frame. "You're going
to be on top of Steve. The first shot, it's going to be of your back. You'll

be covered." They continued for several minutes, detailing every moment of the scene.

"They were very kind," Hutchison said. "It was one of those things where it's a lot of stress because you don't know what to expect. In the end, I was certainly okay with it."

For the record, Hutchison wore nylons that covered her butt and a bit of cloth to hide her breasts. "You can't see that from the back. I felt I had some modicum of modesty, and Steve was covered too," she said.

Before the sex scene, which was filmed on a different day, Hutchison asked Joel if she could improvise a few words. He said, *sure, go ahead.* So during the filming, Hutchison encourages Buscemi to orgasm: "Awwww right. C'mon, I'm hearing bells. C'mon. Well, all right. Well, where are ya? Huh?"

"That was my idea of a northern Minnesota gal that moved to the Cities and thought she was just above the fray," Hutchison said. "She's not walking the streets. But this is her way of kinda talkin' dirty."

In Hutchison's mind, the escort was named Debbi Johnson and came from rural Otter Tail County, not far from the big city of Fergus Falls. She's adamant that Debbi would not spell her first name with an "e" on the end and that, when written, above the "i" would be a circle, or maybe a heart, but definitely not a dot.

Before the sex, Hutchison and Buscemi's characters sip champagne while suffering through an awkward conversation. As José Feliciano strums his guitar in the spotlight, Showalter ignores her question about his line of work and she ignores his gross joke about the old "in and out." The Coens never go to a close-up of either actor; they stay on a medium shot so we can see the characters' lack of connection.

It's a technique Martin Scorsese employed to great effect in *Goodfellas*, his 1990 mob movie. After Joe Pesci tells a humorous story at a bar to a table full of mobsters, Ray Liotta laughs uproariously with the rest of the gang, and then says to Pesci, "You're a funny guy." That line prompts Pesci to confront Liotta. "What do you mean, I'm funny?" Liotta fumbles to explain, and then goes quiet, unsure what to say while Pesci keeps pushing. The hoodlums around them all gradually fall silent. Pesci persists: "Funny how? I mean, what's funny about it?" Throughout the increasingly tense exchange, Scorsese never cuts to a close-up. The shots of Pesci and Liotta are medium shots. Included in the frame are the other men around them, who are getting more and more tense watching the confrontation. We see one hoodlum glance down. Another scratches his face. They're nervous. They don't know what's going to happen.

Pesci continues: "I'm funny how? I mean, funny like I'm a clown? I amuse you? I make you laugh? I'm here to fucking amuse you?" Following a final, "How the fuck am I funny? What the fuck is so funny about me? Tell me! Tell me what's funny," Liotta finally gets that his friend is pulling his leg and blurts out, "Get the fuck out of here." Pesci laughs. And everyone breathes a sigh of relief and joins in the laughter. Pesci was just fucking with Liotta. Everything is okay.

Thelma Schoonmaker, Scorsese's longtime collaborator and film editor, explains the power of the medium shot. "There are no close-ups at all because Marty wanted to show what was happening to the people around Ray Liotta and around Joe Pesci," she said. "It starts out very funny and

Michelle Hutchison (Escort) and Steve Buscemi (Carl Showalter) during their scene at Chanhassen Dinner Theatre, which served as a stand-in for the Carlton Celebrity Room. (Photo by James Bridges)

people are laughing. Then pretty soon, things get a little scary, then scarier and scarier. You see on the faces of the people around them, they are really beginning to get worried. . . . You don't always have to have close-ups. Sometimes a medium shot or a wide shot is just as good."

In the awkward scene between Showalter and the escort at the faux Carlton Celebrity Room, the medium shot allows us to watch Hutchison's eyes dart between the stage and her client. As Debbi, Hutchison isn't exactly hanging on Buscemi's every word.

"She's bored shitless with him," said Jane Brody, the local casting director. "She just can't handle it one more day. She's thinking, 'I've got to get out of this business.' [Hutchison] just brings so much to the role. In the hands of another director, that would never have happened. It all would have been about Steve. He would have had every frame in that scene. They let people act."

The Coens also make unconventional casting choices, choosing a face Hutchison herself describes as funny, with one eye that's slightly closer to her nose than its partner. "I've been told, 'you're attractive,' which is nice for 'you're not really pretty' in a weird way," Hutchison said. "I know I don't look like everybody else."

Brody pretty much agrees.

"Another director, if it was a hooker, would have made her sexy and gorgeous," Brody said. "Hooker means sexy and gorgeous. But Michelle, while she is sexy and gorgeous, brought so much more story to it just because of her cynicism, ennui, boredom. Because of who she is, she created in this tiny, little role the world of a hooker who doesn't want to be in the business anymore."

FEBRUARY 1, 1995

The first day of February delivered cloudy skies and a high temperature in the middle thirties, slightly above freezing. That day's schedule called for a pair of outdoor shots at a bar and at the drive-thru of a fast-food joint. But there was still no snow on the horizon. So line producer John Cameron asked the special effects team to produce "snowfall, snow on ground, snowmaker, smoke in bar."

Crew members, twenty-one extras, and three stand-ins reported to the King of Clubs, a workingman's bar in Northeast Minneapolis, at 8 AM, just a few hours after patrons from the night before downed their last drinks. With its pool tables, pull tabs, and dark walls, the King of Clubs was the perfect stand-in for a North Dakota dump in the movie's opening tryst. It's here where Jerry Lundegaard walks in looking as out of place as a pistol at a peacenik convention. Macy as Jerry Lundegaard is wearing a beige parka, thick snow boots, heavy gloves, and a winter fedora. Other patrons are shooting pool or caressing beer bottles. There are two signs above Lundegaard's head when he walks through the door: "EXIT" and "Drunk of the Week Grahm Place."

Adding to the smoky, atmospheric mix is the sound of a jukebox blasting "Big City," a country classic by Merle Haggard. The song reached number one on the Billboard Country Music chart in 1982. Before turning to music, Haggard tried robbing a tavern, got caught, and was sent to San Quentin for three years. Two of his early hits were about prison ("The Fugitive" and "Mama Tried"), but "Big City" is the perfect choice as a metaphor for Jerry's mindset. He's a guy who wants to escape, just like the narrator of the Haggard hit.

> I'm tired of this dirty old city
> And tired of too much work
> And never enough play
> And tired of these dirty old sidewalks
> Think I'll walk off my steady job today

By walking into the King of Clubs with a stolen car attached to the hitch of his Delta 88, Jerry has pretty much walked off his steady job and into the dark netherworld of Fargo, North Dakota. It's where skinny criminals smoke, fret, and guzzle longnecks, waiting for a chance at a free car and easy cash.

A friend of mine once compared *Fargo* to *Chinatown*. Neither movie really takes place in the location for which it is named, but each place is perceived as mysterious and depraved. It's where bad things happen, beyond the watchful eyes of proper society.

FEBRUARY 2, 1995

When he first read the Mike Yanagita scene, Stephen Park couldn't wrap his head around it. The Coens imagined Yanagita as fat and balding, a loner who hit on a pregnant woman at a hotel bar. Park was thin and sported a thick head of black hair. More importantly, he didn't relate to what he read. Mike Yanagita possessed a sense of alienation Park didn't feel. The character felt far away from him and the people he knew.

Why am I being seen for this? Park wondered. He told his agent, nope, he wasn't interested.

A week or so later, the script found its way back to the Los Angeles actor. His agent asked him if he would read it again. And consider auditioning? Park pulled out the scene and read it again. It begins with Marge entering a hotel bar described as "a rather characterless, low-lit meeting place for businesspeople." A voice asks, "Marge?" The voice is described as coming from "a bald, paunching man of about Marge's age" whose "features are broad, friendly, Asian-American."

With this reading, Park ignored Yanagita's physical description and leaned into the emotional trauma. He thought about the other scenes when Mike isn't in the room with Marge, but Marge is thinking about Mike. There's the phone call to her Brainerd home as she's drifting off to sleep. As Norm snoozes, a man from her past calls and asks for her by her birth name: Margie Olmstead. Later, after the drink with Mike, Marge tells a friend about him over the phone as she packs her bags inside a room at the Radisson. Marge learns Mike's been lying. He never married Linda, as he had claimed during their date; she didn't die of cancer. Mike stalked Linda, never married, and lives with his parents.

"A character like this feels far away from me," Park recalled to me. "It took me awhile to get into this character and feel the pain. At first, I felt like I couldn't even do it."

Before *Fargo*, Park portrayed a Korean American shopkeeper in Spike Lee's *Do the Right Thing*. In the 1989 movie, a bespectacled Park, and his dutiful wife, struggles to understand Radio Raheem's request to buy twenty D batteries for his enormous boom box. Raheem, played by Bill Nunn, gets upset when Park's character doesn't understand.

"Twenty, motherfucker," Raheem insists. "Twenty."

Park, as the immigrant shopkeeper, shouts, "Motherfuck you!"

Two years after *Do the Right Thing*, Park joined the cast of *In Living Color*, a sketch comedy show created by Keenen Ivory Wayans. The series launched Jim Carrey's career. Park didn't enjoy as big of a boost, but he did appear in twenty-eight of the show's 147 episodes, often as an immigrant with an accent. His most famous character was Tommy Wu, a huckster who inherited millions from a rich uncle and now entices lazy television viewers to sign up for his get-rich-quick class.

With the *Fargo* script in his hands, Park began to put himself in Mike Yanagita's boots, living as an Asian American in the snow-white Minneapolis suburbs. Park, who was born and raised in a small town in New York, thought about Yanagita's yearning to fit in with his Scandinavian classmates, their culture, their way of speaking. Slowly, a character began to emerge. Park told his agent he'd audition for the role.

"They sent me cassette tapes to hear what the accent should sound like," Park said. "I did it deliberately subtle."

Joel and Ethan cast him anyway.

After Park returned to California, the Coens asked Elizabeth Himelstein to help him punch up the Minnesota accent. They wanted Mike Yanagita to sound as Norwegian American as Jean Lundegaard or my great-grandparents who lived in a sod house on the South Dakota prairie.

Park arrived at the Holiday Inn on I-394 near Shelard Park on Wayzata Boulevard wearing a long sleeve denim shirt and a look of determination. In makeup, a stylist wetted his hair and began snipping. His long, below-the-ear mane was shaped into a shorter, wavier style. Then he slipped on a brown, three-piece suit with a tie and took his place, alone, in a restaurant booth facing the bar and a tiny television set near the ceiling. As the scene begins, Frances McDormand walks tentatively through double doors and scans the bar, searching for her high school friend. When the Coens cut to a shot from her point of view, we see Park from behind, slumped forward. As she approaches in a flowery, beige blouse, they greet each other, and the scene begins in earnest.

Stephen Park gets ready for his makeover to become Mike Yanagita. (Photo courtesy of Stephen Park)

Stephen Park, post-makeover. (Photo courtesy of Stephen Park)

"I remember I had a padded belly," Park told me. "She had her padded thing. I remember our bellies bouncing against each other as I was squeezing her really tight. And she was like, okay, okay, kinda pushing me away. Then we're sitting down and then there's that kind of awkward moment."

Another such "awkward moment" occurs when Park scoots over to McDormand's side of the booth, then loops his arm behind her. "Yeah, I think that I was probably plotting that the whole time, finding the moment to move," Park said, imagining Mike's thought process. "Then I just did it. 'Do you mind if I sit over here?' Then I put my arm around her, just trying to get cozy."

When that fails, Mike makes other attempts to woo Marge. He lies about his wife's death. Although that sparks some sympathy from Marge—she doesn't know it's a lie at this point—she doesn't swoon. So Mike confesses his love to Marge. She's super. He likes her. He likes her so much.

Then he collapses in tears.

Frances McDormand and Stephen Park pose for the camera following their memorable, and memorably awkward, scene together at the Radisson Hotel bar. (Photo courtesy of Stephen Park)

"Once we sat down, then it was really just about me trying to be fulfilled through her to relieve my loneliness and sadness," Park said. "The whole time I was playing this scene I had this sense that he was crying inside . . . he was just crying out of sheer pain and loneliness. I was kinda carrying that with me through the whole scene. At the end, allowing myself to just be exposed."

During filming, the Coens began with the camera over Park's shoulder, looking at McDormand, recording her lines, her reactions. Park was so intense, so real, McDormand asked them to begin having the camera capture Park's lines and reactions sooner than they might have been planning.

As Park worked, Himelstein hovered nearby, urging him to make the vowels longer. "He worked so hard on the accent," she said. "He worked so thoroughly hard, but the more serious he was with it, the funnier it was. I've got to tell you, he went for it. Talk about a master class for me just watching him put this character together. Once he committed to it, he just understood intuitively about the rhythm and he was just a blast to work with."

The scene, which clocks in at exactly four minutes, has become legendary. Nearly every actor I talk to mentions it before I do. Bong Joon Ho, director of the Academy Award–winning *Parasite*, cast Park in his 2013 *Snowpiercer*. The reason: the Korean director dug Park as Yanagita. The scene is regularly cited as odd, hilarious, brilliant, and, some argue, completely unnecessary.

At the time, Park didn't think the scene was particularly funny.

"To me, when I shot the scene, it was just very painful," he said. "Then I remember when the film started screening and I got a call from Ethan. He was like, 'Oh, we just screened it and you were hilarious. It was so funny.' I was like, 'What?' It wasn't until I saw the movie that I could get the humor of it. But I was so inside the character, I didn't capture the humor of it at the time."

chapter 6

Fran Used to Have a
Car Like This

Shooting Continues, But Inside

"I don't know if anyone really laughed at it, but they thought it was funny."

—LARRY BRANDENBURG

"I ate the doorjamb with my face."

—JENNIFER LAMB HEWITT

FEBRUARY 5, 1995

Dieter Sturm was starting to shiver. He'd been on the roof of a parking ramp at Minneapolis–St. Paul International Airport for hours now, pointing a snow gun into the quiet night air. Nearby runway lights flickered, but jets weren't soaring into the sky or landing. It was past midnight, and Sturm, a special effects man from Lake Geneva, Wisconsin, who specialized in making snow for movies, hadn't created a single flake.

For hours, Sturm's air compressors roared, forcing water through hoses connected to a pair of handheld snow guns gripped by men on his team, but the mists of water had failed to transform into fluffy, white snowflakes. It was nearly 3 AM, and Sturm was getting worried.

"It's like we're never gonna get this thing done by the time they get here," Sturm recalled to me.

They, of course, were the Coens. The Brothers were due to arrive around sunrise, ready to film a scene showing a Cutlass Ciera gliding across a sea

113

of snow, then halting to a stop. Steve Buscemi, dressed in a shit-brown outfit, would emerge from the car, then unceremoniously steal a license plate from another vehicle. After that, he'd have a bitchy encounter with a parking attendant.

Without snow, the parking ramp would be a drab, anywhere kind of place. With snow, it would be quintessentially Minnesotan.

Finally, things changed for the special effects man.

"Right around the time I'm thinking that," Sturm said, "we started really making snow. And I'll be darned, by 7 AM call we just finished with covering the entire five acres of that rooftop."

Joel and Ethan took full advantage of the achievement, spending a luxurious thirty-five seconds on a wide shot of the Ciera emerging onto the ramp's roof, then swooping through virgin snow to create a set of curvy tire tracks. At one point during the shot, which had to be accomplished in a single take, the midsize sedan nearly gets stuck in a thick patch of manufactured snow.

"I remember the car coming up the ramp, and then it hits the rooftop and starts driving," Sturm said. "And then all of a sudden it starts slowing down. I'm like, no, no, no, don't get stuck, don't get stuck. Because, you know, it's not perfectly even. So there were a few little drifts here and there. Luckily, he just kept his foot on the gas."

After Buscemi's character steals the plate, he confronts a bald attendant wearing a cheap, clip-on tie. The attendant wants him to pay four dollars—the minimum charge at long-term parking—even though Buscemi was only at the top of the ramp for ten, fifteen minutes. Buscemi balks, saying he's just pulled in. The attendant insists, politely. The men exchange words. Buscemi finally relents, handing the man the cash, but not before insulting him. "You know, these are the limits of *your* life, man," he says, pointing to the tiny booth. "Ruler of your little fucking gate here. Here, here's your four dollars. You pathetic piece of shit."

Peter Schmitz portrayed the airport lot attendant. He'd recently moved to Minneapolis from New York City, having just worked as an understudy on *My Fair Lady*. After the Broadway production closed, he and his wife relocated to the Twin Cities, where she was enrolled in a grad school program at the University of Minnesota. Schmitz nabbed the role of Ghost of Christmas Past in the Guthrie's 1994 production of *A Christmas Carol*. Many of his acting colleagues were trying out for roles in *Fargo* or had already been cast. Schmitz asked his agent to get him an audition. The Coens were curious and sent him a script. Before reading for the role, Schmitz asked Dale, a Minneapolis neighbor, to read the script out loud so he could listen to the local dialect.

"Dale, would you read this for me?"

"Oh geez, I don't know. I've never done this before."

"I know, Dale, it's fine. Whatever you do, it's fine."

Finally, Dale uttered a few lines, including, "What do mean, you decided not to park here?"

That's all Schmitz needed. When he auditioned, the Coens giggled. But not at his performance. At his noggin.

"The Coens saw me and said, 'He's got this really weird head,'" Schmitz said. "It's very long and narrow. They thought that head popping out of a parking lot attendant booth would be startling."

On the day of the shoot, Schmitz reported for makeup, pulled on the uniform pants of the parking attendant, tucked in the white shirt, and put on the black jacket and, yes, the clip-on tie. When he walked to the perimeter of the set and asked for instructions, he was told, "If you could just keep traffic away from the set."

Schmitz politely explained, "But I'm in the scene."

Shortly after settling into the boxy booth, Schmitz flipped on the space heater to warm his toes. As instructed, he opened the window every now and then to comply with requests, including one from the director of photography. "Stop closing the window!" Roger Deakins shouted at him. "I'm focusing on your fucking nose!"

The actual shooting went well, with Buscemi and Schmitz nailing their roles as Mr. Aggressive and Mr. Passive-Aggressive. With each profanity-laced verbal punch from Buscemi, Schmitz countered with a gaping smile or look of polite disbelief.

"I'm like, 'Who the hell is this guy?'" Schmitz said. "He's obviously trying to cheat his way out of paying, so I just keep being nicer and nicer to prove I can out nice him until he agrees to follow the rules because isn't that really the best for everybody?"

Although Schmitz said he didn't lean into the local dialect, he did embrace its underlying duplicitousness. "The movie is about the real aggression behind Minnesota friendly," Schmitz said. "Minnesota nice can really be 'To hell with you, buddy,' but said with a smile."

FEBRUARY 6, 1995

In Jerry's initial meeting with Wade, his father-in-law, to discuss his business proposition, the scene takes place inside the older man's office, and the car salesman is the supplicant. Jerry stands while Wade sits in judgment behind a majestic desk. In their next meeting, the power dynamic has shifted.

Jerry, Wade, and Wade's right-hand man, Stan, share a curved, red restaurant booth as equals. They've gathered to discuss what to do about Jean's kidnapping, whether to call the cops and how much money to hand over to the kidnappers. Jerry, for selfish reasons, doesn't want the police involved. He's lied to Stan and Wade, telling them the price tag for his wife's return is a hefty $1 million, which is $960,000 more than he's promised the kidnappers he's colluded with. Wade wants the cops involved and—cheap bastard that he is—wants to negotiate a lower ransom.

The men are meeting in an Embers Family Restaurant at 7525 Wayzata Boulevard in St. Louis Park. Founded in 1956 by local entrepreneurs Henry Kristal and Carl Birnberg, the family-style restaurant chain used to be a big deal in Minnesota, commonly seen in advertisements on television and radio. The company's "Remember the Embers" jingle wormed its way into local ears, encouraging mom, dad, and the kids to settle in for eggs, pancakes, pie, or the Emberger Royal, one of the nation's first bacon cheeseburgers. (A&W claims to have invented the bacon cheeseburger in 1963, but Embers loyalists point to a 1958 menu highlighting the Emberger Royal, complete with cheese *and* bacon.)

Throughout the scene, as the father-in-law presses Jerry to see things his way, Macy's hands are twisting and pulling on a napkin wrapped around utensils. Macy doesn't remember doing it. "Once you know what the objective is, you get into a metaphorical ring with the other actor and you're duking it out trying to get your way, inevitably someone will say, 'That thing you did with your hand when you put it on your head, that was genius. How did you think of that?' You have no idea what they're talking about."

Meanwhile, the Coens told Larry Brandenburg, the actor who played Stan, exactly what to do with his hands. "We want you to use your fork, pick up a piece of pie, and just hold it there for the whole scene," Joel and Ethan told him. "Don't eat it. Just hold it there so we can see you holding the pie the whole time."

When I interviewed Brandenburg, I confessed to not seeing the fork thing at all. "I know. That's the problem," he said. "No one noticed it. I was holding the piece of pie the whole time and no one noticed."

But I did see Petra Boden, the actor who portrayed the perky blonde cashier who rings up Lundegaard's bill for $2.40. Boden shines when the camera offers us a close-up of her cheery, smiling face.

As Macy pays the bill, Boden chirps, "How was everything, today?"

The Coens return the camera to Macy for a dour frown, then cut back to a close-up of Boden tilting her head and beaming optimism at the bitter salesman. It's yet another exclamation mark on Minnesota exceptionalism.

FEBRUARY 7, 1995

Ken Barlow's weather corner on this day was particularly bleak. "Finally, winter," read the headline on the full page the *Star Tribune* dedicated to chronicling cold fronts, high and low temperatures, weather maps of the United States and the Upper Midwest, and the column featuring weather observations by the television meteorologist.

"Snow is falling today where it shouldn't and not falling where it should," Barlow wrote. "Places such as Atlanta, Ga., and Birmingham, Ala., will see some snow today."

But Minneapolis? It got next to nothing: one-tenth inch of snow.

It was the first, tiniest trace of flurries since the Coens began shooting a movie whose characters were supposed to be seen stomping around in galoshes, scraping ice off windshields, brushing snow off stolen license plates, and hiding hundreds of thousands of dollars in a suitcase in the snow. Luckily, the suitcase wasn't on tap yet. On this morning, the plan was to film Stormare and Buscemi driving to Minneapolis for the kidnapping.

The script called for Stormare to brood and for Buscemi to talk, pretty much nonstop.

"I guess from the first time we met him we thought that this guy would be a good blabbermouth," Joel said. "In real life, [Buscemi's] not a blabbermouth at all. It's always an interesting dynamic, a character who talks a lot and a character who says nothing."

The Coens love this kind of thing.

In *Blood Simple*, Abby chats while Ray tries to sleep. In *Barton Fink*, Barton blathers while the killer endures his boorish monologues. In *The Big Lebowski*, Walter drones while The Dude abides. In *Fargo*, Buscemi punctuates Stormare's silence with a single question.

"Would it kill you to say something?" he asks.

"I did," Stormare shoots back, his eyes on fire.

"No," Buscemi says. "That's the first thing you said in the last four hours."

On this day, Buscemi and Stormare reported to makeup by 8:30 AM and were ready to go thirty minutes later. The tricky part of filming inside the Ciera was controlling what was outside the window. Since Minneapolis lacked snow, the Coens chose to shoot the scene in a mostly walled section of I-35W to obscure that fact. Behind Buscemi and Stormare, we see only flashes of traffic and concrete.

The scene's establishing shot is a dashboard view of the Minneapolis skyline. On the left, we see the glass IDS Center, which Buscemi references in his attempt at conversation with Stormare. The shot is from just south of downtown, which doesn't make sense because the pair is supposedly driving in from Fargo, which is north of the Cities.

But, whatever.

The brief conversation between Buscemi and Stormare is their second pre-kidnapping chat while on the road. In the first one, which was filmed on a different day, Stormare learned that the Coens are hyper-specific about dialogue. With the camera rolling, Stormare lets Buscemi knows he wants to eat breakfast—again.

Instead of saying "Pancakes Hause" as the script indicates, Stormare corrects the apparent error and utters "Pancake Hause." Ethan noticed.

ETHAN: "Peter? What were you saying there?"

PETER: "I said, 'Pancake Hause.'"

ETHAN: "No, it's 'Pancakes Hause.'"

PETER: "Oh, I thought it was a typo."

ETHAN: "No, no, there are no typos in our scripts."

Years later, Woody Harrelson also tried convincing the Coens to alter dialogue in *No Country for Old Men*. They refused.

✢✣✢

There's a moment when everything goes dark in *Fargo*. Grimsrud has just murdered his third innocent victim. First, the cop. Second, the fat man in the red parka trying to outrun a bullet. Third is the redhead upside down in the fat man's car, breathing heavily, frightened. Grimsrud peers inside the vehicle, stands, then calmly pulls the trigger. As Grimsrud fires, the Coens cut to a dark screen, but the horror of the gunshot echoes, its sound reverberating into our consciousness. Just as it fades into silence, the Coens switch to soothing music, and the screen fades in to an unfinished painting of a Canada goose. Then the camera pans across an array of paintbrushes in glass jars, a stuffed duck, tiny bottles of paint, and books.

We're inside the bedroom of Marge and Norm Gunderson of Brainerd, Minnesota. The couple, played by McDormand and Lynch, is sleeping. The camera continues its pan to McDormand, her head resting on a pillow. After a phone call wakes her, Norm's hairy arm gently falls on her hip, then the couple slowly rises from bed.

The breakfast nook portion of the scene was filmed inside a mansion at 2215 Pillsbury Avenue South in Minneapolis, just north of the Minneapolis Institute of Art, beginning at about 4 PM. Anne Healy, the location scout, was friends with the homeowners. The mansion has a long driveway that extends from the street to the side of the house, allowing the movie crew to park Marge's prowler outside the screen door. The home's impressive exterior is never shown.

When Lynch appeared on set that afternoon, the prop master had a question for him. "We have this spread of breakfast. What would you like to have?"

"Oh no, no, he's not eating," Lynch said of his character. "He made her eggs. He's just going to have coffee."

Joel and Ethan heard the exchange, then jumped into the conversation. "He's not eating?" they said. "He's eating."

McDormand, dressed in her brown Brainerd police uniform, had an opinion too.

"No, he's got up to make her eggs," she said. "He's not eating himself."

The Coens relented—although Norm ultimately gives into temptation.

Inside the breakfast nook, Norm sips coffee while Marge eats. When she shoves off, he pulls the scrambled eggs and toast to his side of the table and digs in.

Norm eats a lot in *Fargo*. In addition to polishing off his pregnant wife's breakfast, he is seen enjoying the Arby's lunch in the cop shop and the piles of meatballs and hot dish at the Scandinavian smorgasbord; he's also eating Old Dutch potato chips in the bedroom. In the six scenes featuring Norm, he's eating in four of them.

"I think the story showed he had a certain level of sympathetic eating to her pregnancy," Lynch told me. "Men have a tendency to gain more weight during their wives' pregnancies than they do. I certainly felt that was true of a guy like Norm. He was an empathic kind of person. Self-centered, but empathic."

McDormand agreed. "Norm was much more pregnant than Marge was, in a way," she said. "It was important for me that it was just a fact of Marge's life. And I think it was just as important for Joel and Ethan that it was more a visual aspect of the character than something that was referred to. Do you know what I mean? Kind of dramaturgically there was this idea that the pregnancy of the future involved Norm and Marge's life. That they were the caretakers of the future in amongst all the craziness and the tragedy and the bizarre aspects of the movie."

Added McDormand, "Marge and Norm have hope for the future."

For Norm, that hope isn't just about becoming a father or wolfing seconds. It's about breathing life into paintings of ducks. It's about the brushstrokes that make a mallard or a goose soar. It's about beating the Hautmans, the juggernaut duck stamp painters referred to twice in the movie, first at the police station while Norm and Marge are eating Arby's and again in the movie's final scene. While the two are in bed, Norm tells Marge he captured second place in the duck stamp competition.

"It's just the three-cent," he says.

"It's terrific," Marge counters.

"Hautmans' blue-wing teal got the twenty-nine cent," he says. "People don't much use the three-cent."

In real life, duck stamps are sold by the US Fish and Wildlife Service, not the US Postal Service. Buyers don't put them on envelopes to mail letters; they purchase the stamps to raise funds for habitat preservation. That said, the competition is real and so are the Hautmans, a brood of seven children who grew up down the block from Joel and Ethan in St. Louis Park. Three of the five boys, James, Joseph, and Robert Hautman, developed into successful painters, winning nearly half of the federal competitions between 1987 and 2017. Mark Hautman, a brother who doesn't paint ducks, hung out with Joel as a kid and appeared in one of their Super 8 movies. Another Hautman—Amy—worked with the oldest Coen at the Embers on I-394.

"It's funny," Ethan said. "Our mother would send us clippings over the years about how they'd won some competition, and their mother would send them news of whichever movie we'd just made. So that's how Norm came about."

Each year, the US Fish and Wildlife Service sponsors the Duck Stamp Contest. Artists choose from among five species, then submit paintings to the competition. A reproduction of the winner's painting becomes the Federal Duck Stamp, which is sold to stamp collectors and duck hunting enthusiasts to raise money for wildlife habitat preservation. In 2017, Robert Hautman's acrylic painting of a pair of mallards, one with its green head jutting forward and its wings spread wide and proud, not only captured first place; it earned perfect scores from five judges.

In the weeks leading up to principal photography on *Fargo*, Lynch and set decorator Lauri Gaffin made separate visits to Robert Hautman's studio. Lynch discussed painting technique and duck stamp competition details;

Gaffin lusted after detritus lying around the studio, including Hautman's unfinished painting of a Canada goose.

"I'd have paid to get them to put it in there," Hautman told me. Instead, the Coens paid him about two grand for the privilege.

Robert attended the Minneapolis screening and the after-party at Bryant Lake Bowl, a hipster bowling alley in the Lyn-Lake neighborhood. The Coens hadn't told him that his name would pop up as a plot point. When he heard Norm say, "The Hautmans are entering a painting this year," Robert giggled.

"Like we're one entity," he said. "They're such funny guys."

FEBRUARY 8, 1995

Before making their way to the Minneapolis suburb of Eden Prairie to film inside a sprawling house that would serve as a stand-in for the home of Jerry, Jean, and Scotty Lundegaard, the Coens recorded a pivotal scene at the production office for Fargo Pictures, Inc. The St. Paul space was big enough for the crew to construct the occasional set, including a bathroom for this day's shoot.

After masked intruders interrupt Jean's knitting and television watching, she bites into the hand of the Swede, then scurries upstairs to hide behind a shower curtain. As the Swede looks in the medicine cabinet for unguent, he notices the shower curtain and guesses correctly that Jean is hiding there, but before he has a chance to react, she bolts from the bathtub. In her fear, she doesn't go around the flimsy plastic; she goes through it, gets tangled up, and tumbles down the stairs in a moment of dark comedy typical of many Coen films. *We shouldn't be laughing at this*, we think, at the very moment we are laughing at this.

The stuntwoman behind the plastic curtain had never tumbled down a flight of stairs before. Jennifer Lamb Hewitt had been hired by the film's stunt coordinator, Jery Hewitt. They'd met on *The Young Indiana Jones Chronicles*, a television series, started dating, worked together on *The Hudsucker Proxy*, fell in love, and married. When the Coens hired Jery for *Fargo*, he asked his bride to join him in Minnesota.

Raised in suburban Philadelphia, Jennifer grew up a tomboy and a tumbler. She competed in gymnastics, flipping her body into the air and landing on her feet. But she abandoned the sport at age thirteen; her knees couldn't handle the constant pounding. Then she acted in plays, majored in theater in college, moved to New York, and grabbed tiny acting roles before—and this is every stuntperson's favorite line—she fell into stunt work.

Jery told me the same thing. He fell into stunt work.

Before Jennifer the stuntwoman hurls herself downstairs wrapped in a shower curtain in *Fargo*, she first has to run like hell from the shower, flail around the bedroom, and then fall.

"I was basically taped and stapled into the shower curtain," she told me. "I was very much blind." Before filming, she counted the steps from the tub through the bathroom door and into the bedroom, and practiced the blind run six times. When it came time to shoot the scene, plans changed.

"They moved me out of the tub and put me on an apple box next to the tub," Jennifer said. "And I didn't mark it again. And—action!—I went tearing and I ate the doorjamb with my face."

The slight change from tub to apple box altered everything. After hitting the doorjamb, she fumbled her way into the bedroom and nearly collapsed. She claimed to be fine, but evidence suggested otherwise. A bump the size of a deviled egg was bloating on her forehead. The Coens sent her to the hospital. She returned to the set and, several days later, successfully chucked herself down the stairs. When I watched the movie again, I could see her bum bouncing backward off the banister at the beginning of the fall. That was intentional, she told me. It slows the tumble and adds a touch of realism. The Coens asked for another take, but ended up using the first attempt.

As for the forehead bang on the doorjamb? More than two decades later, Jennifer can still see traces of it. The slight imperfection is a pleasant reminder of working on a film she loves.

"That's my *Fargo* dent," she said.

FEBRUARY 9–14, 1995

On February 9, cast and crew settled into an Eden Prairie home to record multiple scenes over the course of five days. The two-story, 3,760-square-foot house with an attached three-car garage served as the home of Jerry, Jean, and Scotty Lundegaard. The set decorator filled it with signifiers of suburban tranquility: Sunny Delight next to Scotty's cereal bowl, a brick fireplace, a crocheted throw on a sofa, house plants neatly lined up on a credenza, a massive side-by-side refrigerator adorned with family photos, and an inexplicably large number of decorative pigs. The carpets, the fridge, the woodwork, the dining room table, the telephone attached to the kitchen wall are all shades of brown and beige.

Although the location list suggests both interior and exterior shots were planned, the Coens never show us the outside of the house, likely due to the lack of snow. We do see a hint of snow when Jerry returns from his date with the kidnappers in Fargo. As he opens the door, it's dark outside and there's a smattering of white stuff on the ground. He's wearing his winter uniform of beige parka, dark brown fedora, and winter boots. Thick, brown gloves dangle from one of the coat pockets. It's as if his mother attached them so he wouldn't lose them during recess. When he enters, he stomps his feet and hollers, "Hon!"

Macy remembers getting very specific instructions for whenever his character crosses the threshold. "There are a couple of things that Joel and Ethan wanted that I thought were really charming," he told me. "One of them was, as soon as you walk in the house, you gotta stomp your feet to get the snow off. God bless them, that's sort of the music of living in the North."

Kristin Rudrüd, a native of the actual city of Fargo, North Dakota, portrayed Macy's wife, Jean Lundegaard, the anxious woman with the feathered blonde hair at the center of the household. Rudrüd didn't move far from home to attend college; she simply slipped across the Red River to Moorhead State University (now Minnesota State University Moorhead), where she majored in theater. After graduation, she studied at the London Academy of Music and Dramatic Art, and then in New York City with Kristin Linklater, author of *Freeing the Natural Voice: Imagery and Art in the Practice of Voice and Language.*

"Kristin [Linklater] used to say, 'I never trust a person who always has a beautiful voice. They're hiding something,'" Rudrüd told me. "With her training, your voice becomes more and more reflexive. More like a reflex of what's going on inside."

When we first see Rudrüd in *Fargo*, she's chopping celery in the kitchen. After Macy's greeting, she responds with a chirpy, "Hi, hon! Welcome back!" As he enters the kitchen with a bag of groceries, she asks, "How was Faar-goh?" Rudrüd's voice nearly cracks as she splits the word "Fargo" into two syllables. That was intentional.

When Rudrüd started working on the role, she thought about the stoic Nordic women she'd known all her life. When a stoic Nordic woman is asked how she is, the answer is always, "fine, fine," followed by a porcelain smile designed to conceal emotion. That was the beginning of Rudrüd's creation of Jean Lundegaard.

Next came an inspiring social encounter. While she was exercising in an aqua aerobics class, another woman yelled at Rudrüd from across the pool. In a rushed, high-pitched, quivering voice, the other swimmer said, "Say hi to your mom!" Rudrüd heard it immediately.

That was Jean.

"I waved her off and turned to the side of the pool and said, 'Say hi to your mom, say hi to your mom,'" Rudrüd recalls. "Her voice was cracking [in an upward inflection]. She couldn't control her voice."

Rudrüd achieved a similar state of internal terror by speaking, as Jean, not from the gut or the chest or the mouth, but higher still, from the sinus. "When I found that cry, I realized I could be as hard as an opal on the outside, with that brittle 'everything's fine' smile, and her voice would reveal what was going on inside," she said. "By the time [Jean] gets to the 'o' at the end of her first line, 'Hiya hon, how's Far-go?' her voice has cracked up into a cry. So even though she's smiling, that sound agitates a bit of fear response in the audience."

Rudrüd rarely talks to reporters about *Fargo*. While working on a radio documentary that inspired this book, I emailed and called her several times. I asked people who know Rudrüd to encourage her to call. Finally, she did. But it was June 2016, months after the program aired. I called her back, of course. We chatted. Being a stickler for audio quality, I pushed to get her into a studio or at least in front of a professional microphone for a formal interview. She ignored me. I didn't hear from her again for four years. Finally, we talked, just days before the publication deadline for this book. During our two-hour interview, she fretted about how the public might perceive her.

Jane Drake Brody, the local casting director, put it this way. "She's so sensitive an actress that you worry sometimes that you're just asking too much," Brody said. "She is like an open nerve, an open wound. There's this sense of franticness even when she's calm. When you're with her, even when she's calm, she's on the edge."

That nervous energy is also communicated in the way Jean Lundegaard performs culinary duties—chopping vegetables like a cocaine-fueled sous-chef and stirring pancake batter with equal frenzy. It's only when she's watching television and knitting that her mood lightens. In the moments just before masked men burst into her home, Jean is on the sofa, knitting a burgundy sweater. She's wearing pajamas and a warm wool sweater, one she surely knit herself. Her hair is slightly disheveled as she watches *Good Morning*, a TV show hosted by an affable couple. We watch the show through Jean's eyes, seeing not just the show, but also the television console that displays it. This is circa 1987: the console is a big, wood rectangle that sits on the floor, allowing the owner to place objects of importance on top. The Lundegaards have adorned their console with dancing porcelain pigs, a photo of Scotty playing the accordion, and a photo of a man inserting giant red letters on a movie marquee showing, somewhat ironically, *It's a Wonderful Life*.

Steve Edelman and Sharon Anderson portrayed the fictional hosts of *Good Morning*. They're a bubbly television couple in yellow aprons who chatter about making "Holidazzle Eggs" in a mock kitchen and encourage viewers to sign up for a cruise on the Nile River. In real life, Steve and Sharon starred as hosts of *Twin Cities Today*, a daily morning show, from

1976 to 1980 and *Good Company* in the afternoons from 1982 to 1994. Both shows aired on KSTP-TV Channel 5, the local ABC affiliate, and were ratings powerhouses for parent company Hubbard Broadcasting. Steve, a man with angular features and wavy, dark hair, came to the Twin Cities after working as a reporter and anchor in several cities, including Seattle and Columbus, Ohio. He pitched KSTP president Stanley Hubbard on the idea of a locally produced, lighthearted morning show that would follow ABC's *Good Morning America* and keep housewives like Jean Lundegaard glued to their sets. Hubbard took a chance on Steve, who then set out to find a cohost. He auditioned forty locals before finding Sharon, an actor at Old Log Theatre in Excelsior, and a woman with a bright smile and an infectious laugh.

More than four decades after they began working together, I asked them about their origin story. Steve did most of the talking, until I asked him what he was looking for in a cohost.

Silence.

Then Sharon answered for him: "A wife."

Three years after *Twin Cities Today* went on the air, the pair married in December 1979 at an outdoor ceremony at Lutsen Resort on Lake Superior.

Sharon also noted Steve's other requirement for the job of *Twin Cities Today* cohost: "Someone who laughed at you and found you wildly amusing." Listening to the pair banter, it was easy to see why they were such a hit. They really like each other, and they're funny in a homey, lightly teasing sort of way. About their television interactions, Steve said, "I was the king of walking down a blind alley looking for humor, and Sharon would pay it off." In the UCLA draft of *Fargo*, the Coens penciled in Bill Carlson, legendary anchor at WCCO-TV, for the chirpy television personality. Carlson was a part of the Coens' childhood, first appearing on the air in 1959, just a few years after Joel and Ethan were born. While best known for reading the news, Carlson also interviewed celebrities such as Jimmy Stewart, John Wayne, and Tom Cruise for entertainment segments. Carlson, who died in 2008 at age seventy-three, and his real-life wife, Nancy

Nelson, also a television anchor, auditioned for *Fargo*. But the Coens preferred the younger, perkier made-for-television couple.

"I just remember cruising into the audition," Steve said. He greeted Joel and Ethan with a cheery "Okay guys, what's up?" Then he and Sharon performed. "I felt just great. If we make it, fine. If we don't make it, great. I felt very relaxed. . . . I don't think before or since I've felt so loose."

The pair drove to the KARE 11 TV studios in Golden Valley to film the scene. Showing up at the offices of a former competitor was weird, they thought, but in the end it didn't matter. The Coens instructed *Fargo* makeup artists to poof up Sharon's hair bigger than usual. In the movie, it's a glorious blonde mountain of fluff. As they donned *Good Morning* aprons and strode in front of the bright lights, they felt at home, even though they were instructed to address each other using fake names. Steve introduced Sharon as "Kristine Carlson," perhaps an ode to Bill. As the horrific kidnapping begins to unfold in the film, we can hear Sharon referring to Steve as "Dale." Steve upped the ante on the first take, emphasizing the Minnesota accent by elongating his vowels.

STEVE: "I thought it would be a send-up and an exaggeration of the culture, so I did it really broad."

SHARON: "I didn't think it was that broad."

STEVE: "On the first take, I exaggerated it. One of them came up to me, I don't know which one, and said, 'Why don't you do it again, and this time just do it the way you would normally do it on your show.' I said, 'Oh, you mean we were hokey enough just the way we were?'"

"So we did the second take, and that was it. We were gone."

Steve and Sharon confirmed, in unison: "We were hokey enough just the way we were."

Rudrüd contributed to the scene before even walking on set the morning of the kidnapping shoot. After reading the script, she convinced the Coens to alter Steve's line about the Nile River cruise. Instead of simply encouraging TV viewers to join them on the trip, Rudrüd rightly noted that a real Minnesotan would urge people to "come with."

Her insight fell on deaf ears.

"They said, 'Come with what?'" said Rudrüd, recalling the Coens' response. "And I said, 'No, it's just 'come with.'" Eventually, The Boys got it. In the end, Steve Edelman as Dale, *Good Morning* cohost, declares, "We want all of you to come with. And that's the truth. Pbbbbt!" Ending a sentence with that preposition is very Minnesota / North Dakota.

At about that moment in the movie, the masked Steve Buscemi climbs up the deck, places his hand on the glass patio door, peers inside, then smashes a crowbar through the glass, shattering an innocent woman's life. Before filming, the Coens asked Rudrüd for a Janet Leigh, *Psycho*-like scream. But horror movies frighten Rudrüd, so she avoids them, even Hitchcock classics. So, to communicate her fear, Rudrüd uttered a mix of a guttural "uggggh" and a few brief screams as she runs upstairs to the family bathroom.

The bathroom scene—with its ripped telephone cord, the Swede muttering "unguent," and Rudrüd hiding behind a shower curtain—was filmed elsewhere. The bathroom at the Eden Prairie house was too small to allow the cast and crew to squeeze inside. For the shot of kidnapper Carl Showalter knocking in the flimsy bathroom door, Buscemi thought it would be funny to go in sideways, face first, as if he was flying. So he had a crew member pick him up and bust it open that way. Everyone laughed. For a while, the vibe on the set of *Fargo* was about two wacky guys doing nutty things.

That mood gave McDormand pause.

"When we first started working on it, the crew was so enamored with Carl and Grimsrud, the two bad guys, that I started thinking maybe Marge is the bad guy and they're the good guys," she said. "I wasn't really sure."

⁂

Tony Denman, despite losing his fictional mother, emerged physically unscathed from his *Fargo* experience. Denman played Scotty Lundegaard, the teenage son with the expressive eyebrows. Like nearly every teen, Scotty just wants to do his own thing and not be bothered by doting parents. His grades are average, but Jerry and Jean believe he's capable of doing better. One morning over breakfast, Jean breaks the news to Scotty: "We don't want you going out for hockey." Scotty offers up a defense: "It's just an hour." Then the phone rings. Jean picks it up, tells Jerry it's for him, and as Jerry grabs the phone, Scotty delivers his big line . . .

"Look Dad, there's no fucking way—"

Denman was pumped at the idea of delivering that retort to his fictional father.

"I remember being really excited about being able to drop the f-bomb," he told me. In the days leading up to the shoot, the fifteen-year-old walked around his real-life suburban Minneapolis house uttering, "Look Dad, there's no fucking way, there's no fucking way" over and over. When his folks protested, Denman told them, "Hey, I'm just getting into character here."

That was a lie.

Denman never really tried to get "into character." He just did his best at being a kid. "I don't remember ever thinking about the backstory," he told me. "I didn't sit down with the Coen Brothers and talk about it. I think they just wanted a kid. They just wanted me to be a natural, kind of asshole kid."

Denman could do asshole. He could also do teenager. Because he was one (a teenager, I mean), just fifteen years old. When he got the role, his first thought was how cool it would be to miss school. When he arrived on set, Denman didn't worry about interacting with other actors or fret about the huge number of adults futzing with lights, cables, and cameras. Nope. He zoomed in on the snacks. "I just remember looking at the craft services table and thinking, 'Look at all the food! This is incredible! If this is part of the job, I'm in!'" he said, adding, "I ate a lot of gummy bears."

To Denman, Scotty was simply a boy who was really into hockey and, as evidenced by the posters in his bedroom, the arena rock band Whitesnake and the Accordion King, a fictional polka musician.

"There wasn't a lot going on in Scotty's head," Denman said.

That changed when Scotty's mother disappeared. After Jean is kidnapped, Jerry is so consumed with trying to cover up the crime that he seems to have forgotten about his son. When Jerry finally gets around to paying him a visit, Scotty is sitting on the edge of his bed clutching a stuffed animal and rocking slightly. He's worried about his mom. He wants to call the police. But Dad persuades him to keep quiet.

"No one can know about this thing," Jerry Lundegaard tells his son. "We gotta play ball with these guys."

Denman remembers every detail of that teary moment.

"It was in a really tight room," he said. "I was sitting in there with Bill [Macy]. He was just being really cool and patient. Joel Coen was sitting behind the camera with his long, flowing, curly hair, watching and nodding. Everybody's quiet. And Joel said, 'This sweater you're wearing, your mom made this sweater for you. It's your favorite sweater and now she's not here.'"

Mom isn't home because Dad hired men with black ski masks and crowbars to kidnap her, and they've taken her to a cold, abandoned cabin and tied her to a chair. And what was Mom doing at the very moment these criminals crashed into her life? She was caring for her family, knitting another sweater, likely for her only son. And what was Dad doing to try to get her back? As Scotty fretted in his bedroom, Jerry stood in the doorway, trying to sell him a domestic version of TruCoat, a glossy undercoating of lies.

"Macy himself has a cynical sense of humor," Brody said. "He is *not* the innocent. At all! There is no innocent in him. So when he is playing the innocent, there's this wonderful contrast between who he is and what the role is."

Off-screen, Macy offered Denman a life lesson, which he took to heart.

"We were in my trailer and I think I was finishing up my homework or something and Bill came in and we were talking and getting ready for the scene," Denman recalled. "We had gone over some lines, and they came and knocked on the door and said, 'Alright, we're ready for you guys.' I got up and took my wallet which I had on me and I put it down on the table, and Bill Macy looked at me and said, 'Son, you always carry your wallet on you no matter what.' I said, 'Oh, wow. Okay.' So I put my wallet back in my pocket and to this day, I always have my wallet in my back pocket."

Added Denman, in an upbeat manner, "So there you go!"

FEBRUARY 15–19, 1995

Carving up a corpse with a wood chipper is a bloody mess. Which is why Paul Murphy began with the idea of cutting raw chicken and pork into tiny pieces. The special effects coordinator figured the flying meat would look like human flesh when thrust out the side of the chipper.

It didn't work.

"If you would have seen all that meat flying out of the chipper, it would have been too much," he told me.

Besides, Joel Coen was more focused on color than chunkiness. He wanted a sea of red in the snow at the cabin by the lake. "I want a good portion of this hill covered with blood," Joel told Murphy.

Murphy's explanation for Joel's request: "The leg was probably the last thing that was shoved through the chipper. The whole body would have went through before that. So that's why he wanted that big wide swath of red."

But to the St. Paul native and former marine, this wasn't very Coensian. In earlier films, mayhem flashed by quickly, typically requiring just a smattering of fake blood to sell a scene. This time, the Coens wanted the camera to linger on the horror of the moment. They wanted viewers to see what happens when a corpse is shoved through a machine designed to devour tree limbs. To achieve the pool of blood in the pristine white snow, Murphy turned to propylene glycol, a reddish-orange coolant. He added a little black dye to the liquid to give it a more blood-like richness. Then his crew added the mixture to six fifty-five-gallon drums.

"We ran a hose to the out spout of the chipper, and then we pressured the tank and all of that came flying out as the leg went in," Murphy said. "We had to cover quite a bit of area. We went through three of [the drums], which was quite a bit."

Murphy remembers being stressed out throughout the shooting of the climactic scene. "We had to make a huge amount of snow every day," he said. "We were making snow at night, then shooting the next day. We were burned out up there."

The wood chipper itself was purchased at a store, its dangerous guts ripped out so cast and crew wouldn't lose a limb during filming. It was also given a new name and a paint job.

"Joel and Ethan wanted the machine to feel both utilitarian and familiar," said Rick Heinrichs, the movie's production designer, who won an Academy Award on *Sleepy Hollow* in 2000. "We researched various wood chippers based on what size would frame up well for Peter Stormare. We had to hide the brand name because, after all, what company would give permission to have their potentially deadly yard implement put to apparent deadly use? There was a chipper brand called the Wood/Chuck on the market, so I called ours the Eager Beaver, painted it caution yellow, and put logos and hazard stickers all over it."

The Brothers tossed around other names for the chipper. "At one point it was called the Eager Sphincter," Ethan recalled. "Or the Iron Sphincter."

Cast and crew spent three working days inside and outside the tiny, yellow cabin on Square Lake in Washington County, not far from the Wisconsin border (there was a two-day break wedged between the second and third day). Among the many tasks was recording Marge inside the prowler, an establishing shot of the cabin, a hooded Jean bounding blindly through the snow, Carl slamming the television, and Grimsrud axing Carl, which led to Carl's insertion into the chipper. The daily call sheet included this instruction for the grisly scene: "Carl's Wardrobe from Sc. 107 for dummy, Pant dbls for Grimsrud." Accounts differ on how smooth the chipper scene went.

In a 2016 interview with *Entertainment Weekly*, Stormare claims it was his idea to grab a log to push the leg into the chipper, then toss the log at Chief Gunderson when she confronts him. "I remember this vividly because I'm a country boy. I said, 'I can't push it down with my hand, unless I'm a moron.' So I took a piece of firewood. Then I said, 'I can use this as a weapon when she draws her gun. Maybe I can knock her out with it.'"

In truth, the Coens outlined Stormare's actions clearly in the script: "Grimsrud works on, eyes watering. With a grunt he bends down out of frame and then re-enters holding a thick log. He uses it to force the leg deeper into the machine." After Chief Gunderson makes her presence known and, with her gun pointing at him, yells for Grimsrud to put his hands up, the script reads: "Grimsrud stares. With a quick twist, he reaches back for the log, hurls it at Marge and then starts running away."

In the end, the directors got their climax. Marge confronts Grimsrud— and his heinous, murderous secret—shoots him in the leg, then drives off with the perp handcuffed in the back of her prowler, wondering how

Peter Stormare between takes during the climactic scene at the snowy cabin in
the woods on frozen Square Lake. (Photo by Lauri Gaffin)

anyone could be that evil. "And it's a beautiful day," she says to the passive
and impenetrable killer as she glances in the rearview mirror.

FEBRUARY 23, 1995

On the morning of February 23, 1995, the *Star Tribune* reported on *Fargo* as
if Minnesota's largest newspaper was suddenly the *Hollywood Reporter*. Its
gossip columnist, Cheryl Johnson, tried to nix rumors that The Brothers
were pondering a trip north. "There seems to be some kind of 'disinformation' campaign about what's going on on the *Fargo* set," she wrote,
using her pen name C.J. "The movie . . . is not moving to North Dakota
because of lack of snow here."

Just a day earlier, the *Strib* had predicted a high temperature of forty-
six degrees, melting the meager 1.2 inches of snow from a week earlier.
During four weeks of principal photography on *Fargo*, the National
Weather Service at Minneapolis–St. Paul International Airport reported

just one significant snowfall. Mostly, it was day after day of clear skies, no precipitation, or trace amounts of snow. At one point, meteorologist Ken Barlow pointed out that the winter of 1994–95 was the region's warmest since 1942.

In addition to a national weather map, the newspaper also printed a Midwest map with Minnesota at its center. That map showed high and low temperatures for border cities, including Grand Forks, North Dakota. Careful newspaper readers like Joel Coen undoubtedly noticed how the temperature there always seemed to be ten degrees colder than it was in the Twin Cities.

FEBRUARY 26–28, 1995

Moviegoers love Marge. She's the pregnant superhero of *Fargo*. She tromps through the snow to investigate a murder. She adores her dunderhead of a husband who falls asleep in a bed covered with potato chips. She's sweet to the not-so-bright deputy who mixes up the license plates. She gently brushes off the old high school friend who has a massive crush on her. Through it all, Marge Gunderson is just plain nice.

"I love the way she was so kind with her detectives, who were not very good cops," Macy told me. "I love the way she was the smartest person in the room in almost every single scene and yet she had such respect for everyone and treated people with such kindness."

Ethan Coen begs to differ.

"I always thought she was the bad guy," he said. "I kind of found her a little bit alarming, as did Fran. We were all surprised people liked her quite as much as they did. There are admirable things about her, but she's definitely sure of herself to an alarming degree. Certainly not given to introspection.

"I related to Steve Buscemi's character more. He seems like the classic sane person in an insane land."

When I heard Ethan say these words, I was surprised too.

But then I remembered how, during the movie, I wasn't just cheering for Marge; I was cheering for Carl Showalter too. Throughout the film, Carl tries to connect with Minnesotans. And consistently fails.

At the nightclub, Carl tries to engage in pleasantries with an escort in a low-cut black dress and poofy hair, asking if she finds her work interesting. She responds, with disdain, "What are you talking about?" At the airport parking ramp, the attendant won't give him the courtesy of allowing him to pass through the gate without paying. The state trooper refuses his bribe. After the murders up north, Jerry gives him guff on the phone.

"He's the one person who is not local," Ethan added. "He's sort of an alien in the landscape. . . . He's refreshingly chatty and direct."

During three nights of filming in late February, Carl's downward spiral begins in a big way: the funny-looking man from out east takes a bullet in the face. The *Fargo* crew had rented the top of the Minneapolis Club parking ramp, located at the corner of Eighth Street and Third Avenue, for the evenings of February 26, 27, and 28. It's here where Carl confronts Wade, the gruff father-in-law who shows up with a briefcase full of cash and a loaded gun.

On both days, Buscemi arrived for makeup ninety minutes before shooting was scheduled to begin. In the arc of the film, his character had just suffered a smackdown from Shep Proudfoot, so Buscemi's face needed cuts and bruises near the eye. That would take some extra time. Harve Presnell, the actor portraying Wade, rolled in a half hour before the 6:30 PM set calls.

At this moment in the movie, Buscemi's character had endured all he can. Carl is expecting Jerry to arrive alone with the money. When the other car arrives to the ramp, Carl is dumbfounded. It's not Jerry. It's a tall, oafish man in a puffy green jacket.

"Who the fuck are you? Who *the fuck* are you!?"

Presnell begins mumbling words his character has been rehearsing, including "Where's my damn daughter? No Jean, no money."

Carl yells back, "Fuck you, man. Where's Jerry? I gave simple . . . fucking . . . instructions."

Then Carl shoots Wade in the chest. As the victim slowly tumbles backward onto the snowy pavement, Carl yells three things in quick succession. "Happy now, asshole? [pause] What's with you people? [pause] You fucking imbeciles!"

The first comment is directed at the stranger with the briefcase who is bleeding in front of him: "Happy now, asshole?"

The second thing Carl yells ("What's with you people?") is the result of days of encounters with passive-aggressive Minnesotans. The New Yorker has had it with smug yokels.

And the third thing Carl yells is an exclamation point on the second thing: "You fucking imbeciles!"

Those second and third statements reflect how the Coens feel about Minnesota. They fled to New York. They made a movie that pokes fun at Minnesota, in which many Minnesotans are portrayed as simpletons and buffoons. Carl's bullet into the gut of the man who controls the I-394 mafia, the man who refused to lend his son-in-law funds for a real estate deal, the man who is a hockey obsessive, the man who insists on doing it himself despite specific orders is the Coens' bullet into the gut of Minnesota. The fact that Minnesota (embodied as the father-in-law) fires back with a bullet into Carl's face shows an attempt at revenge, but a nonlethal, failed attempt. It's the father-in-law, not Carl, who dies, alone, on top of a cold slab of concrete.

The action happens fast, and while it's easy to miss the message, it's there, waiting for those who take the time to listen to Carl's words.

And Carl, might I remind you, is through fucking around.

❊❧

Before the ubiquity of the automated pay machine made the job nearly obsolete, parking garage attendant was one of the dullest jobs in America. It offered little pay and zero prestige. The parking lot attendant spent his working life inside a narrow cell. In the winter, an electric space heater with glowing orange electrodes kept frostbite away from the attendant's feet. The rest of his body shivered. When a driver arrived, the parking lot attendant slid open the window, inhaled exhaust fumes, and asked, "May I have your ticket please?"

This was the job Don "Bix" Skahill wanted.

In fairness, Skahill wanted the job of a *fictional* parking lot attendant. To be more exact, the job of a fictional *night* parking lot attendant in *Fargo*. The job of *day* parking lot attendant at the airport (Mr. King Clip-On Tie) had already been cast. Peter Schmitz got that gig. Skahill, *Fargo*'s office production assistant, had read the script and noticed a nameless character with one line. He asked around and learned the role hadn't been cast. So he set his sights on it. It wasn't much, but it was a way to get noticed, and when you're an office production assistant with grander ambitions, getting noticed is essential. That's because the least prestigious job on a movie is office production assistant.

"It's the lowest of the low," Skahill told me.

Mostly, the office production assistant is stuck inside the office, making copies, answering phones, brewing coffee. On the rare occasions when the office production assistant leaves the office, it's to buy snacks for more important people or to shuttle actors to and from the airport. Before *Fargo*, Skahill had worked as an office production assistant on nearly twenty movies, including *Crazy in Love*, a 1992 cable television rom-com filmed near Seattle. That forgotten effort starred Holly Hunter and Bill Pullman. As the production got underway, Skahill was tasked with picking up Frances McDormand, who had a supporting role in the movie, at Sea-Tac Airport. At the time, Skahill drove a ratty sedan with a busted driver's door. To keep the door from falling off, he looped a rope over the roof and through the car's interior. As he escorted McDormand to the car, he warned her of its general shittiness. She told him not to worry. When they reached the vehicle, McDormand saw the busted driver's door and said, "I used to have a car like this."

Skahill, a doughy man, climbed in through the passenger door, then the lithe McDormand followed him inside.

A few weeks later, Skahill heard that Joel and Ethan Coen were coming to visit the set. Skahill got his bosses to let him pick up The Brothers from Sea-Tac. Watching *Blood Simple* as an Iowa teen had inspired him to pursue a career in film; his goal was to write and direct. Skahill begged everyone in the office to lend him a vehicle. No dice. When he met the Coens, he kept his gushing to a minimum and explained how embarrassed he was about the condition of his car. When the Coens saw his junker, Joel shrugged.

"Fran used to have a car like this," he said.

Shortly after *Crazy in Love*, Skahill quit the film business. On a commercial shoot, a director had told him to spray-paint a lawn green. As he misted artificial color on the not-green-enough grass, he thought, *What am I doing with my life?* He quit, switched gears, and enrolled in a graduate creative writing program. Before Skahill had finished his first semester, a friend called and asked if he wanted to work with the Coens. As an office production assistant.

Had it been any other director, he would have refused. But the Coens? Absolutely.

At the Fargo Pictures production office in St. Paul, Joel and Ethan often walked by Skahill's desk, heads down, deep in thought. That wasn't unusual. In fact, it is deeply Coensian. William Preston Robertson, a writer and childhood friend of Ethan's, put it this way: "Joel and Ethan, by nature, are not what you call 'gabby types,' and to that end, one of the things they do when building their production team, as best I can tell, is to select people with whom they communicate well so they don't have to talk much."

One day, Skahill poked his head into the directors' twelve-by-twelve, windowless office.

"Hey, I think I can play the night parking attendant."

Neither Coen looked up.

Finally, Ethan said, "Well, you have to audition."

"When are the auditions?"

"Surprise us."

So the next day, Skahill bounced into their office again and spoke the single line attributed to the night parking lot attendant. "May I have your ticket please?"

Ethan's response: "Brighter. More happy."

Skahill repeated the line, this time in a higher tone of voice. "May I have your ticket please?"

"Okay," Ethan said. "You can do it."

On the evening of February 28, Skahill pulled on his costume, a brown jumpsuit and black earmuffs. With his black glasses and cherubic face, he looked the part of an amiable loser ready for his shift at the Centre Village Parking Ramp in Minneapolis, where the scene was filmed. Then he got nervous. Just before the camera rolled, he made a confession to Donald Murphy, a second assistant director whom everyone called "Murph."

"I don't know about this," Skahill said.

"What do you mean?" Murph asked.

"What if I fuck this up?" Skahill said.

"It's too late," Murph replied. "You're in makeup. We have to shoot it."

In the movie, Skahill is seen asking a bloody Steve Buscemi for his ticket. Buscemi's character has just killed Wade Gustafson on the top of the ramp, but not before the old man got off a single shot that went through the funny-looking man's cheek. Buscemi wasn't present for Skahill's movie moment. Instead, the office production assistant uttered his line directly into a camera mounted inside a car. As the car approaches, the audience sees the ratty little attendant's booth and Skahill from Buscemi's point of view as the driver. The camera pans left as the car approaches the booth. On the first five takes, that unusually complex camera move (for *Fargo* at least) didn't work. Finally, it did. And Skahill chirped his line. But it wasn't chirpy enough. After the take, Ethan walked up to Skahill.

"How was that?" Skahill asked.

"Fine," Ethan said.

"I don't think I'm doing a very good job," Skahill said.

"No, it's fine. Maybe brighter," Ethan said.

He did it again. The Coens called cut. And that was it.

But Skahill's night wasn't over. Next, he had to lie on the ground, inside the cramped booth, covered in fake blood, one booted leg still resting on a swivel chair as the camera car rolled by recording Jerry Lundegaard's point of view as the car salesman, having followed his father-in-law to the meeting site, discovers the horrific consequences of his actions: a dead parking lot attendant.

"They're so fucking cheap, they didn't have a mannequin," Skahill said. "I had to actually lie on the floor for like an hour in the cold."

Still, Skahill's brief cinematic encounter with the Coens was worth it. Skahill felt so blissed, he refused to wash up before leaving the set. As he crawled into bed next to his snoozing wife, the twenty-something was still wearing makeup and fake blood.

chapter 7

Vast, Flat Countryside

Shooting Outdoors

"Peter Stormare needs to wait until I'm dead until he picks at my eyeball and says stuff, cause this is the truth."

—J. TODD ANDERSON

"Cold snow gives you a crunchy, squeaky sound."

—SKIP LIEVSAY

MARCH 6, 1995

Wade is rich; Jerry is striving. Wade could help, but he doesn't. When Jerry asks Wade if he can show him a business proposal, Wade balks. When Jerry suggests the deal could be real good for Wade's daughter and grandson, the older man grunts.

"Jean and Scotty never have to worry."

After rejecting Jerry's business proposal out of hand, Wade later changes his mind, calls his son-in-law, says the numbers look pretty good, and tells him to stop by the office. Jerry is surprised and excited. ITT Financial, an office tower near Betty Crocker Drive and General Mills Road in Plymouth, served as Wade's office.

When Jerry enters Wade's inner sanctum, Macy adds a bounce to Jerry's step. This meeting could change everything for him. But there's nowhere for Jerry to sit. He glances around, searching in vain for a chair at the seat of power. He finally rests his butt on the arm of a sofa and begins to discuss the proposed deal.

Wade, played by Harve Presnell, sits impassively behind a massive desk. As a young man, Presnell performed as a singer with a deep baritone, first in operas, then in the movies, most famously as a cowpoke with a soaring voice in *Paint Your Wagon*, a 1969 musical western starring Lee Marvin and Clint Eastwood. Although he landed some television roles in the interim, *Fargo* was Presnell's first appearance on the big screen since *Paint Your Wagon*. After *Fargo*, he secured numerous screen roles, including in major movies like *Saving Private Ryan* and *Face/Off*. He died in 2009 at age seventy-five.

In Minnesota, during the winter of 1995, Presnell fretted about not sounding Nordic. So he turned to Larry Brandenburg, the actor who portrayed Stan, his business advisor, for advice. Before moving to Los Angeles, Brandenburg had grown up in Wabasha, Minnesota. "[Presnell] constantly asked me how do you say this or how do you say that," he told me. "But mainly, the Coens just needed him to be gruff and old, and he did that really well."

Before auditioning, Brandenburg chuckled as he read the script. "I laughed my ass off," he said.

After winning the role, the Coens cautioned Brandenburg against trying to inject humor. "Don't try to be funny," they said. "The character is funny on its own. If you try and make him funny, you probably will fail. Be as straight as you can possibly be when delivering your lines. Have that okay look on your face that you're on board but you don't know what you're doing."

During Jerry's pitch, Stan backs up his boss, the man behind the desk, both in words and tone. He tells Macy's character: "We're not a bank, Jerry." And he mirrors Presnell's gruff demeanor. In his role as a tough-as-nails businessman, Presnell tells Macy, "I assume, if you're not innarested, you won't mind if we move on it. Independently."

Brandenburg nods in affirmation. And Macy, whose eyes have been moving between Presnell and Brandenburg as he absorbs the bad news, clenches his jaw and hangs his head in defeat.

At that, the Coens cut to an aerial view of a nearly desolate, snowy parking lot. Silently, a single figure emerges into the lower part of the frame. It's Jerry, heading to his car.

Roger Deakins, the film's cinematographer, remembers it this way: "It was early in the day and, luckily, it was cloudy," he said. "The snow had been laid in overnight by our effects team and, as we were arranging where the hero car would go, I commented to Joel that the shot looked good with just the one car and the footprints. We had arranged for some 75 or 100 cars for the shot, but we didn't use them."

As Jerry nears the vehicle, the Coens cut to a view from the car's back seat. We watch as Jerry enters the car, closes the door, and exhales, sending a puff of warm breath through the inside of the chilly vehicle. He picks up a red ice scraper and exits the vehicle. The Coens cut to a medium shot of Macy as he begins scraping ice off the windshield.

"They were pretty specific about me losing my shit," Macy told me. "I guess I did a take or two, and it was probably Ethan who said, 'No, man. Go for it, lose your mind here.' So I just kept ratcheting it up. I think I ended up breaking two or three ice scrapers."

During postproduction, Ethan had more advice, this time for Skip Lievsay, the film's supervising sound editor. He told Lievsay that this entire sequence—Jerry slogging toward the car, slumping inside, getting out to scrape the windshield—was tricky. Ethan, film nut that he is, used an obscure reference from *The Missouri Breaks* to make his point. The 1976 western features Marlon Brando, Jack Nicholson, Randy Quaid, and Harry Dean Stanton as horse thieves. In one scene, most of the gang is galloping up a hill to nab horses from the Royal Canadian Mounted Police.

"I don't know why they had to put Canada all the way up here," Quaid quips. Then his tone shifts as he worries out loud about the task ahead. "The closer you get to Canada, the more things'll eat your horse," he says. The fictional horse thief is clearly nervous about the notion of stealing horses from cops.

For Ethan, this idea of Canada as dangerous territory is a metaphor for any difficult task one dreads or that needs to be carefully sorted out. The sound design for Macy's ice scraper scene is one such task. So before Lievsay and his team started to match sound with images, the younger Coen told them, "We're getting close to Canada, boys."

Lievsay, a 2014 Oscar winner for his work on *Gravity*, told me the scene is an underappreciated sound moment. For Jerry's trudging through the parking lot, Lievsay had access to an on-site recording of Macy's footsteps. To that, he stirred in sounds of his own snowy steps, captured on a frosty day outside his East Coast home. Snow recorded on warm days differs from snow recorded after a big temperature drop.

"Cold snow gives you a crunchy, squeaky sound," Lievsay said.

To heighten the desired squeakiness, Lievsay tossed a bunch of cornstarch in a plastic bin and recorded boots stomping through that. "It makes a very squeaky sound," he said. "We did that to sweeten the footsteps."

For the sound of the red scraper struggling to crack the ice on Jerry's windshield, Lievsay mixed multiple ice scraping recordings to create a crunchy combo that conveys the sound of plastic against a thick coat of frozen snow.

"It wasn't hard to do. We just needed good recordings to convey the tempo of the craziness," Lievsay said.

When the scene, which clocks in at just under one and a half minutes, was shown to the Coens, complete with Lievsay's sound mixes and elements of composer Carter Burwell's haunting score, the horror of Canada seemed like a distant danger.

"Once we got that right, they were very thrilled and very happy," Lievsay said.

March 7, 1995

After flailing in a parking lot the previous day, William H. Macy's assignment on the cloudy day of March 7, 1995, was to portray a cornered Jerry Lundegaard inside a dreary motel getting arrested by North Dakota state troopers.

The brief scene, which is second to last in the finished film, begins with an establishing shot from across the street of the Hitching Post Motel in Forest Lake, Minnesota. A snowplow chugs across the screen and along the road in front of the U-shaped, snow-covered motel. Then these words appear: "Outside of Bismarck, North Dakota." After the cut, we see the troopers and an old guy with a set of keys outside room number 7. They knock and ask "Mr. Anderson" (Lundegaard's alias, it turns out) through the closed door if he's the owner of the burgundy car parked out front.

We hear a faint, falsely chipper "just a sec" as Jerry stalls for time. After the old guy with the keys unlocks the door, the troopers burst inside and see the car salesman, dressed only in a white T-shirt and boxer shorts, run into the bathroom and try to climb through the window. Before he can escape, they grab him and toss him face-first on the bed.

Moments earlier, we watched Chief Gunderson nab Gaear Grimsrud on a frozen lake in the woods. Handcuffed inside the prowler, the Swede broods silently. Jerry Lundegaard's reaction to being arrested is very different. As the troopers throw him onto the bed and pull his arms behind his back, Macy wails like a man caught in a bear trap.

That would be Macy's last scene for *Fargo*.

MARCH 8, 1995

In movie productions, scenes are filmed out of sequence all the time, which is why a few days after *talking* about having had sex with the Little Fella and the Marlboro Man, Hooker #1 and Hooker #2, played by Larissa Kokernot and Melissa Peterman, reported to work knowing they'd have to ride and be groped by Steve Buscemi and Peter Stormare.

A Super 8 motel in Shakopee served as a stand-in for the interior of the Blue Ox Motel, the fictional truck stop in the movie where the two kidnappers have their tryst with the two sex workers. (The exterior of the Blue Ox was the Stockmen's Truck Stop in South St. Paul.) In the bed on the left side of the screen are Kokernot and Buscemi. In the bed on the right side of the screen are Peterman and Stormare. A nightstand separating the two beds is cluttered with a dimly lit green lamp and empty beer bottles. Before filming began on the closed set (meaning only absolutely necessary crew members were present), Kokernot and Buscemi chatted about Brooklyn, Buscemi's hometown. Under the other set of bedsheets, Peterman and Stormare were just getting to know each other. Until this day, they'd never met. As the scene begins, the camera records Kokernot bouncing on top of Buscemi and Stormare pretending to wrestle toward orgasm with Peterman.

Visually, the most memorable element is Kokernot's ponytail, which twirls in a circle as she moves her hips up and down, simulating the act.

During the first take, Joel was mesmerized by Kokernot's hair. "Hey, Larissa, your ponytail is doing this thing where it's going around in a circle," he said. "Can you make it do that more?"

Sure, Kokernot answered.

On the second (and final) take, Kokernot didn't think about her body, the cameras, or Buscemi. "All I thought about was my ponytail," she said. "It was great because that's what I needed, something to focus on in this really weird, awkward scene and I'd be done."

After we watch the couples in the act, the screen fades to black and then fades up to show Kokernot-Buscemi in one bed and Peterman-Stormare in the other, staring at a television. We hear the opening horns of the theme song from *The Tonight Show Starring Johnny Carson* and Ed McMahon's voice introducing Carson, the king of late-night talk shows from 1962 to 1992. The actors' faces are lit by the glow of the television. Originally, Joel and Ethan imagined all four sitting up in bed, topless. But Kokernot and Peterman weren't told this at casting or after winning their roles as Hooker #1 and Hooker #2. They weren't told at all.

After filming their scene at the Loch Ness Lounge earlier in the shoot, Kokernot and Peterman had returned to their trailers to find a legal document known as a "nudity rider." After reading it, Peterman's heart began to race. She walked over to Kokernot's trailer.

PETERMAN: "Did you get one of these to sign?"
KOKERNOT: "Yes."
PETERMAN: "What are you going to do?"
KOKERNOT: "I'm not going to sign it."
PETERMAN: "Really?"
KOKERNOT: "I just don't feel like this was very clear."

Peterman agreed, but she found the idea of confronting the Coens terrifying. What if the directors decided being topless was essential? Would the Coens fire them and find new actors to play the hookers, exposed boobs and all? That was a risk the women were willing to take, not only because the nudity rider surprised them, but because being topless wasn't essential to the scene.

"If the joke is they are vegged out and watching *The Tonight Show*, that doesn't help that joke," Peterman said. "I don't get it."

When the pair talked to Joel, Kokernot spoke.

"If we had had these conversations about your vision during auditions or even before we started shooting, I think I would feel differently," Kokernot said. "But because we're being asked to sign it after we've already shot this [other] scene, it just doesn't feel good to me."

Joel relented. "That makes sense," he said. "We'll figure out a way to make the shot work."

More than two decades later, Kokernot believes the Coens were trying to do a bait and switch. "[Joel] didn't ever say that, but I felt like that was kind of the idea," she said. "I feel like it was a strategy to get us to sign it, that we would shoot this other scene and we would all be so happy and excited to be a part of it because it had gone really well that he would be like, 'Now we're going to do a nude scene,' and we would all be like, 'Okay, cool.' That was actually the thing that made me feel not good about it."

In the end, for the brief post-coitus, television-viewing scene, Kokernot and Peterman remain covered. To Peterman, having a bedsheet—even a nasty Super 8 bedsheet—pulled over her breasts is just more real.

"As a girl, it's not something you do anyway," she said. "Even if it's your partner of twenty years, that's not how you sit comfortably."

MARCH 9–10, 1995

The Coens surrendered. They'd been filming in Minneapolis and its suburbs for six weeks, and not a single snowstorm had swept through their hometown. The experience was deeply frustrating.

"It drove the lads nuts," Macy recalled.

"Production is the most stressful part," Joel said. "There's so much that can go wrong that is beyond your control. Circumstances can make your life miserable or make you make compromises that you wish you didn't have to make. When you're writing, you never feel forced to compromise."

Lack of snow wasn't a compromise they could make on this picture. So cast and crew decamped to a Holiday Inn in Grand Forks, North Dakota. Located 315 miles northwest of Minneapolis, Grand Forks is home to the

University of North Dakota and Grand Forks Air Force Base. Heading north wasn't easy.

"That was a huge move for them," said Paul Murphy, special effects coordinator. "Logistically and financially, it throws everything out of whack."

The Brothers had vital outdoor scenes yet to tackle. They hadn't shot Showalter and Grimsrud's encounter with the state trooper, the officer's execution, or the murder of the innocents in the snow. They hadn't filmed Marge and Deputy Lou's investigation of the murders. They hadn't shot exteriors of the Paul Bunyan statue or a blinking traffic light on a deserted street in downtown Brainerd (later filmed, but not included in the final cut). And they hadn't found the perfect place for a bloody Steve Buscemi to bury a briefcase full of cash in the snow. That and many of the outdoor sequences required the emptiness of the Great Plains.

No mountains. No trees. No animals. No traffic. No people.

"One of the things we talked about with Roger Deakins," Joel once told a reporter, "was the idea of not being able to see where the horizon line is, where the land ends and sky begins. Originally, we were talking about doing shots that looked down from a high place that appeared to be almost the same as shots that looked up."

The Coens abandoned the shots from above, but the slate-gray sky is often seen oozing into the horizon line. During the initial investigation of the roadside triple homicide, as Marge nearly ralphs into the snow due to morning sickness ("Well, that passed"), Deputy Lou stands next to a state trooper squad car and stares dimly into the distance. To his left is a row of telephone poles. To his right is a farm field covered with snow. The gray landscape seems to continue to infinity, merging with the gray sky.

North Dakota's geography also influenced the film's composer, Carter Burwell. "I wanted to contrast the smallness of their humanity with the endless white landscape by playing them with fragile solo instruments: harp, celesta, and hardanger fiddle," Burwell noted. "The hardanger—native to Scandinavia—is a fiddle with sympathetic strings that add a shimmering glowing drone to the played notes."

MARCH 11, 1995

The two-lane highway east of Grafton, North Dakota, is a ribbon of asphalt surrounded by miles of empty space. For Joel and Ethan, it was the perfect place to film Chief Marge Gunderson's murder investigation. The scene's closing shot closely matches the description in the published script: "The police car enters with a whoosh and hums down a straight-ruled empty highway, cutting a landscape of flat and perfect white."

The plan for the day's shoot was twofold: record Marge's take on the crime scene, then spend a few hours documenting Carl burying the ransom money next to a fence. At about 5:30 AM, Frances McDormand, Bruce Bohne, and James Gaulke climbed on a crew bus idling outside their Grand Forks hotel for the one-hour drive to Highway 17, where the investigation would be filmed. After an hour in makeup, the trio was ready to start by 7:30 AM.

Gaulke had the easiest—if most depressing—assignment. As the murdered state trooper, his job was to play dead. Notes from *Fargo's* daily call sheet instructed makeup artists to prepare "blood and 'dead look'" for him.

The investigation scene begins with Gunderson emerging from a Brainerd Police squad car, tugging mittens over her hands, and clomping over to her number two, Deputy Lou. She's wearing snow boots, brownish-gray uniform pants, a brown police coat, and a brown police hat with earflaps and a shiny badge. She greets Lou, played by Bohne, with an upbeat "Hiya, Lou." He hands her a Styrofoam cup of hot coffee.

As the pair began shuffling toward the crime scene, Bohne figured he'd hang out next to McDormand as she investigated. When he started to make his way into the snow with his fictional boss, Joel stopped him.

"No, no, no. You let her do the work," Joel said. "You just stand there and watch her."

Joel pointed to the side of the road, indicating where he wanted Bohne positioned. Bohne obeyed. As McDormand inspects corpses, finds clues, and makes conclusions, Bohne is an observer, dutifully waiting to see what happens, cup of joe in his hands. He's not quite Barney Fife stupid, but he's not the most colorful sunflower on the prairie.

Watching it later, Bohne understood why Joel ordered him to stay put.

"Of course, when I saw it in the theater, I cracked up! It was too funny that he just let the pregnant woman do all the work, and he just stood there holding the coffee," he told me. "[The Coens] just have that way of looking at things."

As the chief does her work, Deputy Lou offers bland encouragement. About half of the lines he utters are "Yah" or "Oh, yah?" That's not how his lines begin; that's the *entire* line. When he's not affirming Marge, Deputy Lou offers up sizzling questions like "You had breakfast yet, Margie?" or "Yah? Well, what now, d'ya think?"

Bohne played Deputy Lou with a mix of confusion and misplaced self-confidence. "He was a little conflicted because, on the one hand, the natural order of things did not dictate that a woman be his boss," Bohne said. "On the other hand, he knew that she was much more capable than him. Whenever he was with her, he was a little bit careful, but a little bit, I don't know if 'cocky' is the right word. He wanted to let her know that he was sure of himself even though he wasn't sure of himself. That's Lou's secret. He's not quite sure what's going on all the time."

Like when he tells Chief Gunderson that the perpetrators' plates begin with the letters D, L, R. She gently disagrees, reminding him that DLR is shorthand for dealer plates, like for a newly purchased car: "I'm not sure I agree with you a hunnert percent on your policework there, Lou," she tells him. Despite this mild rebuke from his boss, Bohne believes that Deputy Lou enjoys Marge Gunderson. Heck, he calls her "Margie" most of the time.

"He did like her a lot," Bohne said. "Everybody liked her. I think he felt really comfortable with her despite his misgivings about his own place in life."

By 11 AM or so on the morning of the outdoor shoot, the crew pivoted to the scene of Carl Showalter hiding the cash, which comes much later in the film. The short but memorable scene showcases *Fargo*'s distinct color palette. As Buscemi runs from the car across the snow to a fence, we see flashes of brown and red against the stark whiteness of the snow. The car, clothes, hair, and fence are brown. The snow is white. And the blood is red. Blood covers his jaw, neck, and clothing. The color scheme isn't unique to this scene; it's just at its most vivid here. Throughout the picture, the characters are bathed in brownish hues; beige police uniforms, Jerry Lundegaard's tan winter getup, Gaear Grimsrud's brown leather duster, and Carl Showalter's brown, not-ready-for-winter jacket dominate the wardrobe. The stuff around them is brown too: stolen cars, prowlers, beer bottles, briefcase, kitchen telephone—all shades of brown.

There are a few exceptions. Jean Lundegaard, the dutiful mother, wears a plum-colored sweater on the day of her disappearance. The men whose plotting leads to her death, Jerry Lundegaard and Carl Showalter, are connected by red ice scrapers. As her husband chips away at winter in a lonely parking lot, he does so with a red ice scraper. And when Carl buries the ransom money in the snow along a desolate highway, he digs the hole with a red ice scraper.

MARCH 12, 1995

Bain Boehlke didn't pay much attention to movies. He dreamed of the stage, an imaginary world he'd been a part of since he was a boy. In 1991, five years before his appearance in *Fargo* as Mr. Mohra, the old man in the parka who talks to the cop, Boehlke started a theater company. The Jungle, a humble ninety-nine-seat theater in south Minneapolis, was a place to stage plays written by international greats and homegrown Minnesotans alike—from Sam Shepard, Edward Albee, and Maxim Gorky to Kevin Kling and Jim Stowell. Boehlke often designed the sets, including intricately detailed reproductions of shabby hotel rooms; professorial digs dusty with tenure, books, and booze; or claustrophobic jail cells.

A few years after the Jungle opened, Minneapolis actors began whispering to each other about the return of Joel and Ethan Coen to Minnesota to film their sixth movie. Actors called their agents, eager for a chance to audition. Boehlke, who also worked as a director and actor at the Jungle, didn't hear those rumors. He wasn't even sure who the Coen Brothers were. But to secure a place in movie history, Boehlke had an advantage over the others. He was born in a small town just ten miles from the Canadian border.

"Warroad was so remote," Boehlke told me, describing the place of his birth. "I grew up with a pair of skates. In the summer you walked; in the winter you skated."

Not many outsiders found their way to Warroad. And in the forties and fifties—Boehlke was born in 1939—not many locals ventured to big cities. The people, and their way of speaking, remained crystallized. "I have the authentic Minnesota accent," he said.

So when other actors auditioned for the role of the small-town bartender but couldn't achieve the desired vocal affect, Boehlke claims they graciously recommended him to those in charge of casting. Eventually, he auditioned for and got the part. "It fit my whole deal like a glove," he recalled.

Boehlke understands small-town ways. Like Mr. Mohra, he knows how outsiders are perceived by locals (suspiciously), how bars are community centers (not seedy places to find hookers), how people do the right thing (mostly), and how conversations about weather serve as social lubricant.

In the published screenplay, Mr. Mohra is simply "Man," and the police officer, played on-screen by Cliff Rakerd, is "Gary." The Coens describe them as standing "stiffly, arms down at their sides and breath streaming out of their parka hoods." The next sentence is even more specific and nails the Minnesota demeanor: "Each has an awkward leaning-away posture, head drawn slightly back and chin tucked in, to keep his face from protruding into the cold."

Mr. Mohra is a bartender who lives in a humble ranch house painted a murky yellow. It's on the edge of a small town, adjacent to a grain elevator and railroad tracks. His "whole deal" is to tell the officer what happened at the bar one night, which wasn't much, but he's doing it because he's supposed to. Because his wife told him to call it in. So he did.

Like Mike Yanagita at the Radisson, Mr. Mohra doesn't exactly propel the plot forward. Like the hookers at the strip club, his description of one of the kidnappers is unhelpfully vague. The best he can muster is "little guy, kinda funny-lookin' . . . in a general kinda way."

The scene begins with Officer Gary Olson pulling up across from Mr. Mohra's home. Boehlke, as Mr. Mohra, has the hood of his parka pulled over his head, thick gloves, and big, rubber boots. Given the unseasonably warm weather that day in Hallock, Minnesota, the outfit was unnecessary. The snow was melting—there are big puddles in the street in front of Mohra's house—so instead of handing Boehlke a shovel, a *Fargo* crew member handed him a broom.

"I thought, 'Who are these people?' No self-respecting Minnesotan sweeps their driveway in the winter," Boehlke said. "It's just unheard of."

Boehlke remembers whisking through the scene in a single take. He doesn't remember meeting the Coens. Nothing about the shooting of the scene impressed him. "I didn't think it was a real film," he said. "I thought it was sort of an indie film. No one asked me if I knew my lines. We didn't rehearse it, you know."

Even when the film appeared in theaters a year later, Boehlke wasn't especially impressed. He skipped the Minneapolis screening for cast and crew. He avoided opening weekend. A couple of months later, he was at the cinema to see a different film and caught a trailer for *Fargo*. He couldn't believe his eyes.

"I was shocked when I saw the preview because it looked just like a real movie," he said. "I thought it was going to look like a home movie."

The praise soon began to roll in. A family in Copenhagen sent a note to him saying they often performed Mr. Mohra and Officer Olson's scene before breakfast. A friend read a *Chicago Tribune* article proclaiming Boehlke's cinematic moment as one of the best cameos in American film history.

Boehlke is flattered by the praise, but he wants to make two things clear. One, he wants it known that he would have preferred to hold a shovel rather than a broom for the scene. "I always bring it up so people know I didn't choose it," he said.

And two, the body disposal via wood chipper always seemed to him more of a Badger State thing. "I think the film has more to do with Wisconsin than Minnesota," he said, chuckling. "Because they have all those grisly murders in Wisconsin. This is Minnesota Nice here. . . . They have Ed Gein and all that stuff, you know."

MARCH 13, 1995

Paul Bunyan, the mighty bearded lumberjack in a plaid shirt, is an icon of Minnesota's Northwoods. With his sidekick Babe the Blue Ox, the mythical Bunyan felled forests with a giant ax, creating civilization where nature once stood. The Red River Lumber Company invented Paul and Babe in 1914. Others added to the story, including W. B. Laughead, author of 1922's *The Marvelous Exploits of Paul Bunyan.*

As the teenage creators of the *Lumberjacks at Play* home movie, the Coens naturally wanted a lumberjack for their made-in-Minnesota cinematic release. The Boys tucked in a reference to Paul and Babe in Jerry Lundegaard and Marge Gunderson's first scene together. After Marge asks if any cars are missing from the car dealership parking lot, Jerry dodges the question, puffs his cheeks as if he's about to explode, and changes the subject.

"Brainerd?" Jerry asks.

"Yah, yah," Marge replies, smiling. "Home of Paul Bunyan and Babe the Blue Ox."

"Babe the Blue Ox," Jerry repeats, stalling for time.

"Yah, you know, we got that big statue up there."

Brainerd's Paul Bunyan statue is a twelve-foot-tall re-creation of the fictional lumberjack. He's got the beard, the plaid shirt, and the blue work pants, only he's sitting on a tree stump, a massive mitt in the air, waving like he's desperate for visitors. A friendly, seated giant was definitely not going to work for *Fargo.* Joel and Ethan wanted a menacing badass with a weapon on his shoulder. So they asked production designer Rick Heinrichs to make one. With their own Paul Bunyan, the filmmakers could place him in any setting and light him from any direction.

Heinrichs loved the challenge of creating his own take on the mythical lumberjack, and he looked to other larger-than-life statutes and roadside attractions in Minnesota and neighboring states for inspiration. "You're in the middle of this vast, flat countryside, and you have these whimsical attractions," Heinrichs told me.

Heinrichs's statue was carved out of foam and divided into several pieces—base, lower half, upper half, head, and ax—to make it easier to

The Paul Bunyan statue that appears in the film was created by production designer Rick Heinrichs. (Photo by Jim Benjaminson)

transport. On this day, the Coens spent a chunk of time filming Paul Bunyan, in darkness and sunlight. The nighttime version appears just before the murders of the state trooper and the unwitting bystanders. A chilling score plays as the camera pans from black sky to the top of Paul's massive head, down his muscular torso, past his enormous feet, to the base of the statute, which reads "Welcome to Brainerd. Home of Paul Bunyan. Est. 1871." The lighting highlights Bunyan's baleful face and piercing blue eyes.

The directors wanted their Paul Bunyan to reflect the creepiness of both the landscape and the story. "There was something unreal about the landscape we really wanted to capture: the starkness of the snowy landscape, the inability to see the horizon," Joel said. "That was very important, as was the mythic, Paul Bunyan–style, tall-tale thing that runs through the movie. Bringing in that larger-than-life, folk-tale aspect seemed a nice, appropriate counterpoint for what is otherwise a very human-scale story."

That juxtaposition is at its most stark in one of the film's final scenes, when Chief Gunderson is driving Grimsrud to jail. As she's thinking out loud about his murderous streak, the Coens cut to a close-up of the cold-hearted killer. He turns his head, and from the back seat of the police car he sees Paul Bunyan, standing majestically—or menacingly—by the side of the road with an ax on his shoulder, an ax not unlike the one the stoic Swede plunged into the little fella's skull just a few hours earlier.

MARCH 14–19, 1995

From the back seat, we hear muffled whimpering from Jean Lundegaard, the woman who just wanted to cook for her loved ones and knit sweaters in front of the television. She's underneath a tarp, hands tied, trapped in the back seat of a car. The kidnappers are driving her to a secluded cabin. She's frightened. And she's probably freezing, because the last time we saw her she was wearing only pajamas, a knitted top, and a shower curtain. Grimsrud, the Swedish badass with the dyed blond hair, finds her sobbing unnerving.

"Shut the fuck up," he yells at her. "Or I'll throw you back into the trunk, you know."

The next seven minutes of *Fargo* are the movie's turning point.

"This is where everything goes to shit," said Skip Lievsay, the film's sound designer. "It's the darkest hour. This is the part we find there is no limit to this movie."

Everything that could go wrong, goes terribly wrong. The kidnappers get pulled over by a state trooper. The Swede shoots the trooper in the head at point-blank range, and then murders a pair of innocent bystanders who drive by and gawk at exactly the wrong moment. The Coens filmed this sequence over several nights in rural Pembina County, North Dakota, a ninety-minute drive north of Grand Forks. One of the nights was dedicated to murdering the state trooper. Another night was focused on killing the witnesses. Still other evenings were spent on car chase sequences and dragging a body off the dark, deserted highway in a scene that is strikingly similar to one in an earlier Coen Brothers movie.

"As we were shooting that scene, Ethan and I looked at each other and we both said, 'It seems like we've been here before.'" Joel recalled. "There's an almost identical scene in *Blood Simple*. It's a complete accident."

Ethan shrugged at the memory. "We don't generally worry about repeating ourselves," he said. "Being original and always doing the new thing is incredibly overrated."

On the night Grimsrud offs the bystanders, Stormare left the Holiday Inn at 4:30 PM, then settled into makeup at 6 PM. The sun fell below the horizon about fifteen minutes later. As darkness covered the countryside, filming began.

J. Todd Anderson, a friend of the Coens, played "Victim in Field," one of the drive-by gawkers who gets whacked. (Instead of acknowledging Anderson, the Coens poked fun at Prince by using a horizontal version of his glyph in the credits.) A storyboard artist and filmmaker from Dayton, Ohio, Anderson began working with Joel and Ethan on *Raising Arizona*, sketching their cinematic vision on white placards. These storyboards are shot-by-shot visual representations of the script, allowing crew members access to the inner workings of the Coensian mind. Working with storyboards helps to slash costs, too, as that kind of planning minimizes the

need to shoot a scene from many different angles; it also minimizes the
need for Joel and Ethan to speak during shooting, always a bonus for the
reticent filmmakers.

In his brief star turn, Anderson, dressed in a red parka, red Elmer Fudd
hat, and red and gold scarf, watches Buscemi drag a dead cop by his arm-
pits into a snowdrift. The storyboard artist's mouth drops in a crooked,
nearly slack-jawed, I-can't-believe-I'm-seeing-this manner.

"The gawking scene went fine," Anderson told me. "Maybe two or
three takes."

Getting murdered was tougher.

After realizing he's an eyewitness to mayhem, Anderson's character hits
the gas and flees, but soon wipes out, flipping the car in a field of snow
with his fictional (and real-life) girlfriend, played by Michelle Suzanne
LeDoux, in the passenger seat. The Swede chases them down. As movie
watchers, we don't see the crash. We arrive when Stormare does. The car
is upside down, lights still on, one of its wheels spinning. We watch as
Anderson emerges from the car and flees on foot into the snowy field.

The overturned car of the eyewitnesses to Gaear Grimsrud's grisly murder of a
state trooper on a snowy North Dakota highway. (Photo by Jim Benjaminson)

As the Coens prepared to film the scene, they spent a few minutes prepping Anderson.

"You're bad, J. Todd. you're bad," Joel told him. "You're leaving her behind. You're a coward. You're a coward."

Added Ethan, "You're a nice guy, J. Todd. But you're a coward."

Not one to leave anything open to interpretation, the older brother stuck the knife in further. "You're leaving her," Joel said. "She's almost dead. You're leaving her for that Swede to kill her."

With that note, Anderson climbed into the overturned car and waited for Joel's command to come in on the walkie-talkie.

"Get out of the car, J. Todd!" Joel yelled. "Run!"

Anderson pushed open the door, climbed out of the car, and ran. Anderson's next job was to detonate a squib, a tiny explosive device sewn into the back of his red parka, then collapse face-first into the snow. He needed to squeeze the bulb in his hand to ignite the squib, then fall as if he'd been shot. The first take sucked. So did several subsequent takes. The timing wasn't working the way Joel and Ethan wanted.

Each new take required a new red jacket with a fresh squib and pristine snow, meaning the crew had to move to a new spot that hadn't been mucked up with J. Todd's footprints from previous takes.

"You gotta remember, I storyboarded the scene, so I'm supposed to know what I'm doing," Anderson said. "We did it again and again. It seemed like four times. Pretty soon we're running out of coats. The crew was not happy. It was cold. . . . We're gonna have to do something, you know?"

Anderson climbed back into the car for yet another try. He's nervous, clearly. Just like on previous takes, a couple of crew members help him into the car. But this time, on secret instructions from the filmmakers, they pack a bunch of snow against the door, making it tougher to push open.

A few moments later, Anderson hears Joel yelling through the walkie-talkie: "GET OUT OF THAT CAR, J. TODD! GET. OUT. OF. THAT. CAR."

I've never heard him talk like that before, Anderson thought. *I better get out, and quick.* So he pushed against the door, but it wouldn't budge. He shoved it. It still wouldn't open. He panicked. Finally, he rammed the door with his shoulder and staggered out into the snow. He ran as fast as he could until Joel yelled again. "And now with the plunger!"

Anderson squeezed the device in his hand and fell to the ground with a thud.

Cut. Take. It worked.

"What they did, they tricked me," Anderson said, laughing.

After shooting Anderson in the back, the Swede turns his attention to the girlfriend, still trapped in the car. LeDoux, dressed in white leggings, white sweater, and plum parka, looks up helplessly as the killer peers inside the vehicle. We hear the car pinging from the door left open by the fleeing boyfriend.

"It's almost like a double dip because it is a familiar thing," said Lievsay, who added the dinging sound during postproduction. "Most people automatically ID it. But then they're like, 'Hey, wait a second, what's going on here? Why are we hearing that? The car's upside down and it's still running. There's all this other stuff going on that's so much more important than those dings. Why are they playing that?'"

Why indeed, I ask Lievsay.

"I believe it's an infuriating reminder from the Coens that this could happen to you," he said. "It's only a tiny inch from what would happen if you'd have looked the other way."

It's Hitchcockian, I say.

"You should tell them that," Lievsay replies. "I would never admit that to them. I'd never hear the end of that."

I laugh. *Would they think that's a compliment or would they give me hell for it?*

"They would be sheepishly acknowledging the compliment."

Of course they would, I say.

"Don't forget, they're them."

MARCH 22, 1995

The Picture Car is a big deal when a movie is being made. When shooting ends, not so much. In *Fargo*, the Picture Car was a tan Oldsmobile Cutlass Ciera. Jerry towed it to the King of Clubs. Reilly from GMAC Financing was obsessed with its VIN. Blood splattered the interior when Grimsrud shot the trooper in the head on a two-lane highway outside of Brainerd.

Then it was Don "Bix" Skahill's turn behind the wheel. Skahill, the jowly production assistant, had spent most of the previous three weeks holed up inside the drab Holiday Inn next to I-29 in Grand Forks, North Dakota. So when the film's transportation supervisor came looking for someone to drive the Picture Car to Minneapolis, Skahill shot him a puppy dog look.

"I was anxious to get home," Skahill told me.

The journey began quietly. As Skahill slid the key into the ignition and flipped it forward, nothing happened. No engine roared to life. Not even the sound of an engine *trying* to roar to life. Nothing. He got a jump, pulled onto the road leading to the highway, and the Ciera died. He scurried back to the Holiday Inn, asked for another jump, and got it. The car began idling again, but it lacked confidence.

"What is wrong with that car?" Skahill asked. "It's not charging itself."

The kidnappers' Oldsmobile Cutlass Ciera, behind the scenes during filming in Pembina County, North Dakota. (Photo by Jim Benjaminson)

The man with the jumper cables shrugged his shoulders, agreed with Skahill's assessment, and offered him the following advice: "Don't stop." The drive from Grand Forks to Minneapolis is close to five hours, longer than most people care to go without a toilet break. As he headed south in the Ciera, Skahill was determined to keep pushing forward. But the more he thought about not being able to pee, the more he convinced himself he had to pee. He knew it was all in his mind, but he couldn't help it.

"If I pee in the Picture Car, I am gonna look like a real dumbass," he said.

So he eased the car onto an off-ramp, where it promptly died. Within moments, a cop car pulled in behind him, and at this point Skahill remembered he's inside a car dripping with blood and displaying illegal license plates. When the officer asked for an explanation, he stuttered.

"C-C-Coen—Coen Brothers movie—I'm sure you've heard—All this blood is fake—"

"Son, get out of the car."

The cop escorted Skahill to his prowler and locked him inside. Luckily, the person at the movie's St. Paul production office vouched for Skahill and his unlicensed Ciera. The cop set him free and even jump-started the car. The next hundred or so miles were uneventful. Then darkness fell and Skahill had to turn on the lights, which sucked power away from the engine, which slowed everything down. So he turned off the lights and closely tailed another car, figuring the other driver's lights would show him the way to Minneapolis. That went well for a while, but soon darkness enveloped Skahill's ride and his mood.

The cop. The engine. The lack of a toilet. The lack of lights. It was all too much.

So he pulled over and called for a tow. Soon, the brown Cutlass Ciera had its front axle in the air again, just like in the movie's opening scene when it pulls into the King of Clubs.

chapter 8

Post-*Fargo* *Fargo*

Reviews, Awards, and the Chipper's New Home

"I paid $6 for this trash."

—JANE NEMITZ

"Not everyone in Minnesota wants to laugh at themselves."

—MICHELLE HUTCHISON

Ethan Coen's high school buddy tried to warn him.

"Jesus Christ! I implore you, as your friend who cares about you and wants to see you do well in life, don't make *Fargo!*" William Preston Robertson told him. "It's the weirdest, most bizarre, most inaccessible of all the things you've written! Even your most diehard fans aren't going to know what to make of *Fargo!*"

Robertson was the guy who recorded funny-sounding Minnesotans for the Coens.

"You're whittling down your audience from the already marginal subset of egghead art-house moviegoers to only the members of the subset who live in or are familiar with upstate Minnesota! You're making this movie for a demographic of seven people, tops! And what happens if one of them is sick or out of town when your movie opens?"

At this, Ethan laughed.

"Do not make *Fargo!*" Robertson continued. "It's career suicide! Do not make *Fargo!*"

By 1996, it was too late.

Fargo was in the can. It had been shot, edited, and mixed and was now ready for a March 8 limited release. In the days leading up to its premiere, Gramercy Pictures screened the movie for industry insiders in Beverly Hills and Los Angeles.

Back in the heartland, the Mann Suburban World Theatre in Minneapolis hosted a cast and crew screening on February 26. Michelle Hutchison, who brought the role of escort to life, occupied an aisle seat next to her parents under the twinkling stars on the cinema's ceiling. Frances McDormand caught her eye.

"Oh Michelle, what a great job," McDormand said. "Are you so excited?"

"Yeah," she said. "They spelled my name wrong."

In the credits, someone had added an "n" to Hutchison's last name. Hutchison didn't intend to make McDormand feel bad; she just wanted her to know.

"No!" McDormand said. "That's your father's name. That's horrible."

A few minutes later, Joel stopped by Hutchison's seat, acknowledged her father, and inquired about the consequences of the error.

"Is he gonna kick my ass?" Joel asked.

Hutchison's dad chuckled, and according to the actor, he loves repeating the story to anyone who'll listen. The punch line: "Joel Coen was worried I was going to kick his ass!"

Bruce Bohne, aka Deputy Lou, was at the screening too. He'd seen a rough cut, but nothing more. As he watched the completed film, with music, sound design, and a smooth edit, he was impressed. "Needless to say, I was pretty blown away," he said.

Unlike some actors who say they can't watch themselves on-screen, Bohne was able to enjoy the movie without being self-critical. "When my character gets the dealer plate wrong and gets reprimanded, I even laughed at that," he said. "It was like I was outside of myself. I wasn't necessarily looking at me doing the character; I was looking at the character. I decided that I did good and didn't embarrass myself in a Coen Brothers movie."

When McDormand watched the film, a fresh appreciation emerged. "With Marge, it was only when I finally saw the movie with an audience that I realized she was so funny. I didn't play her as comic. Unless it's broad

GRAMERCY
P I C T U R E S

and
THE MINNESOTA FILM BOARD
invite you and a guest to the
Cast & Crew screening of

a homespun murder story

Monday, February 26, 1996
7:00 P.M.

MANN SUBURBAN WORLD THEATRE
3022 Hennepin Ave.
Minneapolis, MN

ADMIT TWO

Seating is limited. You must present this ticket for admission.

Special thanks: *Mann Theatres*   *Bryant-Lake Bowl*
                   Nemer, Fieger & Associates

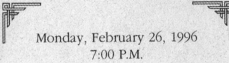

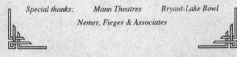

The hottest ticket in town on February 26, 1996: the
cast and crew screening of *Fargo* at the Suburban
World Theatre in Uptown Minneapolis

slapstick, you can't approach characters that way; the laughs really come from the editing process. So I just tried to respect her, make her behavior believable, as I would any other character."

In the weeks leading up to *Fargo*'s release, Ethan fantasized about retiring, claiming he and Joel might quit after making ten films. Then he'd buy a porkpie hat and drive around Los Angeles and attend screenings. Joel played along, quickly imagining what others might whisper behind his younger brother's back.

"That old guy used to make movies in the eighties and nineties," Joel joked. "He's a real pain in the ass, too. Guy is a fucking bore."

Ethan continued the riff, imagining himself tottering around California in his sunset years with a hearing appendage. "That's my fantasy. Just me and my ear horn."

❖

In the pre–Rotten Tomatoes era, newspaper movie critics possessed clout. Great reviews could lift a film; sour ones could spike it. Apparently unthreatened by the power of the review, the Coens once called critics "ugly, bitter people, fat and acned for the most part, often afflicted with gout, dropsy, and diseases of the inner ear."

On March 8, 1996, those critics' reviews of *Fargo* were published on newsprint nationwide.

"The filmmakers have taken enormous risks, gotten away with them and made a movie that is completely original," wrote Roger Ebert in the *Chicago Sun-Times*. The influential critic predicted that McDormand would nab an Academy Award nomination, calling her performance "true in every individual moment, and yet slyly, quietly, over the top in its cumulative effect." His colleague across town, Gene Siskel of the *Chicago Tribune*, loved it too, declaring *Fargo* "the first great American movie of the year."

Janet Maslin of the *New York Times* praised the film's writing, acting, and cinematography: "*Fargo* has been hauntingly photographed by Roger Deakins with great, expressive use of white-outs that sometimes make the characters appear to be moving through a dream. Roads disappear, swallowed up in a snowy void, making *Fargo* look eerily remote."

But Joe Morgenstern of the *Wall Street Journal* trashed it. "People who don't respond to the work of Joel and Ethan Coen often say that their movies are distanced and therefore cold," he wrote. "I'm one of those people." Although he praised the performance of William H. Macy, the critic hated getting hit on the head with jokes.

"[The Coens] can never leave well enough alone," Morgenstern continued. "Here is a phrase that's funny, they tell us through tiresome repetition. There is a moment that's weird or absurd or picturesque, they tell us with eccentric camera angles, editing rhythms or insistent, extreme close-ups. I mean, aw, geez, lots of their stuff is real good, and I mean real, real good, but I'd much rather sort it out for myself."

Ads promoting the movie featured an embroidered image of a corpse, facedown in the snow. The tagline: "A Homespun Murder Story." One could easily imagine Auntie Ruth, sipping coffee and nibbling on lefse, carefully threading the needle as she created the twisted picture.

The same weekend that *Fargo* premiered, American cineplexes screened a trio of other, mostly forgettable films. *Homeward Bound II*, *The Birdcage*, and *Hellraiser: Bloodline* appeared on 2,119 screens, 1,950 screens, and 1,465 screens across the country, respectively. *The Birdcage*, a comedy starring Robin Williams and Nathan Lane, attracted the most moviegoers, earning $18.3 million at the box office that weekend. *Homeward Bound II*, a Disney feature about lost dogs, raked in $8.6 million, while the *Hellraiser* sequel brought in $4.5 million for Miramax.

By comparison, *Fargo* was a blip on the cinema landscape, earning $717,665 on its first weekend. But it did that business on just thirty-six screens—an average of $19,935 per screen. A *Los Angeles Times* box office analyst reported the movie "did extremely well."

One place where *Fargo* was highly anticipated was in the film's namesake city. North Dakotans—and some Minnesotans from across the Red River to the east—could barely contain their excitement. The line for the city's first screening snaked outside the Fargo Theatre, an 870-seat movie palace. Margie Bailly, manager of the theater, told me that some customers grew impatient.

"Budging in line, that kind of thing," she said. "It was not Fargo nice. No. It was not. Maybe not fisticuffs. That would be a little strong. I would say, some major shoving."

During the show, Bailly sat in the rear of the house and observed.

"There was a lot of laughter during the film," she said. "I watched people watching the film. And then they left. We don't talk about it right then. We wait until we get to a safe place, then we say what we really think."

What many said at home wasn't positive. Locals bitched about the dialect, claiming it was exaggerated. A couple of decades later, the FX series inspired by the movie earns similar reactions from locals. "I'm from #Fargo. No we don't really talk like that. Bye" read one tweet. Another typical social media response: "We don't talk like that, fuckers."

It wasn't just the movie's accent that got people's goat. It was all that snow.

"I think people felt insulted that their weather was really, really insulted," Bailly told me. "[The filmmakers] think we're just unintelligent, sort of snow-shoveling people."

Garrison Keillor, host of the popular public radio program *A Prairie Home Companion*, also found the movie distasteful. "You had a lot of time to see where you were going and wishing you didn't have to," the Minnesota native whined. Ross Raihala, then columnist at the the *Forum*, in Fargo, North Dakota, called it "violent, potentially ethnically offensive, not even about Fargo and just plain old weird."

Ralph of Fergus Falls, Minnesota, wished he'd stayed at home. "I left that movie feeling violated and lied about," he told KSTP AM listeners during a two-hour call-in show dedicated to the movie. "The Coens should be ashamed."

My favorite angry local was Jane Nemitz of Nisswa, Minnesota. In a 214-word screed to the *Brainerd Dispatch*, she let the Coens have it.

"This movie is one poor, dismal attempt to entertain," Nemitz wrote. "The movie tried to incorporate kidnapping, body mutilation, beating and two ridiculous scenes taken from other films and all put into this one movie. There really was no story—just events with fadeouts that look like it was produced using a home video camera."

Added Nemitz, "Also, the young couple behind us left after three-fourths of the movie was over."

Had Keillor, Raihala, and Nemitz read *Positif*, a French film journal, they would have been really pissed. An article on "Les frères Coen" featured this exchange:

> *Positif*: "What are your connections with the characters in *Fargo*, who for the most part seem somewhat retarded?"
>
> JOEL COEN: "We have affection for them all and perhaps particularly for those who are plain and simple."
>
> ETHAN COEN: "One reason for making them simpletons of a sort was our desire to go beyond the Hollywood cliché of the villain as a kind of super-professional who has perfect control over everything he does. In fact, in most cases, criminals belong to social classes that are not well equipped to succeed in life, and that's the reason why they get themselves caught so often."

Fargo did have local defenders.

Cole Carley, executive director of the Fargo-Moorhead Convention and Visitors Bureau at the time, enjoyed the movie while sipping Diet Coke, munching popcorn, and popping DOTS. "You had about as many people that hated the movie as liked it," Carley told me. "The people that hated it were kinda taking it personally. And we'd have to tell them it wasn't a documentary. It was a movie. They made this up. Okay?"

In early March 1997, shortly after *Fargo* received seven Academy Award nominations, the City of Fargo purchased a full-page ad in *Variety* praising Joel and Ethan Coen. "You have produced a fine, entertaining film and we earnestly hope you are justly rewarded on Oscar night," wrote Fargo mayor Bruce Furness.

The local support continued later that month, as hundreds of North Dakotans streamed into the Fargo Theatre to watch the live Academy

Awards simulcast. Kristin Rudrüd, the actor who portrayed Jean Lunde-gaard, presided over the evening.

Later, when the movie was released on video, Carley bought copies to pass out at conventions. His marketing philosophy for North Dakota's biggest city was simple. "Just say the name," he said.

Some people up Brainerd way felt the same way as Carley about the whole name recognition thing. The city's chief of police, Frank R. Ball, found the picture entertaining, despite the exaggerated accents, which he called the "fer-sure, you betcha thing."

"You might say this movie's put the name Brainerd all across the nation," Ball said. "So I say we should ride that wave. If you should get some noto-riety, you should make hay with it."

In the weeks after the film's release, curiosity seekers phoned the Brainerd police, wondering if Marge Gunderson worked there and whether the crimes depicted in the movie really happened. One of them was Tim Madigan, a *Fort Worth Star-Telegram* columnist who grew up in Crookston, Minnesota, about seventy miles north of the city of Fargo. He watched the movie near his new home in Texas, more than a thousand miles south of Fargo.

"As I watched, I was stricken by nostalgia for that barren winter land-scape, so flat and white and unending that it sometimes induces vertigo in the uninitiated," he wrote in the *Star-Telegram*. "I remembered those tentlike parkas and the mammoth winter footwear we called bunny boots."

Long-distance calls to Brainerd spiked. Madigan reported that four or five people telephoned the police department daily about the veracity of the kidnapping-for-hire, triple-homicide story. It was such a curiosity, the Minnesota Bureau of Criminal Apprehension dug into its archives looking for cases.

"This is major fiction," said Kathleen Leatherman, a statistician for the agency. "There were no officers killed in 1987. There were two homicides in Crow Wing County [which includes Brainerd] in 1987, one an infant killed by a parent and the other a 76-year-old man. There's nothing that even vaguely relates to these circumstances."

That didn't deter Ethan from fueling the ruse. On April 2, the *Brainerd Dispatch* published a story featuring interviews with Chief Ball and the younger Coen Brother. Ball told the reporter the kidnapping and murders never happened. Ethan claimed they did, but refused to offer details. "I could tell you, but then I'd have to kill you," he quipped.

❖❖❖

Fargo created a different kind of stir within the industry. Those people loved *Fargo*. The Screen Actors Guild nominated McDormand and Macy for awards. (Frances won; Bill didn't.) The American Cinema Editors nominated Joel and Ethan, as Roderick Jaynes, for its top award. Joel nabbed best director at Festival de Cannes, the world's most prestigious film competition. Three days before Christmas, Gene Siskel called *Fargo* one of the year's best films—backing up an assertion he had made less than three months into the start of the year—saying it stood up to repeated viewings and calling it "visually stunning, frequently hilarious." Oscar buzz was intensifying.

On February 11, 1997, Arthur Hiller, president of the Academy of Motion Picture Arts and Sciences, and actor Mira Sorvino announced the Oscar nominees. *The English Patient* snared nine nominations. *Shine* and *Fargo* pulled down seven nominations each. *Fargo* was nominated for best picture, best director, best original screenplay, best editing, best cinematography (Deakins), best actor in a supporting role (Macy), and best actress in a leading role (McDormand).

The flood of attention seemed to catch The Boys off guard. Instead of just making movies for themselves and a small army of fans, Hollywood was sniffing around. Brad Pitt. Tom Hanks. People wanted to know. *Who the hell were these guys?*

"The truth is, Joel and Ethan themselves were blindsided by *Fargo*'s success," wrote Robertson, who was on the set of *The Big Lebowski* with the Coens when the Oscar buzz was at its most feverish. "In the weeks prior to the Academy Awards, two more miserable-looking creatures had never trod the earth's crust."

"We had no idea *Fargo* was going to do any business at all," Ethan said.

❖❖❖

Unlike nearly every other actor in Hollywood, Frances McDormand lacks vanity.

The day before the 1997 Oscars, she wore sandals to the Independent Spirit Awards ceremony. And why not? It was held under a tent on a beach. Samuel L. Jackson of *Pulp Fiction* hosted the event. *Fargo* was up for multiple awards. The Coens, McDormand, Macy, and Deakins all scooped up trophies. The film took home six awards in all. Before leaving the event, McDormand jammed the awards into a gym bag, then inadvertently knocked it off a table.

The next night, there'd be no sandals or exercise bag. Or kids, thanks to the filmmakers' parents. Rena and Edward Coen agreed to babysit Pedro, the son of Joel and Frances, and Buster, the son of Ethan and Tricia Cooke. The little ones were two and one year old at the time.

"We're going to be in Los Angeles then anyway for a course Ed's teaching, so why not?" Rena recalled telling her sons.

Mom didn't expect *Fargo* to win best picture. *Too offbeat*, she said. But she really wanted McDormand to bring home an Oscar. *She's great*, Rena added.

Ten days earlier, *Hollywood Reporter* chronicled *Fargo*'s worldwide haul. Thirteen months after its debut, the movie had earned $45.5 million, including $22.9 million in the United States and more than $1 million in France, Germany, Spain, Australia, and the United Kingdom. That surprised pretty much everyone, including Ethan. "What're you going to do, you know? I mean, if a movie like *Fargo* succeeds, then clearly nothing makes sense, and so, you know, you might as well make whatever kind of movie you want and hope for the best."

At the awards, the power trio sat together in plush red theater seats near the stage. Joel's long, black hair was pulled into a ponytail. He wore a black tuxedo and occupied the aisle seat so he could stretch his long legs every now and then. Frances sat beside him in a sleeveless blue dress. On the other side of Frances was her brother-in-law, sporting a Jewfro, beard and mustache, black suit, white shirt, gold tie, and pocket square.

Once presenters began opening envelopes in front of a packed Shrine Auditorium and millions of television viewers, Rena's predictions proved prescient. The movie got beat out for best picture. And a handful of other awards too. But it won two categories: best original screenplay and best actress in a leading role. Actor Jodie Foster handed Joel and Ethan their Oscar. The Boys made forgettable speeches, but when Joel gave a shout-out to the cast viewing party taking place at costume designer Mary Zophres's house, people there screamed with delight.

When McDormand won, she cradled the shiny prize, swallowed hard, looked up briefly, and began. "It is impossible to maintain one's composure in this situation," she said. "What am I doing here?" Some audience members giggled uncomfortably. "Especially considering the extraordinary group of women with whom I was nominated—we five women who were fortunate to have the choice, not just the opportunity, but the choice to play such rich, complex characters."

McDormand continued with a plea to Hollywood for more roles for women and to cast women based on talent, not box office appeal.

What's great about her brief if opinionated speech is she clearly doesn't care about the next role or whom she pleases. Whether onstage at the Academy Awards or in front of a movie camera, McDormand puts it out there.

"She completely submerges herself," said Jane Drake Brody, the acting coach, about McDormand. "She has no vanity. She does her job, and she doesn't care how she looks.

"[McDormand] herself is very complex but with an absolute dirt will of iron," Brody continued. "She's a dirt woman. She has a will of iron. Her choices are always about winning and fighting so hard and loving. Those two things are often hard to get from the same actor.

"She will not be stopped."

❈

After the Academy Awards, Milo Durben knew he had something more than a wood chipper on his hands. The dolly grip had bought the yellow chipper with the black-and-white safety stripes used in the film—the one that pulverized Carl Showalter's corpse.

He bought the chipper to clear branches and brush scattered around his twelve-acre horse farm in Delano, Minnesota. But now he figured he might have something more than that.

On *Fargo*, Durben, a talkative man, worked alongside cinematographer Roger Deakins. As a dolly grip, it was his job to build the infrastructure to execute fancy camera moves dreamed up by The Boys and Deakins. The only thing was, unlike the Coens' *Blood Simple* or *The Hudsucker Proxy*, *Fargo* had very few fancy camera moves. So Durben mostly hung around Deakins, watched Ethan chew on coffee stir sticks (the younger Coen had recently quit smoking), and collected his day rate. When the production moved north to Grand Forks and other locations near the Canadian border, he and other crew members collected extra cash to help pay for incidentals. Durben squirreled away his per diem.

Then stuff went up for sale.

This happens on movies. To recoup part of the cost of assorted props, the production unit sometimes sells items to the highest bidder. On *Fargo*, another crew member approached the dolly grip and told him, "Milo, the chipper is for sale." Durben, a man with a fresh $200 of per diem in his pocket, wanted it. After calling his wife to get approval, he headed over to the production office and made an offer on the chipper.

"Here's two hundred bucks."

"We want five hundred bucks or best offer."

"Well, here's your best offer. Two hundred bucks."

"Ah, c'mon, c'mon."

"No. Two hundred bucks."

Durben got the chipper.

After the machine's guts were restored to its interior—they'd been removed for safety reasons during filmmaking—the wood chipper roared to life again.

"I bought the wood chipper because I needed it on the property here," Durben told me. "I didn't buy it for memorabilia sake."

When the movie began screening a year later, people couldn't stop talking about the film's most gruesome scene. Its star wasn't the criminal disposing of a leg or the cop with a gun. The star was an inanimate object owned by thousands of homeowners around the country: the humble wood chipper.

The legend of the *Fargo* wood chipper grew slowly. In 1996, Durben and a friend hoisted the yellow power tool onto a flatbed trailer for Delano's Fourth of July parade, which the small town bills as "Minnesota's oldest and largest" celebration of its kind. The chipper served as a promotional tool for Dwayne's World, a local video store owned by Durben's buddy.

In the years after *Fargo*, Durben worked as a dolly grip on other movies, including *A Simple Plan* (1998), *Election* (1999), and *About Schmidt* (2002). When chatting with crew members on those films about his previous gigs, Durben not only would note his credits; he also would be sure to sneak in a mention of his prize possession. The reaction was usually immediate and gleeful. One guy got so excited he dialed a friend on the spot and insisted Durben talk to him.

"Tell him you own the chipper. Tell him you own the chipper," the man said, handing Durben his phone.

"I'm Milo. I own the chipper from *Fargo*."

When considering his weird claim to fame, Durben shakes his head in wonder. "Really? Are you kidding me?" he said. "I still play that card on a job. 'I was on *Fargo*. I bought the chipper.' People just get so excited."

As the chipper's legend grew, Durben stopped using it to clear brush and tucked it away in a shed next to a snowblower. It made occasional appearances at fundraising events. When Joel and Ethan returned to Minnesota to shoot *A Serious Man* in 2008, Durben seized the moment.

"I walked right on the set with the wood chipper, and no one stopped me," he said. "I had them smiling and giggling, and I was making them laugh. I literally had their attention for forty-five minutes."

Then Durben shoved a Sharpie at The Brothers and asked them to autograph the chipper. They happily complied. A year later, Joel told a *GQ* reporter about Milo and the chipper, saying Durben lived in a "small village" and "puts it in the town's Fourth of July parade."

In honor of the film's fifteenth anniversary in 2001, KARE 11 television produced a feature story on Durben and the *Fargo* wood chipper. A day later, an excited staffer from the Fargo-Moorhead Convention and Visitors Bureau telephoned to say the organization had been looking for the original chipper but couldn't find it anywhere. Would he, Milo Durben, want to come to Fargo and put the chipper on display?

Soon Durben and his wife were enjoying a weekend at the Hotel Donaldson, Fargo's sleekest lodging, and free admission to local museums. "They gave me the keys to the city," he said.

The Fargo-Moorhead Convention and Visitors Bureau team liked the autographed Eager Beaver so much, they wanted to showcase the chipper in a refurbished grain silo just off of I-94. A staffer offered Durben $15,000. He liked the price, but the tax associated with selling the chipper? That he hated.

"I'm going to have to pay capital gains on this," Durben told the staffer. "Can you cover the capital gains?"

So the Fargo boosters bumped up their offer to $17,000 to ease Durben's tax burden. Durben acquiesced. Years later, the chipper—along with a shooting script and other collectibles bought from Durben—are on display at the city's convention bureau. Tourists bop in and get their photo taken with the chipper, proudly displaying bomber hats, like the one worn by Grimsrud in the grisly scene, provided by the affable North Dakotans who work there. When I stopped by for an obligatory photo with the most famous power tool in movie history, the blonde woman behind the counter told me visitors sometimes plop their babies and dogs into the top of the chipper and laugh.

❖❖❖

There's no chipper in the original television version of *Fargo*. But there is a Marge Gunderson, a Deputy Lou, ice fishing houses, a meat loaf, and a murder in a snowy shopping mall parking lot. Yah, before Noah Hawley's successful adaptation of *Fargo* debuted on FX in 2014, a pair of seasoned television veterans wrote and filmed a pilot for CBS. The network rejected it, sending it to the scrap heap of discarded shows.

The 1997 effort, which aired on cable in 2003, starred Edie Falco as Marge and Bruce Bohne reprising his role as Deputy Lou. The one-hour drama begins with a man, a dead car battery, and that snowy parking lot. A woman drives up, wordlessly connects jumper cables to the man's car battery, then slays him with a shotgun blast. And then a second blast, for good measure. The show features many of the same elements as the movie. Norm is a painter. Marge is pregnant. He fusses over his duck paintings. She solves crimes. The show's climax is the baby's birth.

"We weren't really involved," Joel said. "I can't say that we weren't happy that it died."

Although the show fizzled, the Coens kept rolling, making a new movie every couple of years. In 2001, the same year Billy Bob Thornton and Frances McDormand starred in *The Man Who Wasn't There*, Joel and Ethan consented to a prestigious *Playboy* interview. By the mid-aughts, *Fargo* was a pop-culture touchstone. When stuck outside Dunder Mifflin's fictional Scranton building in *The Office* one day in 2005, Jim asks his colleagues what movies they'd take with them to a deserted island. Pam included *Fargo* among her five desert island movies. Jim's response: "Oh, definitely in my top five."

Also in 2005, Writers Guild of America West members voted *Fargo* as one of the Top 101 screenplays ever. Sure, *Casablanca*, *The Godfather*, *Chinatown*, and *Citizen Kane* secured the top slots, but *Fargo* slid in at #32, ahead of *Goodfellas* and *Midnight Cowboy*. A year later, the Library of Congress added *Fargo* to the National Film Registry. Not everyone agreed that the Coens' sixth film should be part of the canon. In Annie Baker's *The Flick*, a Pulitzer Prize–winning play about movie geeks sweeping up popcorn at a local cinema, Sam and Avery debated their favorite movies since 2000. Sam is trying to convince Avery that The Brothers deserve merit because of *No Country for Old Men* and *Fargo*.

"First of all, *Fargo* was '96," Avery says, shooting him down. "Second of all, those are all pretty good movies. Those are interesting movies. But those are not like like like like . . . profound commentaries on, like—"

A new generation discovered *Fargo* in 2014, the year FX began airing Noah Hawley's reimagined version of the story with a ten-episode series. Instead of a pregnant cop, the heroine was a single mother who loved her father. Instead of a car salesman paying bad guys to kidnap his wife in a get-rich-quick scheme, an insurance salesman murders his wife in the basement of his house out of anger and resentment. Everything about this *Fargo*—in its inaugural season at least—hinted at the 1996 movie without imitating the original. And it caught on, attracting about one million viewers per episode. Each season had a new setting, new characters, and a new time period. It attracted a rotating roster of well-known actors, such as Billy Bob Thornton, Kirsten Dunst, Chris Rock, Ewan McGregor, Mary Elizabeth Winstead, Ted Danson, and Jason Schwartzman, among others; even Bruce Campbell, the hero of *The Evil Dead* films, makes an appearance as Ronald Reagan. The Coens didn't write or direct, but they are credited as executive producers. And you better believe they got paid.

"They are top-level talent," said Elsa Ramo, a Los Angeles entertainment attorney. "There are a dozen or two dozen [directors] that sit at that level. They didn't just hit one out of the park. When we think of Martin Scorsese, and people like that, they stand alongside that level."

As writers, directors, and producers of the original *Fargo* movie, Joel and Ethan got paid a fee just so FX could make the damn thing. It's a rights deal. The Coens own the rights; *Fargo* FX is a derivative of the original. One has to pay the original artist. But that's not all. As executive producers of the FX show, Joel and Ethan also receive a per-episode fee. Each new season, Ramo said, brings a pay bump, likely five percent. In 2020, FX launched season four, giving the Coens a total of forty-one executive producer payments, with potentially more in the future.

To Don "Bix" Skahill, money isn't the point. It's simple human decency. After wrapping production on a Hollywood movie, the director thanked him for his work and promptly messed up his name, saying, "Thanks, Biz."

"That fucker doesn't even know my goddamn name."

The Coens aren't like that. "To this day, if they see me across the room, they'll say hi to me."

Timeline

JUNE 2, 1919
Edward Coen, Joel and Ethan's father, is born.

FEBRUARY 22, 1925
Rena Neumann Coen, Joel and Ethan's mother, is born.

FEBRUARY 15, 1952
Joel and Ethan's older sister, Deborah, is born.

NOVEMBER 29, 1954
Joel Daniel Coen is born in Minneapolis.

JUNE 23, 1957
Frances Louise McDormand is born in Chicago.

SEPTEMBER 21, 1957
Ethan Jesse Coen is born in Minneapolis.

1979
Ethan Coen completes *Two Views of Wittgenstein's Later Philosophy*, his senior thesis at Princeton University.
Ethan Coen moves to Manhattan.

MAY 14, 1980
Soundings, a short film by Joel Coen, released.

1981
Fear No Evil and *The Evil Dead* horror movies released. Joel Coen is credited as assistant editor on *Fear No Evil* and assistant film editor on *The Evil Dead*.

1982
Frances McDormand graduates from Yale School of Drama.

OCTOBER 12, 1984

Blood Simple screens at New York Film Festival and earns a *New York Times* rave. The film, starring John Getz, Frances McDormand, Dan Hedaya, and M. Emmet Walsh, is released in theaters in January 1985.

1987

Raising Arizona released. The Coen Brothers' second film stars Nicolas Cage and Holly Hunter.

MAY 15, 1988

The *New York Times* reports on a Connecticut pilot accused of killing his wife, then pulverizing her corpse in a wood chipper. The headline: "Everything but a Body in Murder Trial."

SEPTEMBER 21, 1990

Miller's Crossing released. The Coen Brothers' third film stars Gabriel Byrne, Albert Finney, and Marcia Gay Harden.

OCTOBER 2, 1990

Ethan Coen marries Tricia Cooke, a film editor.

MAY 18, 1991

Barton Fink screens at Festival de Cannes and wins the Palme d'Or award for Best Picture. Joel Coen is named best director at the prestigious French film festival.

AUGUST 21, 1991

Barton Fink released. The Coen Brothers' fourth film stars John Turturro and John Goodman.

MARCH 11, 1994

The Hudsucker Proxy released. The Coen Brothers' fifth film stars Tim Robbins, Paul Newman, and Jennifer Jason Leigh.

OCTOBER 25–28, 1994

John Cameron, *Fargo* line producer, meets with the Minnesota Film Board to discuss needs for an upcoming film by the Coen Brothers.

NOVEMBER 2, 1994

Fargo script, at 104 pages, is registered with the Writers Guild of America.

NOVEMBER 14, 1994

Fargo Pictures, Inc. creates an original business file with the Minnesota secretary of state.

JANUARY 14, 1995

Fargo script, revised. 113 pages.

JANUARY 20, 1995
Fargo script, revised again. 113 pages.

JANUARY 22–23, 1995
Fargo principal photography begins.

MARCH 9–10, 1995
Fargo crew leaves Minneapolis for Grand Forks, North Dakota.

MARCH 20, 1995
Fargo crew returns to Minneapolis.

MARCH 21, 1995
Fargo principal photography ends.

FEBRUARY 28, 1996
Preview screening of *Fargo* at Charles Aidikoff Screening Room in Beverly
Hills.

MARCH 4, 1996
Special preview screening of *Fargo* at GCC Beverly Connection in Los
Angeles.

MARCH 8, 1996
Fargo released. The Coen Brothers' sixth film stars William H. Macy, Frances
McDormand, Steve Buscemi, and Peter Stormare.

MAY 21, 1996
Joel Coen wins best director at Festival de Cannes.

OCTOBER 1, 1996
PolyGram releases *Fargo* on video. According to a press release, *"Fargo* point
of purchase merchandise includes a standee theatrical poster, *Fargo* snow
globe and a hanging *Fargo* license plate."

DECEMBER 1996
The Minnesota Film Board and Minnesota Governor Arne Carlson give the
Golden Chair award to Joel and Ethan Coen.

DECEMBER 22, 1996
Gene Siskel, *Chicago Tribune*, lists *Fargo* as his favorite film of the year.

MARCH 23, 1997
Fargo wins six Independent Spirit Awards for best picture, director, actor,
actress, cinematographer, and script.

MARCH 24, 1997
Frances McDormand wins the Oscar for Best Supporting Actress for her role
as Marge Gunderson in *Fargo*.

Ethan Coen and Joel Coen win the Oscar for Best Original Screenplay for
Fargo.

MARCH 8, 1998

The Big Lebowski released. The Coen Brothers' seventh film stars Jeff Bridges,
John Goodman, Julianne Moore, and Steve Buscemi.

1998

American Film Institute celebrates its centennial with "100 Years . . . 100
Movies" list of best pictures. *Fargo* sneaks in at #84, just below *Platoon* and
just above *Duck Soup*. Ten years later, *Fargo* is removed from the AFI list.

OCTOBER 18, 2001

Rena Coen dies.

SEPTEMBER 10, 2003

Fargo television pilot airs, starring Edie Falco as Marge and Bruce Bohne as
Deputy Lou. Kathy Bates directs.

2005

Writers Guild of America names *Fargo* to its list of Top 101 Greatest
Screenplays.

DECEMBER 27, 2006

US Library of Congress adds *Fargo* to the National Film Registry.

NOVEMBER 21, 2007

No Country for Old Men released. The Coen Brothers' twelfth film stars
Tommy Lee Jones, Javier Bardem, and Josh Brolin.

AUGUST 27, 2012

Edward Coen dies.

APRIL 2014

Season 1 of *Fargo* debuts on FX, starring Billy Bob Thornton and Martin
Freeman.

OCTOBER 2015

Season 2 of *Fargo* airs on FX, starring Kirsten Dunst and Ted Danson.

APRIL 2017

Season 3 of *Fargo* airs on FX, starring Ewan McGregor and Mary Elizabeth
Winstead.

SEPTEMBER 2020

Season 4 of *Fargo* airs on FX, starring Chris Rock and Jason Schwartzman.

Where Are They Now

J. TODD ANDERSON is an actor, filmmaker, and storyboard artist living in Dayton, Ohio.

SHARON ANDERSON and STEVE EDELMAN work as unpaid media consultants to Democratic congressional candidates. They are married, live in San Francisco, and continue to laugh at each other's jokes.

BAIN BOEHLKE served as artistic director of the Jungle Theater in Minneapolis until his retirement in 2014.

BRUCE BOHNE is an actor who regularly appears on television and in movies, including in a reprised role as Deputy Lou in the 2003 television pilot of *Fargo*. He lives in Minneapolis.

LARRY BRANDENBURG works as an actor in Los Angeles.

JANE DRAKE BRODY leads acting workshops in Chicago, Boston, and the UK.

STEVE BUSCEMI works as an actor and has appeared in dozens of movies and television shows, including in the Coens' *The Big Lebowski*. He also starred in HBO's *Boardwalk Empire* from 2010 to 2014.

ETHAN COEN and JOEL COEN write, direct, and produce movies. Following their *Fargo* win, they won three Oscars for *No Country for Old Men*. Ethan also writes short stories and plays. Joel adapted *Macbeth* for the screen, starring Denzel Washington and Frances McDormand.

ROGER DEAKINS is an in-demand cinematographer who has won Oscars for cinematography for *Blade Runner 2049* and *1917*.

TONY DENMAN is an actor and producer who lives in Minnetonka.

MILO DURBEN works as a dolly grip.

LAURI GAFFIN works as a set decorator.

ANNE HEALY works as a location scout.

RICK HEINRICHS works as a production designer and art director. In 2000, he won an Oscar for art direction on *Sleepy Hollow*.

ELIZABETH HIMELSTEIN works as a dialect coach.

MICHELLE HUTCHISON is an actor and theater artist who lives in Minneapolis.

LISA KOKERNOT works as a theater director. She cofounded Chalk Repertory Theatre in Los Angeles.

SKIP LIEVSAY works as a sound editor and rerecording mixer for film and television. He won an Oscar for sound mixing on *Gravity* and was nominated for Oscars for sound mixing and sound editing for *Roma*.

JOHN CARROLL LYNCH works an actor. He's appeared in the television series *American Horror Story* and in *The Founder*, a movie about McDonald's founder Ray Kroc.

WILLIAM H. MACY continues to act in movies and television, and since 2011 he has starred in the FX series *Shameless*.

FRANCES McDORMAND is an actor on stage and screen. In addition to her acting Oscar for *Fargo*, she won a second Academy Award for *Three Billboards Outside Ebbing, Missouri*. She also starred in HBO's *Olive Kitteridge* and frequently performs with the Wooster Group in New York City.

PAUL MURPHY is retired from the film industry.

STEPHEN PARK works as an actor.

MELISSA PETERMAN lives and works in Los Angeles. She's best known for her role as the ex-husband's ditzy girlfriend on *Reba*, a television show that aired from 2001 to 2007.

KRISTIN RUDRÜD works as an actor and has lived in New York City and Fargo, North Dakota.

PETER SCHMITZ teaches acting in Philadelphia.

DON "BIX" SKAHILL wrote the movies *Chain of Fools* and *Life without Dick*. He lives in Minneapolis.

PETER STORMARE works as an actor and appeared in the Coens' *The Big Lebowski*, among other films and television series.

DIETER STURM is a special effects coordinator with a focus on making fake snow for movies, often in collaboration with Yvonne Sturm, his wife.

MARY ZOPHRES works as a costume designer. She's been nominated for three Oscars, including for the Coen Brothers' *True Grit* and *The Ballad of Buster Scruggs*.

Endnotes

PREFACE

"evokes the abstract landscape of our childhood": Coen and Coen, *Fargo* (1996), x.

CHAPTER 1: HOMEY AND EXOTIC

"Scenarists are inevitably amateurs, boobies, and hacks": Coen and Coen, *Collected Screenplays 1*, viii.

"We tell the story the way we want": *Playboy*, "Joel & Ethan Coen."

"Native with a Spear": IMDb, *Zeimers in Zambezi*, www.imdb.com/title/tt6261510.

"Vivitar Super 8": St. Louis Park Historical Society, "The Coen Brothers," and *Playboy*, "Joel & Ethan Coen."

"We would shoot one side of the chase": Regis Film Dialogue, "Joel and Ethan Coen."

"For *Lumberjacks at Play*": Brodesser-Akner, "From Their Childhood Friend, How to Better a Coen Brother."

The Banana Film: *Playboy*, "Joel & Ethan Coen."

Would That I Could Circumambulate and *My Pits Smell Sublime*: Lidz, "Raising Minnesota."

Henry Kissinger: Man on the Go: Regis Film Dialogue, "Joel and Ethan Coen."

"It's true that they grew up in a house": Abbe, "The Coen Mother's Pictures."

"The rule is, we type scene A": Goldman, *Which Lie Did I Tell?*, 212.

"Shooting is all most people know": Goldman, *Which Lie Did I Tell?*, 29.

"It's that stupid auteur theory again": Linville, "Billy Wilder, The Art of Screenwriting No. 1."

"Joel was lying on the floor smoking cigarettes": Nayman, *The Coen Brothers*, 61.

"Whatever the movie, [language] is how you work": Smith, "Coens of Silence."

"For some reason the question fascinates": Coen and Coen, *Blood Simple*, v.

"The rule is, you quit rewriting": Coen and Coen, *Blood Simple*, x.

"He takes loping dwarfstrides": Coen, Coen, and Raimi, *The Hudsucker Proxy*, 25.

"The elevator screams into overdrive": Coen, Coen, and Raimi, *The Hudsucker Proxy*, 28.

"The phone pops out of her hands": Coen and Coen, *Fargo* (1996), 24.

"Norm snores away": Coen and Coen, *Fargo* (undated), 52.

"races along the wall-sweat goopus": Coen and Coen, *Collected Screenplays 1*, 510.

"gumballs": Coen and Coen, *Fargo* (1996), 31.

"We've always tried to emulate the sources of genre": *Playboy*, "Joel & Ethan Coen."

"We've always been interested in kidnapping": Biskind, "The Filmmaker Series: Joel and Ethan Coen."

"because we're doing our own thing": Goldman, *What Lie Did I Tell?*, 212.

"We can faintly hear the cry of the fishmongers": Coen and Coen, *Collected Screenplays 1*, 451.

"When I saw *Fargo* the first time": Goldman, *What Lie Did I Tell?*, 221.

"The warmth of that relationship": John Carroll Lynch, interview by the author.

"Both Marge and Norm gave the audience a safe haven": *Minnesota Nice*.

"We got stuck two-thirds of the way through": Regis Film Dialogue, "Joel and Ethan Coen."

"That's child's play": Regis Film Dialogue, "Joel and Ethan Coen."

"I've always told them they write great women": Fuller, "How Frances McDormand Got Into 'Minnesota Nice.'"

"Being a writer myself": William H. Macy, interview by the author.

"She has an inner life that is not immediately evident": Fuller, "How Frances McDormand Got Into 'Minnesota Nice.'"

"I believe I got the role": Isabell Monk O'Connor, interview by the author.

"They came to me and said that [Reevis] looked fantastic": Bruce Bohne, interview by the author.

"Grandma told the story of the large Negress": Coen and Coen, *Fargo* (1996), vii.

"People crawl across this thin crust to arrive": Coen and Coen, *Fargo* (1996), ix.

Chapter 2: This Is a True Story

"How close was the script to the actual event?": Biskind, "The Filmmaker Series."

"Here is my first question": Joel Coen and Ethan Coen, interview by Charlie Rose.

"It scared the hell out of everybody": William Swanson, interview by the author.

"It's completely made up": Roberts, "T. Eugene Thompson Dies at 88."

"Tell me a little bit about the actual case": Macy, interview by author.

"goddamned embarrassing": Coen, Coen, and Raimi, *The Hudsucker Proxy*, viii.

"The utility or interest of a motion picture script": Coen and Coen, *Collected Screenplays 1*, viii.

"Oh, those men" and following: Piper, KSTP-TV press conference.

"From the back seat we hear whimpering": Coen and Coen, *Fargo* (1996), 31.

"We wanted to make it much more observational": *Fargo*, DVD commentary.

"that 'purist' attitude": Ciment and Niogret, "Closer to Life Than to the Conventions of the Cinema."

"blown off in a hunting accident": *Playboy*, "Joel & Ethan Coen."

"to move the camera sometimes": Ciment and Niogret, "Closer to Life Than to the Conventions of the Cinema."

"You're just outside of the conversation": *Fargo*, DVD commentary.

"The camera is tracking forward, past Marty": Coen and Coen, *Collected Screenplays 1*, 11.

"At the cut the music": Coen and Coen, *Collected Screenplays 1*, 24.

"The fact-based nature of the film": Andrew, "Pros and Coens."

"It is a true story, but it might not have happened": *Minnesota Nice*.

"Perhaps the goriest detail": Ravo, "Everything but a Body in Murder Trial."

"I think it changes you": Tony Denman, interview by the author.

CHAPTER 3: I'LL SHOOT YOUR DOG

"I was nothing if not bold": Macy, interview by author.

"It's really a buyer's market": Ethan Coen, interview by Terry Gross (1998).

"It's the most inhumane thing I've ever seen": William H. Macy, interview by Charlie Rose.

"I was called in to read for the young cop": Macy, interview by author.

"Bill, the Coen Brothers have this new film": Bill Schoppert, interview by the author.

"Bill, the Coen Brothers want to see you again": Schoppert, interview by author.

"I found out that they were auditioning in New York": Macy, interview by author.

"No seriously, I'll shoot your dog if you don't give me this role": Brockes, "William H. Macy: May I Be Frank?"

"I was making a joke": William H. Macy, interview by Terry Gross.

"He really showed he wanted the part": Schoppert, interview by author.

"It was a nice opportunity as far as Steve's character is concerned": *Minnesota Nice*.

"I didn't tell anybody in the firehouse": Steve Buscemi, interview by Neal Conan.

"He's a very, very modern young actor": Babski, "Bergman Brings a Restive Hamlet to Brooklyn."

"It sold out because it was a Bergman thing": *Minnesota Nice.*

"I had long hair that was bleached" and following: *Minnesota Nice.*

"We really liked that": Durbin, "The Prime of Frances McDormand."

"I've never had a director in my life" and following: Jane Drake Brody, interview by the author.

"The agent was suggesting": Brody, "Fargo Auditions 1."

"Awesome": Brody, "Fargo Auditions 1."

"Good. One more take, and we'll be where we want to be": Brody, "Fargo Auditions 1."

"When I was at the Guthrie": Lynch, interview by author.

"Don't reveal": Brody, "Fargo Auditions 1."

"Do you know what you should do": Lynch, interview by author.

"He was astonishingly good": Brody, interview by author.

"We'd kind of make fun of [Prince]": Denman, interview by author.

"one of the finest performances by a child": Vaughan, "Delicate Direction Gives Two Capote Stories Life."

"I remember auditioning for it": Denman, interview by author.

"He was just comfortable": Brody, interview by author.

"An open call means": Brody, interview by author.

"We're going to use Tony": Brody, interview by author.

"You know, I just remember thinking": Denman, interview by author.

CHAPTER 4: DANCING IN YOUR MOUTH

"I would have to say, they introduced me to a musical score": Elizabeth Himelstein, interview by the author.

"Everybody in Minnesota talks so stupid, don't they?": Denman, interview by author.

"Michael Rapaport chewed out the front-desk staff": Devie Hagen, interview by the author.

"In the 1990s, Hollywood came to Minnesota": Berggreen, "Minnesota Index."

"Perhaps you'd be happier somewhere else" and following: Hagen, interview by author.

"They were very quiet": Hagen, interview by author.

"I don't think of myself as a movie star": Ellison, "I'd Love to Play a Psycho Killer."

"Want it for Fran": *Fargo* 12/94 production notebook.

"You just cannot imagine how excited" and following: Himelstein, interview by author.

"Through voice and speech": Skinner, *Speak with Distinction.*

"I started to really work on my voice then" and following: Himelstein, interview by author.

"Apparently, John Goodman hasn't done a whole lot" and following: William Preston Robertson, interview by the author.

"It's really dancing in your mouth": Himelstein, interview by author.

"I had spent a lot of time": Bohne, interview by author.

"Getting cast in this movie is a huge deal": Bohne, interview by author.

"What filmmakers always want is more time": John Cameron, interview by the author.

"We thought, we're going to make it really cheaply": *Playboy*, "Joel & Ethan Coen."

"You have to be aware and not kid yourself": Tunison, "Independent Streak."

"All it is is a corridor with a couch": Deakins and Deakins, "Joel Coen."

"The Coen Brothers were very specific" and following: Lauri Gaffin, interview by the author.

"Mary Zophres, the film's costume designer, was also busy buying": Cameron, et al., "Great to Be Nominated, Part Five."

"I asked Ethan why they called it *Fargo*": Macy, interview by author.

"There's something about the name": Denman, interview by author.

"You've seen their body language": Don Skahill, interview by the author.

"Since you're my deputy" and following: Bohne, interview by author.

"I got a call from Liz Himelstein" and following: Larissa Kokernot, interview by the author.

"Marge was the most pronounced accent": *Minnesota Nice*.

"Thank you so much for teaching this": Himelstein, interview by author.

"You do whatever you need to do": Himelstein, interview by author.

American Buffalo excerpt: Mamet, *Plays: 1*, 193.

"Sometimes you get this stylized thing": Haile, "Roots Radicals."

"Wide-eyed, flat-voiced and utterly without guile": Houston, "Now a Hollywood Star."

"Bobby was definitely my first break": Houston, "Now a Hollywood Star."

"The phrase, in fact, has no meaning" and following: Mamet, *True and False: Heresy and Common Sense for the Actor*.

"No one has defined the actor's job better than Mamet": Mamet, *True and False*.

"Oh yah, it's real cold out dere": Himelstein, interview by author.

CHAPTER 5: UNBLEMISHED WHITE

"If I could, I'd have Hooker #2 vanity license plates": Melissa Peterman, interview by the author.

"I was like okay, Marge, a midwestern cop": *Minnesota Nice*.

"It was a beautiful thing": *Minnesota Nice*.

"To prepare, McDormand spent time": Andrew, "Pros and Coens."

"She said the baby would kind of jump up in her belly" and following: Pecchia, "Pregnant, and on Her First Homicide."

"I completely understood his point of view" and following: Macy, interview by author.

"Don't be hasty": Houston, "Now a Hollywood Star."

"How long did it take me to nail it": Macy, interview by author.

"He begins not terribly panicked": Brody, interview by author.

"For whatever reason": Macy, interview by author.

"They fell in love with the place" and following: Anne Healy, interview by the author.

"No doubt about it": Barlow, "Mild and Quiet."

"The costume was truly genius": Kokernot, interview by author.

"They sent us to the makeup truck" and following: Kokernot, interview by author.

"Her mom thinks it's French": Peterman, interview by author.

"I had been kept around": Kokernot, interview by author.

"A lot of actors want to be the best" and following: Peterman, interview by author.

"I'm listening to her talk about the case": Lynch, interview by author.

"My voice was blasted": Bohne, interview by author.

"A lot of times you'll see actors and they'll have one piece of lettuce": Lynch, interview by author.

"Unfortunately, there are sort of aspects of": Adams, "The Brothers."

"This is the last day": Barlow, "Farewell, January."

"But what about the nudity?" and following: Michelle Hutchison, interview by the author.

"There are no close-ups at all": "Thelma Schoonmaker: From 'Raging Bull' to 'Silence.'"

"She's bored shitless with him": Brody, interview by author.

"I've been told": Hutchison, interview by author.

"Another director, if it was a hooker": Brody, interview by author.

"Why am I being seen for this?" and following: Stephen Park, interview by the author.

"They sent me cassette tapes" and following: Park, interview by author.

"He worked so hard on the accent": Himelstein, interview by author.

"To me, when I shot the scene": Park, interview by author.

CHAPTER 6: FRAN USED TO HAVE A CAR LIKE THIS

"I don't know if anyone really laughed at it": Larry Brandenburg, interview by the author.

"I ate the doorjamb with my face": Jennifer Lamb Hewitt, interview by the author.

"It's like we're never gonna get this thing done" and following: Deiter Sturm, interview by the author.

"Dale, would you read this for me?" and following: Peter Schmitz, interview by the author.

"Once you know what the objective is": Macy, interview by author.

"We want you to use your fork" and following: Brandenburg, interview by author.

"Finally, winter": Barlow, "Finally, Winter."

"I guess from the first time we met him": *Minnesota Nice.*

"Peter? What were you saying there?": *Minnesota Nice.*

"Oh no, no, he's not eating": Lynch, interview by author.

"I think the story showed": Lynch, interview by author.

"Norm was much more pregnant than Marge": Frances McDormand, interview by Terry Gross.

"It's funny": Andrew, "Pros and Coens."

"I'd have paid to get them to put it in there" and following: Robert Hautman, interview by the author.

"I was basically taped and stapled into the shower curtain": Hewitt, interview by author.

"There are a couple of things that Joel and Ethan wanted": Macy, interview by author.

"Kristin [Linklater] used to say": Kristin Rudrüd, interview by the author.

"Say hi to your mom": Kristin Rudrüd, interview by Michael Feldman.

"When I found that cry": Rudrüd, interview by author.

"She's so sensitive an actress": Brody, interview by author.

"A wife": Sharon Anderson, interview by the author.

"I just remember cruising into the audition" and following: Steve Edelman, interview by the author.

"I didn't think it was that broad": Anderson, interview by author.

"They said, 'Come with what?'": Rudrüd, interview by Michael Feldman.

"When we first started working on it": McDormand, interview by Terry Gross.

"I remember being really excited" and following: Denman, interview by author.

"It was in a really tight room": Denman, interview by author.

"Macy himself has a cynical sense of humor": Brody, interview by author.

"We were in my trailer": Denman, interview by author.

"If you would have seen all that meat flying out of the chipper" and following: Paul Murphy, interview by the author.

"Joel and Ethan wanted the machine to feel both utilitarian and familiar": Rick Heinrichs, interview by the author.

"At one point it was called the Eager Sphincter": Lidz, "Raising Minnesota."

"I remember this vividly because I'm a country boy": Sullivan, "Fargo's Wood-Chipper Turns 20."

"There seems to be some kind of 'disinformation' campaign": Johnson, "Tiny Tim Gives His Intended the Chance to Wriggle Off Marital Hook."

"I love the way she was so kind": Macy, interview by author.

"I always thought she was the bad guy": Ethan Coen, interview by Terry Gross (2000).

"He's the one person who is not local": Ethan Coen, interview by Terry Gross (2000).

"It's the lowest of the low": Skahill, interview by author.

"Fran used to have a car like this": Skahill, interview by author.

"Hey, I think I can play the night parking attendant": Skahill, interview by author.

"They're so fucking cheap, they didn't have a mannequin": Skahill, interview by author.

CHAPTER 7: VAST, FLAT COUNTRYSIDE

"Peter Stormare needs to wait": J. Todd Anderson, interview by the author.

"Cold snow gives you a crunchy, squeaky sound": Skip Lievsay, interview by the author.

"[Presnell] constantly asked me how do you say this" and following: Brandenburg, interview by author.

"It was early in the day": Deakins, "Fargo Long Shot."

"They were pretty specific about me losing my shit": Macy, interview by author.

"We're getting close to Canada, boys": Lievsay, interview by author.

"Cold snow gives you a crunchy, squeaky sound": Lievsay, interview by author.

"Hey, Larissa, your ponytail is doing this thing": Kokernot, interview by author.

"All I thought about was my ponytail": Kokernot, interview by author.

"Did you get one of these to sign?": Kokernot, interview by author; Peterman, interview by author.

"If the joke is they are vegged out": Peterman, interview by author.

"If we had had these conversations about your vision": Kokernot, interview by author.

"As a girl, it's not something you do anyway": Kokernot, interview by author.

"It drove the lads nuts": Macy, interview by author.

"Production is the most stressful part": Haile, "Roots Radicals."

"That was a huge move for them": Murphy, interview by author.

"One of the things we talked about with Roger Deakins": Biskind, "The Film-maker Series."

"I wanted to contrast the smallness of their humanity": Burwell, "Fargo: Carter's Notes."

"No, no, no" and following: Bohne, interview by author.

"Warroad was so remote": Bain Boehlke, interview by the author.

"I thought, 'Who are these people?'" and following: Boehlke, interview by author.

"You're in the middle of this vast": Heinrichs, interview by author.

"There was something unreal about the landscape": Andrew, "Pros and Coens."

"This is where everything goes to shit": Lievsay, interview by author.

"As we were shooting that scene": *Playboy*, "Joel & Ethan Coen."

"The gawking scene went fine": Anderson, interview by author.

"You're bad, J. Todd": Anderson, interview by author.

"You gotta remember, I storyboarded the scene" and following: Anderson, interview by author.

"It's almost like a double dip": Lievsay, interview by author.

"What is wrong with that car?": Skahill, interview by author.

CHAPTER 8: POST-*Fargo Fargo*

"I paid $6 for this trash": Nemitz, "Letter to the Editor."

"Not everyone in Minnesota wants to laugh at themselves": Hutchison, interview by author.

"Jesus Christ! I implore you": Robertson, *The Big Lebowski: The Making of a Coen Brothers Movie*, 15.

"Oh Michelle, what a great job": Hutchison, interview by author.

"Needless to say, I was pretty blown away": Bohne, interview by author.

"With Marge, it was only when I finally saw the movie with an audience": Andrew, "Pros and Coens."

"That old guy used to make movies": Smith, "Coens of Silence."

"ugly, bitter people": Coen and Coen, *Blood Simple*, ix.

"The filmmakers have taken enormous risks": Ebert, "'Fargo' Delivers: Coens Tale Deliciously on Target."

"the first great American movie of the year": Siskel, "Actors Have Roles of a Lifetime in Daring Comedy 'Fargo.'"

"*Fargo* has been hauntingly photographed": Maslin, "Milquetoast's Deadly Kidnapping Plot."

"People who don't respond to the work of Joel and Ethan Coen": Morgenstern, "Film: 'The Birdcage,' 'Fargo.'"

"*Homeward Bound II, The Birdcage*, and *Hellraiser: Bloodline*": Welkos, "'Birdcage' a Surprise in Small Markets."

"Budging in line, that kind of thing": Margie Bailly, interview by the author.

"You had a lot of time to see where you were going": Karlen, "If the Shoe (Snowshoe) Fits, Well . . ."

"violent, potentially ethnically offensive": Raihala, "'Fargo' is Not for Everyone."

"I left that movie feeling violated": Karlen, "If the Shoe (Snowshoe) Fits, Well . . ."

"This movie is one poor, dismal attempt to entertain": Nemitz, "Letter to the Editor."

"What are your connections with the characters in *Fargo*": Ciment and Niogret, "Closer to Life Than to the Conventions of the Cinema."

"You had about as many people that hated the movie as liked it": Cole Carley, interview by the author.

"You have produced a fine, entertaining film": Furness, "The City of Fargo (The Academy Award Nominated Capital of America) Congratulates the Movie 'Fargo' on Its Academy Award Nominations."

"Just say the name": Carley, interview by author.

"You might say this movie's put the name Brainerd all across the nation": Verhovek, "Hollywood Thinks You Talk Funny, Darn Tootin.'"

"As I watched, I was stricken by nostalgia": Madigan, "Hey, Dis Movie, 'Fargo'; Is Dat Da Real Minnesoda?"

"This is major fiction": Covert, "'Fargo' Events Never Happened, BCA Says."

"I could tell you, but then I'd have to kill you": O'Rourke, "'Fargo' a True Story? Not Hardly. No Such Case Happened Here, Real Police Chief Frank Ball Tells Inquirers."

"visually stunning, frequently hilarious": Siskel, "Actors Have Roles of a Lifetime in Daring Comedy 'Fargo.'"

"The truth is, Joel and Ethan themselves were blindsided": Robertson, *The Big Lebowski*, 16.

"We're going to be in Los Angeles then anyway": Abbe, "Coens Recruit Babysitters for Oscar Night."

"What're you going to do, you know?": Robertson, *The Big Lebowski*, 19.

"It is impossible to maintain one's composure": McDormand, "Frances McDormand Winning Best Actress."

"She completely submerges herself" and following: Brody, interview by author.

"Here's two hundred bucks": Milo Durben, interview by the author.

"Tell him you own the chipper": Durben, interview by author.

"small village" and "I'm going to have to pay capital gains on this": Lidz, "Raising Minnesota."

"We weren't really involved": Lowe, "The Brothers Grim."

"First of all, *Fargo* was '96": Baker, *The Flick*.

"They are top-level talent": Elsa Ramo, interview by the author.

"That fucker doesn't even know my goddamn name": Skahill, interview by author.

Bibliography

Abbe, Mary. "The Coen Mother's Pictures." *Star Tribune*, January 13, 1997.

——. "Coens Recruit Babysitters for Oscar Night." *Star Tribune*, February 12, 1997.

Adams, Jeffrey. *The Cinema of the Coen Brothers: Hard-Boiled Entertainments*. London: Wallflower Press, 2015.

Adams, Noah. "The Brothers." NPR, March 8, 1996.

Allen, William Rodney. *The Coen Brothers: Interviews*. Jackson: University Press of Mississippi, 2006.

Anderson, J. Todd. Interview by Todd Melby. March 15 and March 18, 2020.

Anderson, Sharon. Interview by Todd Melby. August 9, 2019.

Andrew, Geoff. "Pros and Coens." *Time Out*, May 15–22, 1996.

Associated Press. "Pilot Convicted of Killing Wife in Wood-Chipper Murder Trial." *New York Times*, November 21, 1988.

——. "Pilot Denies Disposing of His Wife in Chipper." *New York Times*, June 16, 1988.

Babski, Cindy. "Bergman Brings a Restive Hamlet to Brooklyn." *New York Times*, June 5, 1998.

Bailly, Margie. Interview by Todd Melby and Diane Richard.

Baker, Annie. *The Flick*. New York: Theater Communications Group, 2014.

Barlow, Ken. "Farewell, January." *Star Tribune*, January 31, 1995.

——. "Finally, Winter." *Star Tribune*, February 7, 1995.

——. "Mild and Quiet." *Star Tribune*, January 24, 1995.

Benjaminson, Jim. "Pembina County: 150 Years of History Part 8—Filming 'Fargo' in Pembina County." *Cavalier [ND] Chronicle*, June 14, 2017.

——. Interview by Todd Melby. March 11, 2020.

Berggreen, Kris. "Minnesota Index." *Session Weekly*, May 8, 2009.

Bergman, Ingmar. Official Website. https://www.ingmarbergman.se/en/person/peter-stormare.

Biskind, Peter. "The Filmmaker Series: Joel and Ethan Coen." *Premiere*, March 1996.

Boehlke, Bain. Interview by Todd Melby and Diane Richard. December 7, 2015.

Bohne, Bruce. Interview by Todd Melby. July 30, 2018.

Booker, M. Keith. *The Coen Brothers' America*. Lanham, MD: Roman & Littlefield Publishers, 2019.

"Boy's Role to Be Filled Locally in Minnesota-Filmed 'Fargo.'" *Star Tribune*, January 21, 1995.

Brandenburg, Larry. Interview by Todd Melby. August 2, 2018.

Bridges, Jim. Interview by Todd Melby. July 9 and July 21, 2019.

Brockes, Emma. "William H. Macy: May I Be Frank?" *The Guardian*, June 3, 2011.

Brodesser-Akner, Claude. "From Their Childhood Friend, How to Better a Coen Brother." *Vulture*, February 23, 2011.

Brody, Jane Drake. "Fargo Auditions 1." DVD, undated.

———. "Fargo Auditions 2." DVD, undated.

———. Interview by Todd Melby. July 10 and December 21, 2018.

Burwell, Carter. "Fargo: Carter's Notes." Carter Burwell website. http://www.carterburwell.com/projects/Fargo.shtml.

Buscemi, Steve. Interview by Neal Conan. *Fresh Air*, NPR, November 14, 2000.

Cameron, John. Interview by Todd Melby. December 15, 2019.

Cameron, John, Lauri Gaffin, Skip Lievsay, Thomas P. Wilkins, and Mary Zophres. "Great to Be Nominated, Part Five," *Fargo* panel discussion. Academy of Motion Pictures Arts and Sciences, May 12, 2008.

Carley, Cole. Interview by Todd Melby and Diane Richard. October 17, 2015.

Carr, David. "They Keep Killing Steve Buscemi, but He's Not Complaining." *New York Times*, March 23, 2006.

Ciment, Michel, and Hubert Niogret. "Closer to Life Than to the Conventions of the Cinema." *Positif,* September 1996.

Coen, Ethan. "Two Views of Wittgenstein's Later Philosophy." PhD diss., Princeton University, May 7, 1979.

———. Interview by Terry Gross. *Fresh Air,* NPR, October 21, 1998.

———. Interview by Terry Gross. *Fresh Air,* NPR, December 22, 2000.

Coen, Joel, and Ethan Coen. *Blood Simple*. New York: St. Martin's Press, 1988.

———. *Collected Screenplays 1*. London: Faber and Faber, 2002.

———. *Fargo*. Fargo Pictures, Inc., 1994. (Casting script; accessed at Writers Guild of America Library, Los Angeles.)

———. *Fargo*. Fargo Pictures, Inc., 1995. (Shooting script; accessed at Margaret Herrick Library, Los Angeles.)

———. *Fargo*. London: Faber and Faber, 1996. (Published script.)

———. *Fargo*. UCLA, undated. (Undated script; box 1160 and box 1194 at UCLA Library Special Collections.)

———. *Raising Arizona*. New York: St. Martin's Press, 1988.

———. Interview by Charlie Rose. *Charlie Rose,* PBS, March 21, 1996.

Coen, Joel, Ethan Coen, and Sam Raimi. *The Hudsucker Proxy*. London: Faber and Faber, 1994.

Coen, Rena Neumann. "The Indian as the Noble Savage in Nineteenth Century American Art." PhD diss., University of Minnesota, 1969.

Covert, Colin. "'Fargo' Events Never Happened, BCA Says." *Star Tribune*, March 3, 1996.

Deakins, Roger. "Fargo Long Shot." RogerDeakins.com. https://www.rogerdeakins.com/composition/fargo-long-shot/.

Deakins, Roger, and James Deakins. "Joel Coen." *Team Deakins* podcast, August 2, 2020.

Denman, Tony. Interview by Todd Melby and Diane Richard. May 7, 2016.

Durben, Milo. Interview by Todd Melby. August 14, 2018.

Durbin, Karen. "The Prime of Frances McDormand." *New York Times*, March 2, 2003.

Ebert, Roger. "'Fargo' Delivers: Coens Tale Deliciously on Target." *Chicago Sun-Times,* March 8, 1996.

Edelman, Steve. Interview by Todd Melby. August 9, 2019.

Egloff, Elizabeth. *The Swan*. New York: Dramatists Play Service, 1994.

Ellison, Michael. "I'd Love to Play a Psycho Killer." *The Guardian*, January 26, 2001.

Falsani, Cathleen, *The Dude Abides: The Gospel According to the Coen Brothers*. Grand Rapids, MI: Zondervan, 2009.

Fargo. DVD. Directed by Joel and Ethan Coen. Orion Pictures Corporation, 1996.

Fargo Daily Call Sheets. Provided by John Cameron.

Fargo Final Crew List. Minnesota Film Board. March 21, 1995.

Fargo Location List. Minnesota Film Board. March 21, 1995.

Fargo Production Notes. Gramercy Pictures, 1996.

Fargo 12/94 production notebook. Provided by Julie Hartley.

Fuller, Graham. "How Frances McDormand Got Into 'Minnesota Nice.'" *New York Times*, March 17, 1996.

Furness, Bruce W. "The City of Fargo (The Academy Award Nominated Capital of America) Congratulates the Movie 'Fargo' on Its Academy Award Nominations." *Variety*, March 5, 1997.

Gaffin, Lauri. Interview by Todd Melby. November 2, 2019.

Genzlinger, Neil. "Kristin Linklater, Who Made Actors Their Vocal Best, Dies at 84." *New York Times*, June 16, 2020.

Giese, Donald John. "Who Killed Carol?" *Saturday Evening Post*, September 14, 1963.

Goldman, William. *Which Lie Did I Tell? More Adventures in the Screen Trade.* New York: Pantheon Books, 2000.

Goodfellas. Directed by Martin Scorsese. Warner Bros. Pictures, 1990.

Hagen, Devie. Interview by Todd Melby. November 15, 2018.

Haile, Michael. "Roots Radicals: The Coen Brothers Are Feeling Minnesota in Fargo." *Venice*, March 1996.

Hautman, Robert. Interview by Todd Melby. December 28, 2019.

Healy, Anne. Interview by Todd Melby. October 26, 2018.

Heinrichs, Rick. Interview by Todd Melby. February 12, 2020.

Henerson, Evan. "He's Got It Down Cold. Cast Again as a Shlump, 'The Cooler' Star William H. Macy Is One Hot Property." *Daily News* [Los Angeles], November 25, 2003.

Hennepin County: District Court. An Inventory of Its Criminal Case File No. 48680 (*State of Minnesota v. T. Eugene Thompson*) Documents. Gale Family Library, Minnesota History Center, St. Paul.

Herzog, Arthur. *The Woodchipper Murder.* New York: Henry Holt and Company, 1989.

Hewitt, Chris. "In Really Cold Blood." *St. Paul Pioneer Press*, March 3, 1996.

———. "Some Minnesotans Might Think the Harsh, Bold 'Fargo' Goes Too Far." *St. Paul Pioneer Press*, March 8, 1996.

Hewitt, Jennifer Lamb. Interview by Todd Melby. January 26, 2020.

Hewitt, Jery. Interview by Todd Melby. January 29, 2020.

Himelstein, Elizabeth. Interview by Todd Melby and Diane Richard. November 16, 2015.

———. Interview by Todd Melby. December 6, 2019.

Hodson, Jane. *Dialect in Film and Literature.* London: Palgrave Macmillan, 2014.

Holden, Stephen. "Review/Theater: The Swan; Surreal Love and a Triangle of Needs." *New York Times*, November 16, 1993.

Houston, Gary. "Now a Hollywood Star, William Macy Sees Chicago as His Acting Testing Lab." *Chicago Tribune*, February 15, 1995.

———. Interview by Todd Melby. December 28, 2017.

Hutchison, Michelle. Interview by Todd Melby and Diane Richard. April 29, 2016.

Ivry, Bob. "After 'Fargo,' His Plate Is Overflowing." *The Record*, March 7, 1997.

Johnson, Cheryl. "Tiny Tim Gives His Intended the Chance to Wriggle Off Marital Hook." *Star Tribune*, February 23, 1995.

Karlen, Neal. "If the Shoe (Snowshoe) Fits, Well . . ." *New York Times*, May 5, 1996.

Kauffman, Vanessa. "Minnesota Artist Bob Hautman Wins 2017 Federal Duck Stamp Contest." US Fish and Wildlife Service, September 16, 2017.

Kisner, Jordan. "Frances McDormand's Difficult Women." *New York Times Magazine*, October 3, 2017.

Kokernot, Larissa. Interview by Todd Melby. July 26, 2018.

Korte, Peter, Georg Seesslen, Rory Mulholland, and Michael Kane. *Joel & Ethan Coen*. New York: Proscenium Publishers, 2001.

Lentz, Harris M. III. *Obituaries in the Performing Arts, 2009*. Jefferson, NC: McFarland & Company, 2010.

———. *Obituaries in the Performing Arts, 2017*. Jefferson, NC: McFarland & Company, 2018.

Lidz, Frank. "Raising Minnesota." *GQ*, September 15, 2009.

Lievsay, Skip. Interview by Todd Melby. November 12, 2019.

Linville, James. "Billy Wilder, the Art of Screenwriting No. 1." *Paris Review*, Spring 1996.

LoBrutto, Vincent. *Selected Takes: Film Editors on Editing*. Westport, CT: Praeger Publishers, 1991.

Long, Robert Emmet. *Ingmar Bergman: Film and Stage*. New York: Abrams, 1994.

Lowe, Andy. "The Brothers Grim." *Total Film*, May 1998.

Luhr, William G., ed. *The Coen Brothers' Fargo*. Cambridge: Cambridge University Press, 2004.

Lynch, John Carroll. Interview by Todd Melby and Diane Richard. February 12, 2016.

Macy, William H. Interview by Charlie Rose. *Charlie Rose*, PBS, March 3, 1998.

———. Interview by Terry Gross. *Fresh Air*, NPR, January 30, 2013.

———. Interview by Todd Melby and Diane Richard. October 26, 2015.

Madigan, Tim. "Hey, Dis Movie, 'Fargo'; Is Dat Da Real Minnesoda?" *Star Tribune*, via *Fort Worth Star-Telegram*, April 25, 1996.

Mamet, David. *Plays: 1*. London: Methuen Publishing, 1996.

———. *True and False: Heresy and Common Sense for the Actor*. New York: Random House, 1997.

Maslin, Janet. "Milquetoast's Deadly Kidnapping Plot." *New York Times*, March 8, 1996.

McDonald, William. "Brothers in a Movie World of Their Own." *New York Times*, March 3, 1996.

McDormand, Frances. "Frances McDormand Winning Best Actress." youtu.be/ Phno8FKSl48.

———. Interview by Terry Gross. *Fresh Air*, NPR, May 6, 1996.

Melby, Todd, and Diane Richard. *We Don't Talk Like That:* Fargo *and the Midwest Psyche*. Prairie Public, 2016.

Minnesota Film Board. "Car dealership, cabin in woods." Production Request. October 26, 1994.

———. "A woman sherriff [*sic*] in a small town." Production Request. October 24, 1994.

Minnesota Nice (documentary). MGM HD, 2003.

Morgenstern, Joe. "Film: 'The Birdcage,' 'Fargo.'" *Wall Street Journal*, March 8, 1996.

Murch, Walter. *In the Blink of an Eye: A Perspective on Film Editing*. Los Angeles: Silman-James Press, 2001.

Murphy, Paul. Interview by Todd Melby. October 23, 2019.

Nadel, Ira. *David Mamet: A Life in the Theatre*. New York: Palgrave Macmillan, 2008.

Nayman, Adam. *The Coen Brothers: This Book Really Ties the Films Together*. New York: Abrams, 2018.

Nemitz, Jane. "Letter to the Editor." *Brainerd Dispatch*, April 12, 1996.

O'Connor, Isabell Monk. Interview by Todd Melby. December 14, 2019.

O'Rourke, Mike. "'Fargo' a True Story? Not Hardly. No Such Case Happened Here, Real Police Chief Frank Ball Tells Inquirers." *Brainerd [MN] Dispatch*, April 2, 1996.

Pagani, Susan. "Last of the Embers: The Final Holdout of the Embers Restaurant Chain Keeps the Flames Burning in Fridley." *The Growler*, September 24, 2018.

Park, Stephen. Interview by Todd Melby and Diane Richard. January 29, 2016.

Pecchia, David. "Pregnant, and on Her First Homicide, A New, Quirky Film from the Coens." *The Record* [Bergen County, NJ], March 1, 1996.

Peterman, Melissa. Interview by Todd Melby. September 10, 2019.

Piper, Virginia. KSTP-TV press conference, July 1972. youtu.be/PoKZk730dOo.

Playboy. "Joel & Ethan Coen. A Candid Conversation with the Maverick Filmmakers About Blowing Up Cows and Rabbits, Avoiding the Studio System and Working the Hollywood Baby Pit." November 2001.

Pratt, Kelly. Interview by Todd Melby. August 8 and October 10, 2018.

Preus, Catherine. "Minnesota's Coen Honored at Cannes as Best Director." *Star Tribune*, May 21, 1996.

Puig, Claudia. "Minnesota Maniacs." *Los Angeles Times*, February 25, 1996.

Raihala, Ross. "'Fargo' Is Not for Everyone." *Forum* [Fargo, ND], March 17, 1996.

Ramo, Elsa. Interview by Todd Melby. August 2, 2019.

Ravo, Nick. "Everything but a Body in Murder Trial." *New York Times*, May 15, 1998.

Regis Film Dialogue. "Joel and Ethan Coen: Raising Cain with Elvis Mitchell." Walker Art Center, Minneapolis, September 25, 2009.

Rich, Frank. "Reviews/Theater; Mabou Mines Creates a 'King Lear' All Its Own." *New York Times*, January 26, 1990.

Roberts, Sam. "T. Eugene Thompson Dies at 88; Crime Stunned St. Paul." *New York Times*, September 5, 2015.

Robertson, William Preston. *The Big Lebowski: The Making of a Coen Brothers Movie*. New York: W. W. Norton and Company, 1998.

———. Interview by Todd Melby. September 13, 2019.

Rudrüd, Kristin. Interview by Michael Feldman. *The Whad'Ya Know Radio Hour*, Wisconsin Public Radio, October 20, 2012.

———. Interview by Todd Melby. September 30, 2020.

Russell, Carolyn. *The Films of Joel and Ethan Coen*. Jefferson, NC: McFarland & Company, 2001.

St. Louis Park Historical Society. "The Coen Brothers." Slphistory.org/coen brothers.

Schimke, David. "Lukewarm: Fargo's Arctic Blast Lacks the Complexity of the Coens' Best Work." *Twin Cities Reader*, March 6, 1996.

Schmitz, Peter. Interview by Todd Melby. January 3, 2020.

Schoppert, Bill. Interview by Todd Melby. November 28 and December 4, 2018.

Siskel, Gene. "Actors Have Roles of a Lifetime in Daring Comedy 'Fargo.'" *Chicago Tribune*, March 8, 1996.

Skahill, Don. Interview by Todd Melby. September 5, 2019.

Skinner, Edith. *Speak with Distinction: The Classic Skinner Method to Speech on the Stage*. New York: Applause Theater Book Publishers, 1990.

Skrien, Stuart. Interview by Todd Melby. August 22, 2018.

Smith, Sean K. "Coens of Silence." *Los Angeles View*, March 15–21, 1996.

Strickler, Jeff. "'Fargo' Wins 6 Spirit Awards, Embarrassing the Coens." *Star Tribune*, March 23, 1997.

Sturm, Dieter. Interview by Todd Melby. August 2, 2018.

Sullivan, Kevin P. "Fargo's Wood-Chipper Turns 20: A Brief Oral History." *Entertainment Weekly*, March 8, 2016.

Swanson, William. *Dial M: The Murder of Carol Thompson*. St. Paul: Minnesota Historical Society Press, 2006.

———. *Stolen from the Garden: The Kidnapping of Virginia Piper*. St. Paul: Minnesota Historical Society Press, 2014.

———. Interview by Todd Melby and Diane Richard. January 22, 2016.

Swartz, Max M. "Thompson Murder Story Woven with Details of Bumbling, Greed." *St. Paul Dispatch*, April 24, 1963.

Terrace, Vincent. *Encyclopedia of Unaired Television Pilots, 1945–2018*. Jefferson, NC: McFarland & Company, 2018.

"Thelma Schoonmaker: From 'Raging Bull' to 'Silence.'" *Studio 360*, January 25, 2017.

Tobin, Paulette. "Star of Coen Film Relishes New Role." *Calgary Herald*, April 4, 1995.

Tunison, Michael. "Independent Streak: The Studio Hasn't Been Built That Can Contain the Coen Brothers' Decidedly Uncommercial Cinema of Quirk." *Entertainment Today*, March 8–14, 1996.

Turan, Kenneth. "Grins from the Brothers Grim." *Los Angeles Times*, March 8, 1996.

Vaughan, Peter. "Delicate Direction Gives Two Capote Stories Life." *Star Tribune*, November 28, 1989.

Verhovek, Sam Howe. "Hollywood Thinks You Talk Funny, Darn Tootin'." *New York Times*, April 21, 1996.

Virshup, Amy. "Taking Hamlet by Stormare." *New York* magazine, June 13, 1988.

Welkos, Robert W. "'Birdcage' a Surprise in Small Markets." *Los Angeles Times*, March 12, 1996.

Welsh, John. "Henry Kristal, 75 / Embers Co-Founder Was Industry Leader." *St. Paul Pioneer Press*, December 23, 2007.

Welter, Ben. "Nov. 11, 1940: The Armistice Day Blizzard." *Star Tribune*, November 11, 2015.

Index

About the Author

TODD MELBY is a reporter, documentarian, and podcast producer. In 2016 he coproduced *We Don't Talk Like That:* Fargo *and the Midwest Psyche*, a one-hour documentary about the movie. *Black Gold Boom*, his public media series on North Dakota's oil boom, featured stories of hope and despair. *Spirit and Body Willing: Sex Over Age 70* and *Death's Footprint*, radio documentaries he coproduced with Diane Richard, won national Edward R. Murrow awards. He lives in Minneapolis.